Sketching Interior Architecture

Sketching Interior Architecture

BY NORMAN DIEKMAN AND JOHN PILE

WHITNEY LIBRARY OF DESIGN
An imprint of Watson-Guptill Publications/New York

First published 1985 in New York by the Whitney Library of Design
an imprint of Watson-Guptill Publications,
a division of Billboard Publications, Inc.,
1515 Broadway, New York, N.Y. 10036

Library of Congress Cataloging in Publication Data
Diekman, Norman, 1939–
Sketching interior architecture.

Bibliography: p.
Includes index.
1. Interior architecture in art. 2. Drawing—
Technique. I. Pile, John F. II. Title.
NC825.I5D5 1985 720'.28'4 84-27074
ISBN 0-8230-7450-1

Distributed in the United Kingdom by Phaidon Press Ltd., Littlegate
House, St. Ebbe's St., Oxford

Manufactured in U.S.A.

1 2 3 4 5 6 7 8 9 10 / 90 89 87 86 85

ACKNOWLEDGMENTS

The authors are indebted to the many people who contributed drawings and suggestions. Their help in making this book possible has been invaluable.

Special thanks are offered to Joseph Paul D'Urso, Michael Kalil, Max Protetch, Massimo and Lella Vignelli, and Giuseppe Zambonini for contributing drawings and photographic material for specific projects, and to Jon Naar and Alchemy Color Labs for providing photographs created especially for this book.

Clients whose projects are illustrated include Estelle Brickel, Stephen Brickel, Mr. and Mrs. Ralph Konheim, Mr. and Mrs. Robert Morgan, Mr. and Mrs. Lloyd Morrisett, and Dr. and Mrs. Edward L. Raab.

Institutions that have supplied drawings and permission to reproduce drawings include the Houghton Library of Harvard University; the Louis I. Kahn Collection at the University of Pennsylvania; the Carlo Scarpa Archives, Treviso, Italy; and the Max Protetch Gallery, New York.

Thanks are also due to our editors, Stephen A. Kliment and Brooke Dramer, and to graphic designer Jay Anning. Their encouragement and support have been vital to the completion of this book.

Credits

All designs and drawings in this book are by Norman Diekman, unless otherwise credited. Photographs and drawings have been reproduced courtesy of the following individuals and institutions:

George Cserna, Photographer, New York: 155–157

Joseph Paul D'Urso, D'Urso Designs, New York: 18–19, 44–45, 139–147

Gruppo Editoriale Electa, Milan, Italy: 115

Houghton Library, Harvard University, Cambridge, MA: 50

Wanda Josefson, Designer, New York: 132–133

Louis I. Kahn Collection, University of Pennsylvania, Philadelphia: 13

Michael Kalil, Designer, New York: 54–57, 88–93

William Machado/Norman Diekman, Designers, New York: 46–47, 111

Mitchell/Giurgola, Architects, New York: 95

Jon Naar, Photographer, New York; all photographs by Jon Naar © Jon Naar 1984: 23, 25 (top), 26 (bottom), 29, 31, 61, 127, 128, 134, 136

Doris Nieves, Designer, New York: 121, 131, 137

John Pile, Designer, New York: 35

Max Protetch Gallery, New York: 17, 26 (top)

Carlo Scarpa Archives, Trevignano de Montebelluna, Treviso, Italy: 14–15

Carlo Scarpa Drawings, Collection of Giuseppe Zambonini and the Open Atelier of Design: 39, 52, 53

VAGA New York/SPADUM: 38

Massimo Vignelli, Vignelli Associates, New York: 80–87

Tom Yee, Photographer, New York: 101

Giuseppe Zambonini, Architect, New York: 40–43, 58–59, 113–125, 148–157

Contents

Sketching Interior Architecture

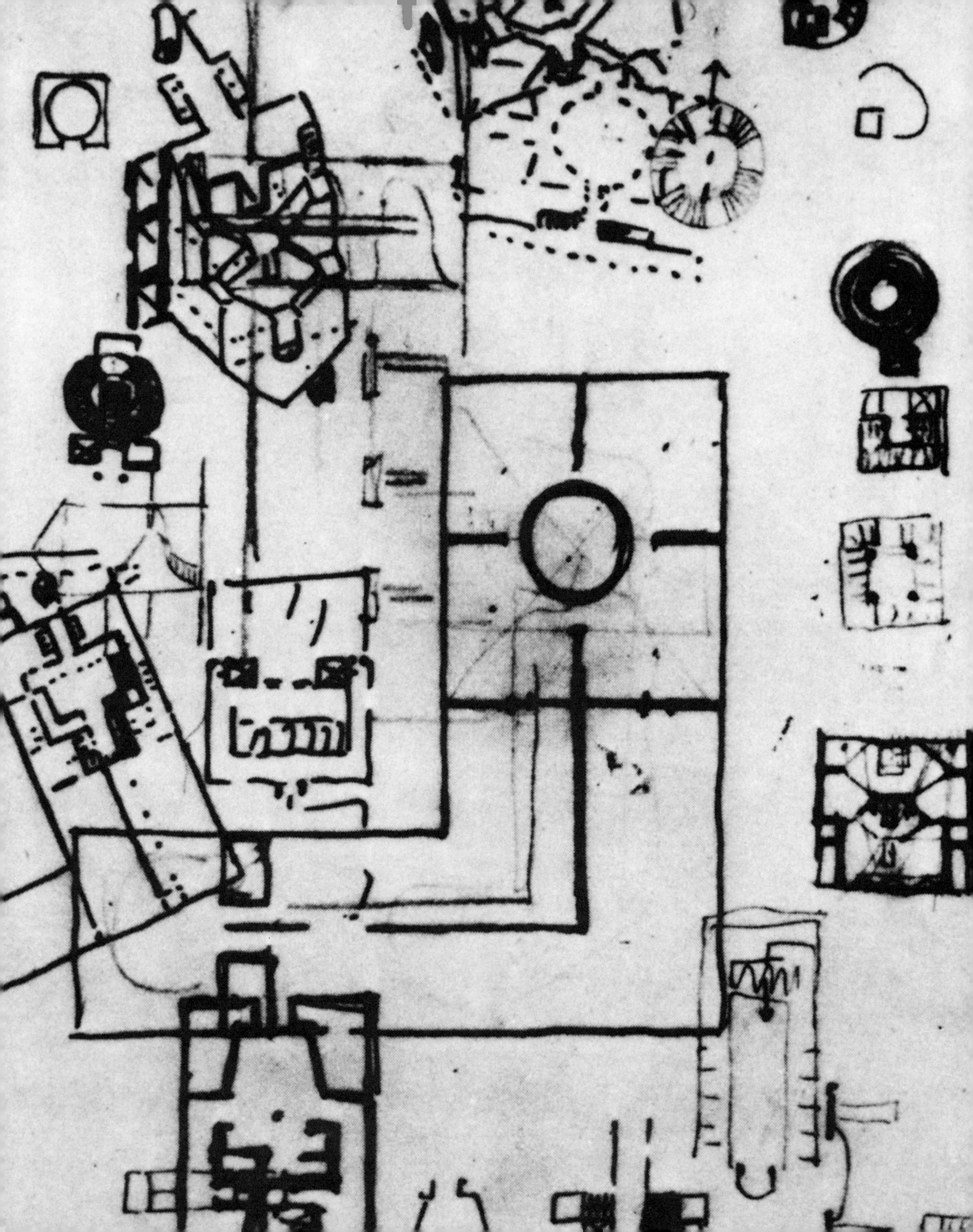

Introduction

Sketching is an activity with a long-established role in the arts. The term has pleasant, even slightly romantic, implications with suggestions of artistic travel to remote places leading to small works, quickly and easily done but with the special charm of directness and informality. A "sketchbook" becomes a unique souvenir; great artists' sketchbooks become treasures with a special value because they give a direct insight into the thought processes that stand behind the artists' work. One thinks of the sketchbooks of William Turner and the notebooks of Leonardo da Vinci, each filled with work that ranks with major paintings in spite of its small-scale and modest form.

Painters have always made sketches—first as a form of quick note taking and then as a way of blocking out, on canvas, the general forms that will become a finished painting. Sculptors make sketches also—often sketch drawings first and then small-scale, three-dimensional sketches in clay or wax—before launching on the laborious carving of stone or modeling at full size for future casting in metal. Interior designers and architects also rely on sketching as a means for rapid visualization and communication more flexible than the carefully made "presentation drawings" and construction drawings that are needed for actual execution of a project. From Joseph Hoffmann to Alvar Aalto and Le Corbusier, architectural sketches have come to be treasured both for their artistic merit and for the information they give about the designer's way of thinking and working.

In recent years there seems to have been a decline in interest in sketching as a technique worthy of special attention. The available books that deal with the subject seem to be addressed to artists or to casual amateurs who want to learn a quick and easy way to make drawings of horses, boats, or some other subject of hobby interest. The camera is probably responsible for discouraging travel sketching; it is so easy to produce a postcard likeness of any scene with the push of a button that the incentive to use pencil and paper has been undermined. Publication of the sketchbooks of Le Corbusier in a large-format, multivolume edition is only one evidence of a rediscovery of the sketch in architectural circles. Louis Kahn, Carlo Scarpa, James Stirling, and many others have produced an increasing flow of sketch drawings that have found their way to publication and so to new attention.

In recent history, the sketch was given great importance in the Beaux Arts system of architectural education. Every major design problem began with a requirement that each student produce an *esquisse*—a sketch made *en loge* (that is, "in the building")—without references, criticism, or other assistance. This quick sketch, made in one day, had to embody the basic idea that the student would develop during the following weeks into a complete design presented in the elaborate drawings that made the Beaux Arts famous. Students were bound to stick to their original concept, for better or for worse, and the esquisse was displayed with the final presentation so that the jury could verify that this had been done. The intention was to ensure that the end product was based on the student's own original concept, to enforce learning through the exercise of developing one theme to its best possible realization, and to encourage the ability to

James Stirling develops his architectural concepts with soft graphite pencil on vellum tracing paper, often with a graph paper grid slipped beneath for controlling the scale. (Courtesy James Stirling Michael Wilford and Associates, London)

Detail of Louis Kahn's study for the Hurva Synagogue in Jerusalem. A bold charcoal drawing technique was used to reinforce the drama of light and power of this majestic space.

find and present a concept in quick sketch form.

The brief "sketch problem" was also a part of that system of architectural education and survives from time to time in modern design training, requiring the student to design and present a complete project in one day entirely without help or use of reference materials. Whether exposed to sketching through such formal techniques of training or not, every designer and architect comes to use sketching of some kind, as do many other professionals involved in some type of creative work that has visual results. An inventor, engineer, stage designer, or fashion designer will almost inevitably turn to sketching as a step on the way from purely mental conceptualization to detailed realization.

In spite of photography, sketching remains an important method of note taking, a way of recording something seen in a way that can emphasize or omit details as desired and so can produce a record with more special meaning than the all-inclusive snapshot. Travel is a traditional part of the architect's training, since it is the only way to have direct experience of a wide variety of historic and modern buildings. Sketching on location not only records what was seen; it leads to a kind of analysis and internal understanding that aids memory but also is itself a special kind of study. The travel sketches of Kahn and Le Corbusier remind us that this interest never disappeared totally, and, with the new interest in study of historic architecture (and the new ease of travel), sketching on location is once again being taken seriously as an important part of design education.

However useful and important, travel sketching is not the primary concern of this book; it is already well covered in any number of books addressed to painters and other artists. Here, our concern is rather with the sketches that are important steps in, actually the very heart of, the process of design. The design process begins with a "problem"—a set of requirements more or less clearly recognized or articulated by the person, group, or organization who is to be the "client" of the designer. Developing clarity about the problem as presented is a well-known and much-discussed first step in any design process. It is often said that a truly adequate statement of the problem will imply a solution that will then be almost inevitable. In practice, problems are rarely so clearly stated and are often not fully clarified and understood until the design process is well along.

Real problems—those with enough substance to require professional attention—are rarely simple. Even the design of one room or a single piece of furniture can turn out to be, when looked at in detail, quite complex. Since the hoped-for "solution" is not to be an abstract statement or formula, but rather a physical, three-dimensional reality, the mental steps from problem to solution involve a process of alternate invention and experimentation or review of three-dimensional forms. The human mind is able to deal with such concepts, but it has limitations in detailed visualization and in memory. Other creative mental work has similar problems. Writing music, poetry, or prose, mathematical work, or developing chemical formulas all make demands on memory that almost require writing down notes—really "sketches" in words or symbols that make it possible to look at the products of thought processes quickly and easily but in a recorded form that permits review, change, and development.

The designer's sketch is a similar step of notation—but notation in a visual form, since the material under development is a physical reality that will become known, understood, and appreciated primarily through visual means. Designed works become known through the other senses as well, of course—touch in particular (the other three senses usually have only minor significance)—but the visual sense has such a strongly dominant role in understanding environmental reality that it can usually stand alone as the means of communicating the ideas that design is concerned with. As soon as a design idea comes to mind, it becomes almost necessary to record it visually so that

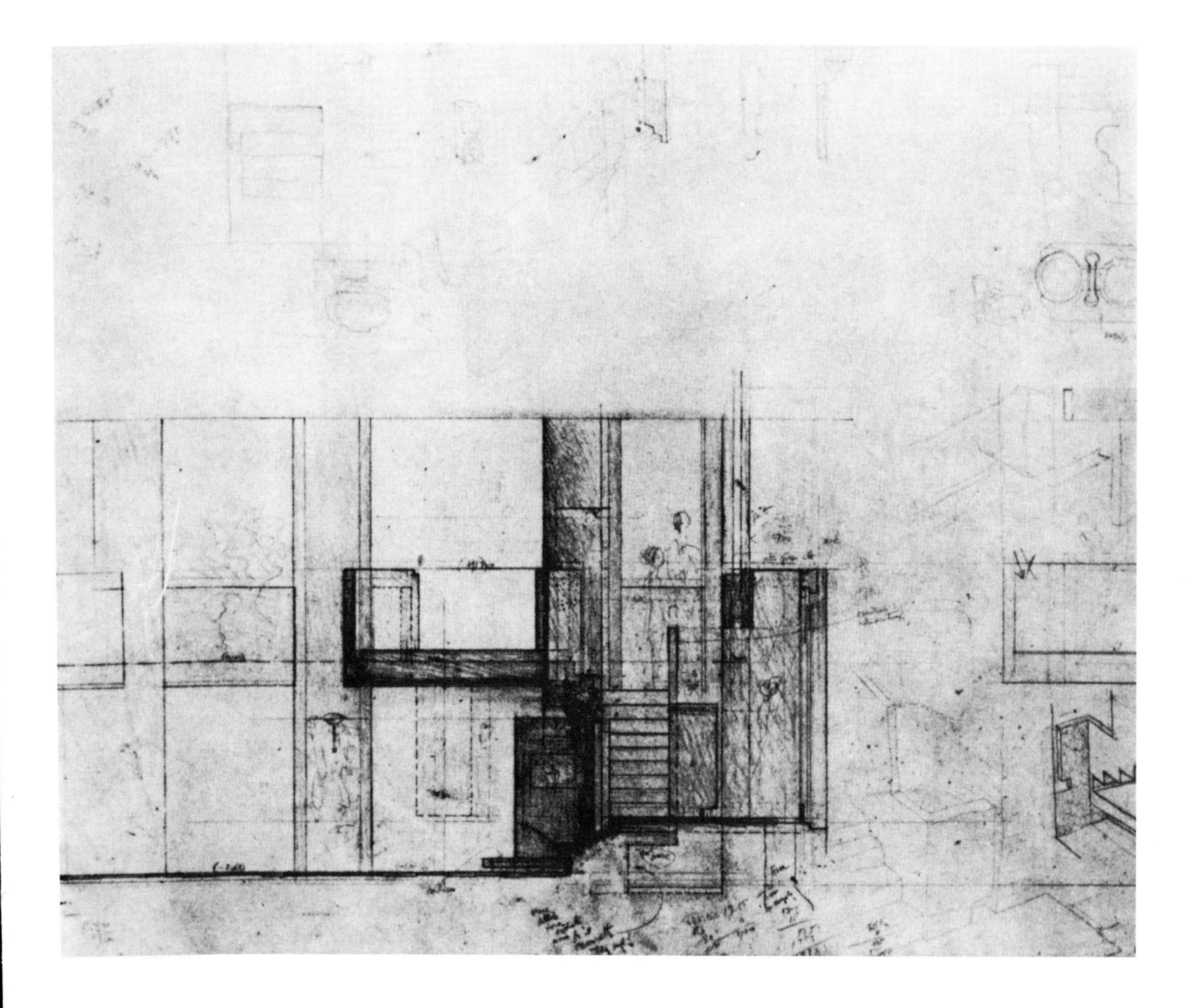

Two design studies by Carlo Scarpa in pencil and colored pencil on ozalid paper. Ideas are extended and random thoughts are spread out across the paper surface as if on a blackboard.

Two views of a sketch model by Frank Gehry for a Beverly Hills residence, 1980–82. (Courtesy Max Protetch Gallery, New York)

it can be given a specificity that strictly mental concepts seem not to have; held for some period of time while other ideas are developed; viewed for revision, development, and self-criticism; and, when appropriate, shown to others for comment and discussion. The making of a series of sketches is thus the very heart of the design process as it is carried on by architects, interior designers, and designers in virtually every other field.

In every design school, teaching depends on a dialogue between student and teacher in which there must be some visual material out on the table for discussion. The student who wants to "talk out" design ideas without sketching is a notorious problem for every design teacher. The teacher or "critic" carries pencil and tracing paper as tools of the trade so that comments can be given substance through a constant flow of sketches that suggest directions that the student is being urged to explore.

In professional practice, the designer depends on sketches, not only to help in the development of ideas, but also as a means to communicate with colleagues, to convey information to other designers and to draftsmen who will convert design ideas into highly specific construction drawings. From time to time, the designer uses sketches as a means of communication with clients. In many situations it is thought best to show clients only formal "presentation drawings" that are as realistic as possible and often quite elaborate. Ideally, presentation drawings require no explanation and are inherently impressive and convincing. In practice, however, it often develops that such drawings, whether convincing or not, are not well understood by the people who must review and approve them. For modest projects (houses and their interiors) and even for larger projects where communication between client and designer is direct and informal, sketches are often a far more effective means of communication.

The ability to sketch while talking is a skill that any designer will find helpful. It is impressive and, in its way, charming to most clients, who enjoy seeing the creative process actually taking place before their eyes. Sketching while talking allows a kind of cooperation along with communication between designer and client that makes for a close, participative relationship. A sketch by Joseph Paxton (later *Sir* Joseph), which he drew on the back of a blotter while riding on a railroad train with Prince Albert, was the genesis of the Crystal Palace of 1851. The original sketch is preserved in the British Museum. Le Corbusier's letter to his client Madame M., illustrated with many charming and informative thumbnail sketches, has become well known and much admired.

In addition to sketch on paper, sketch models in three dimensions have become a widely used way of studying spatial relationship and developing concepts. Notice the sketch models by Frank Gehry illustrated on the opposite page.

It is surprising that sketching is not taught to architects and designers as a formal discipline. In educational institutions in the past, architecture had a close relationship to the other arts. An architectural student was expected to study freehand drawing, painting in water color and other media, and to try a hand at sculpture. Modern design curricula have pulled away from the other arts and drawn closer to technical fields, including engineering. The drawing studied by the typical student today is the drafting with instruments needed for construction documents. Design sketching is left to be picked up in passing, with some minimal guidance from design teachers who may well have had little training in this direction themselves. Current books on architectural drawing seem to emphasize the formal presentation drawing over the more personal sketch.

This book is an effort to fill the vacuum that we believe exists. It is both a collection of fine examples of design and architectural sketching and a manual of suggestions about materials and methods that may be of direct help to the student or professional who is interested in design sketching as a major technique in effective practice.

In this Joseph Paul D'Urso sketch, explosive, quick, and bold felt-tip pen strokes are used to set out ideas rapidly and vigorously. Color is used for accent and highlight only.

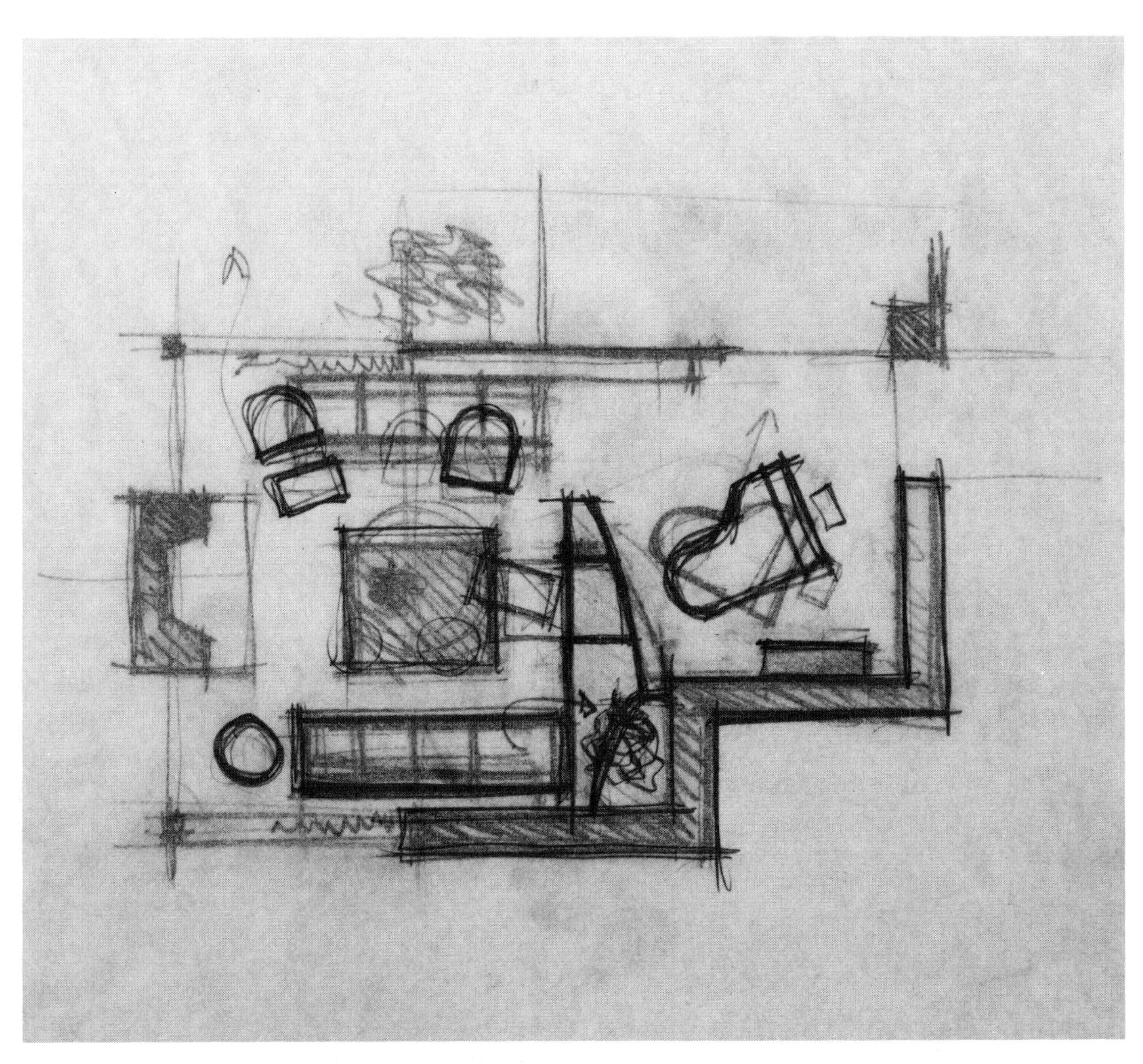

Overlays of tracing paper allow the designer readily to compare previous ideas with new ones.

Soft black pencil and colored pencils on cream trace produce a "Xerox of the mind." (Norman Diekman, designer)

1

Sketching Materials

Sketching is by its nature such a simple and basic technique that tools and materials pose very little problem. Equipment adequate for *some* sort of sketching is virtually certain to be at hand almost anywhere, anytime. This chapter will discuss the simple and available materials and offer some hints about choices that can easily be made; it will also review more specialized materials and tools that are more likely to require a trip to an art or drafting supply store but that can make sketching more varied and, sometimes, more interesting. There are also certain art materials that involve some special technique for use, but that are also quite useful as sketch materials if they are at hand.

Even if one sets out to acquire a sketch kit all new and fresh, the total cost will be modest—as compared to a full setup for drafting, almost negligible. Brand names and prices are not discussed here, since both are subject to change and are not, generally, matters of great importance. The exception will be those few cases where the authors have found a certain product or brand so superior that it seems appropriate to call attention to it. Otherwise, it can be assumed that most available products of a particular kind will prove satisfactory. The basic tools are marking media—most often pencils or pens—while the basic materials are papers of various sorts. These are discussed in order, while more special equipment and media are dealt with last.

PENCILS

Pencils are such a useful commonplace that it is hard to remember that they are a relatively modern invention. The great artists of the Middle Ages and Renaissance had to manage with brush and ink or such awkward substitutes as the silver point, with its sensitive but pale line. Now we take it for granted that pencils are always at hand everywhere. They are probably the most useful of all sketching tools because they are inexpensive and available, they can produce line and tone in great variety and, not of the least importance, they produce a mark that erases easily. Ordinary pencils are fine sketching tools, provided they are *soft* enough. Hard pencils are often supplied for everyday use because their mark does not smear so easily and because they hold a point well and do not break as easily as the lead of a softer pencil. This may be helpful in accounting or when making a shopping list, but it is frustrating when drawing.

A hard pencil makes a pale mark; even when pressed down hard, it is more likely to dig into or tear the paper than to make a clear, black line. Ordinary pencils are marked to show hardness by a number. No. 2 is the hardest grade that will be found useful for sketching. Pencils without a number (those with advertising slogans, for example) should be compared with a no. 2 and discarded (for design use at least) if they are any harder than that grade. Some ordinary pencils will be found to be gritty or easy to break, but an Eberhard Faber Mongol or a Lerman Glider no. 2 will be found a most useful standby for sketching. Keeping a box of a dozen on hand reduces the temptation to make do with an inferior and frustrating alternative. A superb pencil for sketching and general use is the Berol (formerly Eagle) Chemi-Sealed Draughting pencil no. 314—a fine, soft pencil, mysteriously named since it is rarely used for drafting but ideal for sketching. It is usually available only at art and drafting supply shops. Such shops also carry the more specialized pencils made for drafting, which usually will already be at hand at the desk of a working designer or architect.

Pencils designed for art and drafting are manufactured in various hardnesses, which are marked on the pencil. H stands for hard, B ("black") for soft. Such pencils are graded with letters from 9H (very hard) down to H (the hardest grade suitable for general use), through HB and F (medium grades), and so on through B to 6B, softest of all. For sketching, HB, F, B, and 2B will be found useful; the still softer grade is helpful at times, although subject to easy breaking. Dietzgen, Staedtler Mars, and Eagle Turquoise are well-known brands, the last being a special favorite with many users.

The "lead" in the ordinary pencil is, of course, not really lead, but pressed graphite. Its characteristic line has a slight gloss even on matte paper. Other pencils available at art supply stores use different types of lead. Carbon pencil lead (also made in a range of hardness grades) is more like charcoal and produces an intense black line, almost totally matte. Other pencils developed for artists' use have a more waxy, crayon-like lead. There are pencils with wide, flat leads (often sold in hardware stores as "carpenter's" pencils) and pencils with extra thick leads. Black pencils from various colored pencil sets have characteristics different from the ordinary lead pencil.

Colored pencils are also available as sketch media although sketching is rarely done in a full range of color. A few well chosen colors can be useful at times. Primaries (red and blue in particular) and a few neutral or earth

DESIGN

Soft pencils or charcoal sticks give the ability to record design ideas spontaneously; sketches may be changed easily by erasing.

(Photos on page 23 and top of opposite page by Jon Naar)

colors, browns, or tans are good choices. Many available colored pencils are very unsatisfactory, being too hard and having weak color. Berol Prismacolor is an excellent standard brand that is widely available.

Other Media

A number of other media are available as alternatives to pencils. Charcoal is a classic artist's medium, well-suited to large-scale sketching because of its ability to lay down tones of grays and blacks over large areas. Louis Kahn's large plan sketches in charcoal are well known. Since charcoal smears easily, charcoal drawings must be sprayed with fixative if they are to have any reasonable lasting qualities. Crayons, available in a full range of colors, are rarely used in serious work; however, the special type known as Conté crayons—available only in black, white, and the rusty red color called sanguine—are fine sketch media. China-markers are a waxy pencil type that will mark glass, china, or other slick surfaces. They are used occasionally for sketching, although they are available only in a limited color range and almost impossible to erase.

ERASERS AND SHARPENERS

The fact that ordinary pencil line erases easily is one of its great assets. Many pencils come with an eraser on the top end, convenient and useful when new, but easily worn away and subject to hardening with age. A bad eraser can ruin a sketch in a moment, so it is wise to always test on a scrap paper before using a pencil eraser. Risk can be avoided by using a separate eraser of a kind that can be trusted never to harden or cause smearing. Staedtler Mars no. 526 50 is a plastic eraser that has these qualities and also seems to work better than any rubber eraser. Stocking a few (they last very well) is a convenience for every eraser need. When working with charcoal, a "kneaded rubber" eraser is a necessity for introducing whites or lightening charcoal tone areas; it is of little use otherwise.

Pencils need sharpening almost constantly. A good cranked sharpener is a standard need in any studio or drafting room; the electric sharpener is now a frequently seen luxury alternative. Since sketching is often done away from a fixed base, a portable sharpener is also needed. The simple plastic or metal block twist-type sharpener will serve; a good imported version with a long-lasting blade is best if it can be found. Shavings and graphite crumble drop from these sharpeners in a somewhat messy fashion so that various versions with a means of catching this waste have been devised. A simple and generally useful alternative is a simple pocket knife with a sharp blade, usable for hand sharpening with any profile of point shape desired. It takes some practice to become skillful at hand sharpening. This was once a skill that draftsmen took pride in, but now seems lost to the mechanical sharpener.

PEN AND INK

Pens are a traditional sketch tool with excellent possibilities. The most traditional of pens, the quill, was long ago replaced by steel pen points of the sort usually called "straight" or sometimes "crowquill." Points are available in such great variety that it takes some searching and testing to find suitable types. The point is placed in a holder and dipped into ink more or less constantly as drawing takes place. This means that there must be an inkwell or open bottle of ink at hand and demands some skill and care to avoid blots and spills.

To deal with these problems and make pen and ink conveniently portable, the fountain pen was developed and became a popular everyday item of utility. Designers often still use fountain pens; such brands as Osmiroid and the prestigious Mont Blanc are favorites and make pen-and-ink sketching easy and convenient. Old fountain pens can be repaired and restored and may also prove quite useful. Fountain pens must be filled regularly and used frequently to stay in good condition. If neglected, even a good pen will become hard to start,

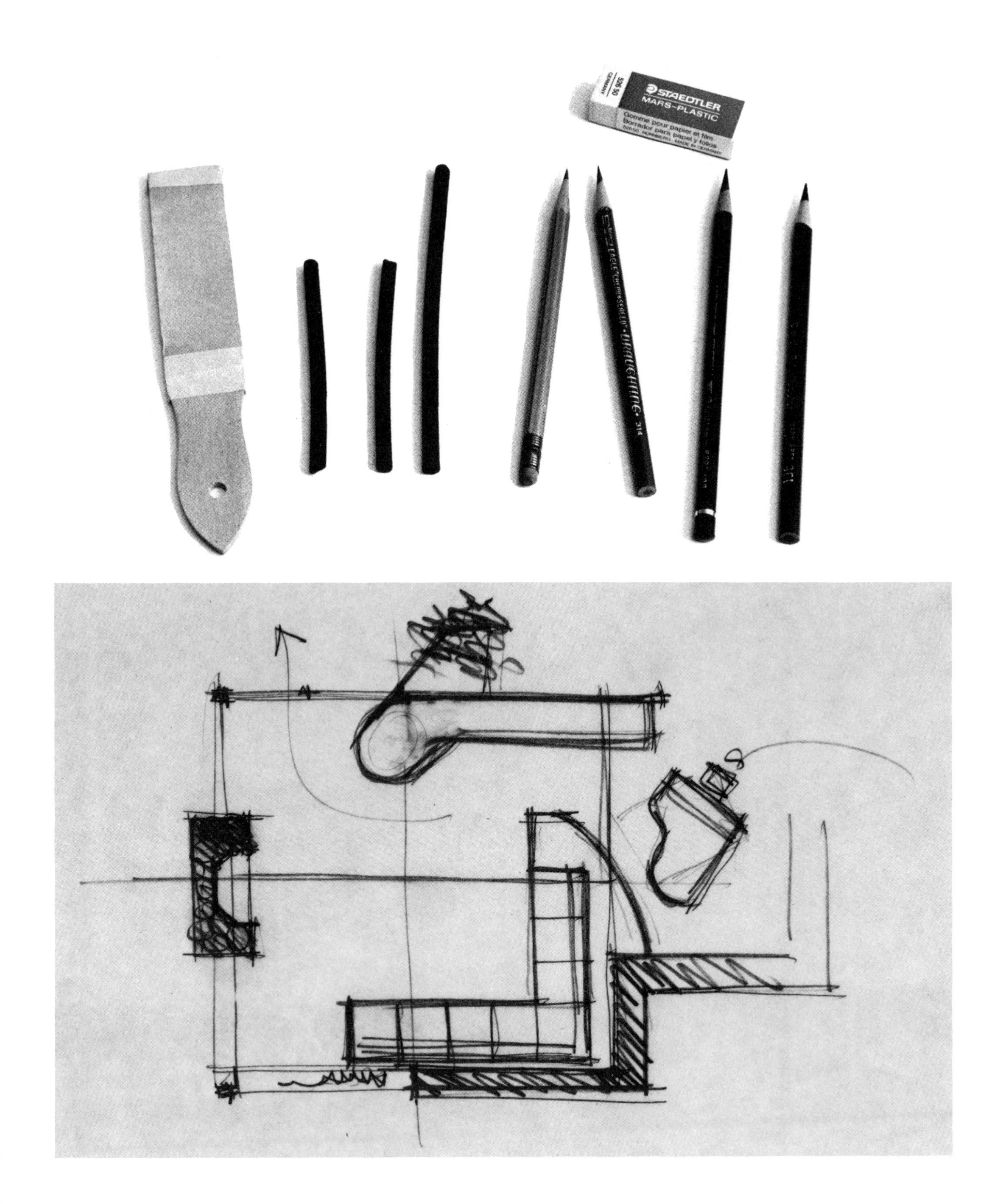
STAEDTLER
MARS-PLASTIC
Gomme pour papier et film
Borrador para papel y folios

GRAY
WARM

will clog, and will finally become useless. To offset these problems, both straight and fountain pens offer a flexibility of line, varying from thin to thick with pressure that makes them a fine art medium destined to remain in use in spite of newer competition.

"Technical" fountain pens used for ink drafting have little use for sketching because they require a different point for each line thickness and are held vertically. Most makers offer a special holder for technical pen point and ink assemblies that make freehand use possible, and some designers who make use of a technical pen set for drafting use this accessory for sketching.

Technical pens, fountain pens, and straight pens all depend on a supply of ink. Ink comes in many types and colors, but it is a good opaque, waterproof black that is most useful. Pelikan and Higgins are well-known makers of fine drawing inks, including special types that are called "nonclogging" and are therefore suggested for use in fountain and technical pens. Unfortunately, in spite of the label, all inks tend to clog pens. Various fluids and gadgets are available to help with this problem. Colored inks are rarely used in sketching, a possible exception being the sepia or brown that gives a certain softness to drawing suggesting the work of "old masters." Inks sold in stationery stores for writing are usually too watery for use in sketching and are most often of a sickly blue or blue-black color. Higgins "Eternal" black writing ink is an exception, a fair compromise between easy flowing and dense black color.

All of the irksome problems of pens and ink have been swept aside by the modern development of ballpoint and felt-tip pens, now familiar to everyone as the most common of writing instruments. Ballpoints may occasionally be useful in sketching, but they tend to "skip" and produce a poor line quality. Felt points, on the other hand, produce an excellent line and are a fine sketching medium. Felt-tip pens do not offer the easily varied line width of older ink pens, but are available with various tip profiles that somewhat compensate for this fault. Better pens are available with replaceable point and ink cartridges, but the cheap, disposable pens are also, at their best, highly satisfactory. The ink dries quickly and so is less likely to blot or smear. Also, it is easy to keep pens of several colors at hand. Flair, Pentel, and Pilot are good brands available with various points described by names such as "hardhead" and "razor point," that are more or less descriptive.

The felt-tip with a wide point usually called a "marker" has become a very popular design medium. The availability of a vast range of color together with almost instant drying is a great convenience. Colors range from subtle to garish in each brand. Large sets, popular for rendering, become quite expensive and are hardly needed for sketching. Choosing a few colors, preferably subtle and muted colors, will provide a compact package that can be helpful in adding color to sketches.

Colored markers are a favorite sketch medium tending to replace water color in modern practice. Design Markers and AD Markers are favorite brands available in a wide range of colors. Staedtler Mars 3600 series markers have a soft, brush-like tip that retains some of the feel of the watercolor brush.

PAPERS

Among materials, paper is the basic and vital necessity. Sketches have been made on almost any imaginable kind of paper. The proverbial sketch on the back of an envelope or menu is produced every day, and there can be a real charm in using odd and unusual papers that come to hand by chance. For more systematic use, several types of widely available paper can be kept on hand. The most obvious of possibilities is normal white writing paper. It is cheap and available, and the standard 8½ × 11-inch size makes for standardization and easy storage and filing. For some hard-to-explain reason, the lined yellow pad (usually legal size) is a great favorite among architects and interior designers. The yellow color and lines seem in some way to give this material an unassuming quality that encourages informality

Robert Venturi used a felt tip pen to quickly sketch his idea of an eclectic architecture. (Courtesy Max Protetch Gallery, New York)

Ballpoint and felt-tip pens are available with various point styles. (Photo by Jon Naar)

Keeping orderly sketchbooks allows the designer to build a small library of ideas for reference and review. (Photograph by Jon Naar)

and an easy flow of sketched ideas.

At the drawing board, the paper most often at hand is some type of tracing paper. The thin sort called yellow or cream trace is on every drafting table and is probably the most used of all sketch papers. Yellow or cream trace is highly transparent, making it easy to "draw over" an earlier drawing or sketch. It is easily torn off the roll and so cheap as to seem totally disposable. Its only faults are that its thinness makes it easy to tear (even with the point of a pencil or pen) and easy to wrinkle or muss. Its yellow tone, on the other hand, seems helpful providing a mild background value against which even a white line will show up. A more sturdy white tracing paper is also usually kept on hand for design work, since it is best for working drawings that will be sent for prints. Roll form is most usual, but cut sheets and pads are also available.

There are many types and many brands of tracing paper, but most users find a favorite and stick to it to avoid endless experiment with different materials. A small roll of white tracing paper is an excellent sketch medium. Some designers and many students (particularly industrial design students) like to keep sketches on a roll in a continuous band with fresh paper on the right, finished sketches rolling up on the left into a "scroll." This way of working develops a continuous record of process, but can make it somewhat inconvenient to refer to earlier sketches. Tearing off each sketch tends to create a tangle of oddly sized bits, easy to muss or lose. A pad of standard size discourages this problem.

Many better papers are good for sketching, although the quality and cost can inhibit the easy flow of ideas and drawings. Good drawing or "detail" paper in sheets can be excellent, while special papers called "charcoal," "pastel," and "water color" paper are most often reserved for the media for which they have been developed. Charcoal and pastel papers have a rough "tooth" and texture and come in many excellent, subtle colors that make the paper a middle tone against which both lighter and darker tones show up well. Water color papers come in a range of texture; the smoother surfaces are fine for pencil or ink as well as water colors. The best of these papers can be quite costly, but set off a presentation sketch in a way that suggests a real "work of art."

More modest special papers include graph paper, available in sheets and pads. A grid in light blue in a familiar dimension (¼-inch squares, for example) helps in sketching to scale and makes it easy to keep horizontals and verticals accurate when sketching without instruments. When copied, the grid will "drop out" (not reproduce) if it is of light tone. Brown wrapping paper is a favorite for large sketches—plot plans, or full-size details—because it is sturdy, cheap, and has a tone that works well with charcoal, black ink or marker, or blunt soft pencil line.

Loose or rolled paper requires a desk or board to draw on, and can be inconvenient to transport away from home base. For travel sketching or noting ideas when away from the drafting table, papers are available in various pad and books developed for these situations. Tracing papers, writing papers, special drawing papers, graph paper, and the special "art" papers are all to be had in these forms. Pads make it possible to tear off sheets to discard failures or to file or mount sketches to be retained. Bound books (sometimes made with highly attractive bindings) encourage the making of a carefully planned sketchbook; however, they can sometimes discourage spontaneity, since removing a page is not easy (it is possible, of course, with a knife or razor blade and a bit of care). Books with perforated pages are a compromise. Books with spiral binding have become a particular favorite; a spiral book can be opened out flat conveniently, and it is easy to tear out sheets. The perforated edge and the rounded lower corners that are often cut to make carrying easier give the torn-out sheet clear evidence of its origin. If sketches are kept away from edges, it is easy to trim these features away, but they can be an annoyance

33"SOFA
KITCHEN 3'8"x72" MAX.

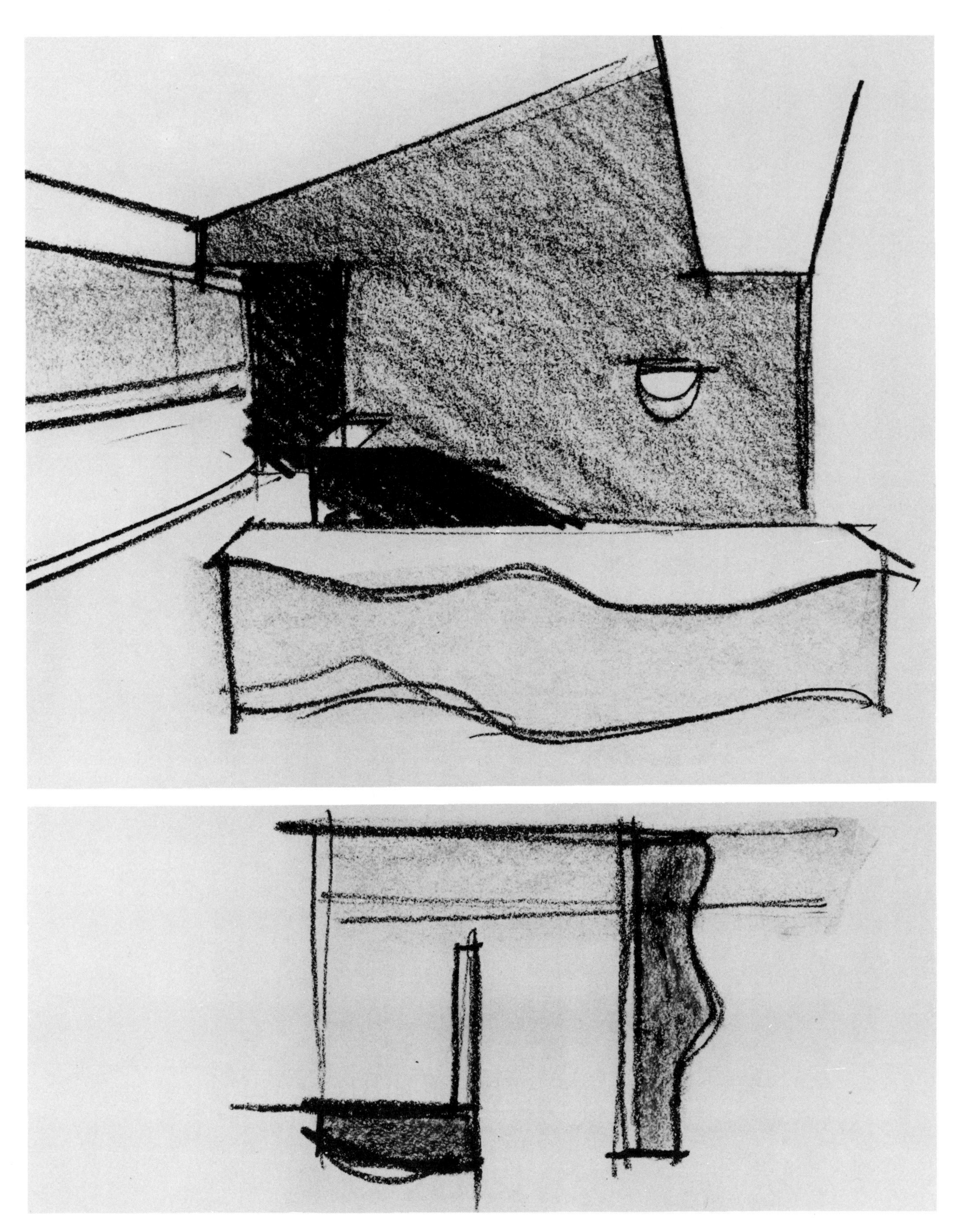

New media and materials continually join the list of familiar sketch materials. The Berol Company recently introduced "Prismacolor Art Stix" in colors coordinated with their colored pencils, making line and tone relationships easy to control. (Photo by Jon Naar)

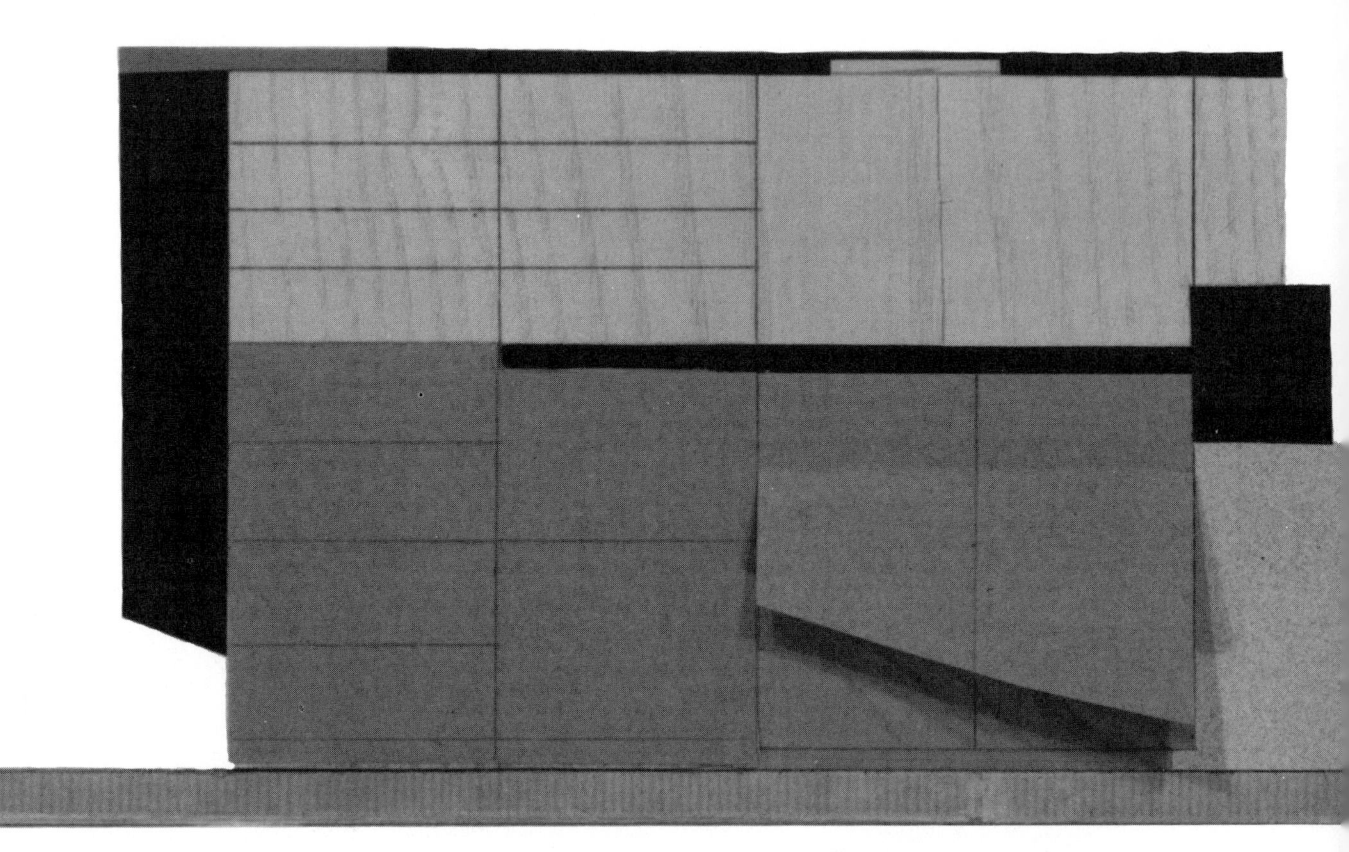

when mounting a sketch that ran to the edges of the sheet.

Water color paper is available in "blocks" with all four edges firmly held down and with a firm board base. This is because water colors cause rippling and stretching as they wet paper. The block limits this problem in the field and in the studio as well. Paper on a block is, of course, firmly held for pencil or ink sketching as well.

OTHER SUPPLIES

Since sketching is ordinarily done freehand, there is no need for drafting instruments. When at the drafting table, it may sometimes be helpful to begin with T-square and triangle, but these tools are not a normal part of a sketch kit. A small straight-edge and a pocket scale may be useful occasionally. At a board, drafting tape will be available if needed. It is wise to plan ahead a bit to have appropriate sketch materials ready for different situations away from the drafting table. Because ideas occur at unexpected times and places—on a train or plane, in a restaurant, or even in bed—some sketch materials, drawing pencils or pens and a sketchbook or pad should always be at hand. Even a few index cards in a pocket can serve when no other materials are handy.

For travel, visits to a project site, or a meeting with a client, it is helpful to have ready a larger pad or book and appropriate drawing materials. It is easy to keep such materials in a briefcase or bag. Travelers often carry a photo gadget bag that can easily hold a few pads or books, drawing tools, and a good eraser. The main point is to make it a habit to *always* have materials close by so as to avoid the frustration of having to search about or borrow when the need develops.

When sketches turn out well, it is often helpful to have a way of displaying them, even if only briefly. A few ready-made mats in various sizes make it easy to display a sketch in an informal but respectful way. Inexpensive frames in which mats can be easily inserted and removed are now widely available. Using a few for a constantly changing display of sketches can help to stimulate a flow of fresh ideas.

SPECIAL PURPOSE MATERIALS

In addition to the usual tools and materials discussed above, some other art materials can be considered for sketching. They will most often appeal to users already familiar with them. Oil paints and acrylics, for example, are possible sketch media, but they are rarely used in design work. Chalks and pastels are useful in sketching, either as a primary medium or as a means of adding tones to pencil or ink sketches. Chalks come in a variety of colors and in various degrees of hardness. Softer grades can be used to lay in areas of color tone or to add highlights, particularly when drawing on paper with a strong color tone. Tailor's chalk is a wide, flat, fairly hard chalk that can produce wide strokes of soft tone in the limited colors available. By placing a textured material under a sketch and rubbing a wide chalk over the top surface, a textured tone can be obtained that is sometimes quite effective.

Pastels are an art medium that can produce "paintings" of fine quality in the hands of an experienced user. The

Scraps of colored papers and a piece of wood veneer cut and assembled to make a collage sketch for a material and color study. (Norman Diekman, designer)

best quality pastels are very soft and are produced in a vast range of colors, including many colors of great subtlety and beauty. A full set of good pastels is both bulky and expensive, but a small selection of good colors can be useful in design sketching. Fixative is necessary if the results are to be stored and kept to prevent smearing. Berol Prismacolor Art Stix are a somewhat harder stick pastel in colors that coordinate with the same maker's Prismacolor pencils. They are useful for laying in flat areas of tone (with the side of a stick) or developing rubbed tones, particularly when used together with the related pencils.

Water color is another art medium with a reputation for being difficult. It was at one time widely used by architects and designers for both sketching and more formal color rendering. First experiments with water color are often made discouraging by use of poor-quality color. Cheap sets of the sort (unfortunately) often given to children are of little use, and even better colors are hard to use when they are supplied in small cakes or pans that give no space for the water that will make them usable.

Good water colors are well worth their price and are best bought in a tube. Some of each color to be used is then squeezed out into a pan or plate. Boxes with empty small china pans are ideal for use with tube water color. The soft paint, when wetted, makes a strong color that can then blend with other colors to produce the "wet" effects that one associates with water color painting. Winsor and Newton colors are generally highly regarded and are well worth their high price, since quantities used are generally small. Rembrandt and Grumbacher are other respected brands. Ready-made sets are to be avoided; colors are best chosen from a color card.

Water color tones can be very effective when added to drawings in other media. The paper should, ideally, be made for water color since ordinary papers will wrinkle from the water, such wrinkling sometimes leads to pleasant sketch effects, however. Using water color away from home base means preparing some sort of suitable box and providing a water container. Blotters may also be useful.

BRUSHES

Mention of water color leads to discussion of one more kind of tool, necessary for water color but also useful with some other media. These are brushes. Ink washes can be a useful sketch medium, as can undiluted ink, black, or color. Both inks and water colors require brushes of fine quality for best results. Cheap brushes sold in sets do not hold color well, do not point at the tip, and lose hairs in a most irritating way. Good brushes are very expensive but, fortunately, few are needed and they will last, with care, almost indefinitely. Three good-quality (Winsor and Newton is again a best brand) red sable watercolor brushes will serve most purposes; nos. 5, 3, and 1 make a good choice. A chisel-shaped brush and a large, flat brush may be added. Good brushes come to a fine point, the point of a large brush just as fine and controllable as that of a smaller brush while the large brush holds a better charge of color. *Never* leave good brushes standing in water; they must be rinsed, shaken out, and left to dry with the hairs projecting out horizontally in open air.

COLLAGE

A remaining, unusual sketch medium should be mentioned. This is collage, the technique of arranging cut or torn bits of colored papers or other materials to form the areas of tone that will make up a sketch. This may seem an unlikely way of producing design sketches, but it can be very effective. A pencil sketch or drawing is usually made first, then cut materials are pasted in place to represent the colors and materials of the finished project. To be ready to use this technique, it is best to have collected a large variety of papers and similar materials in advance. Systems of colors in paper such as Color-Aid are good sources, but a habit of saving bits of good colors that come from packaging, printed materials, and similar odds and ends can supply a fine variety at no cost. Trimming and filing such scraps by color prepares a fine kit of collage materials. Collage also requires a suitable adhesive—library paste is traditional, but household cement such as Duco dries quickly, holds well, and is less likely to cause wrinkles. Collage sketches are best made with a base of mat or illustration board that discourages bending.

Making of sketch models will call for some additional materials, but these will be dealt with in Chapter 7, where the techniques of sketch modeling are discussed.

As with almost all art materials, it will be found that top-quality materials and tools are almost always well worth their price. Sketching, in particular, calls for such modest materials in such small quantities that it is pointless to suffer with bad pencils and pens, inferior papers and pads. Good materials also convey to the user a certain sense of quality—one feels "professional" and will tend to "live up to" the quality of the best available equipment. Good materials are thus not only technical support for good work, but a source of a certain sense of improved morale as well. There is nothing more inviting to work than a collection of good materials laid out and ready for use.

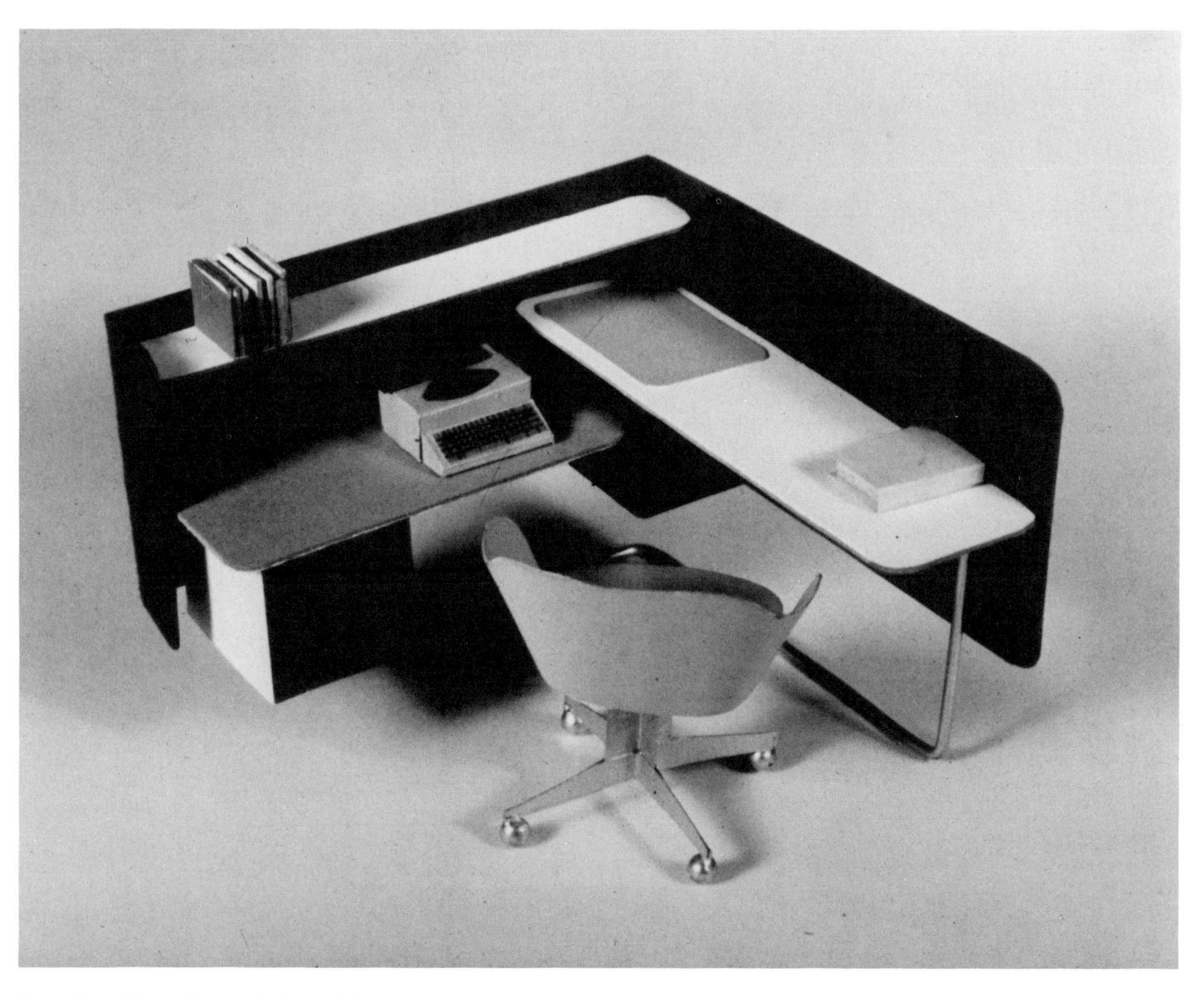

Extension of the collage technique of the preceding pages can lead to full three-dimensional models in paper and wire. (John Pile, designer)

2

Personal Sketching

Of all the kinds of drawings that designers make, none is more personal than the sketch. More finished drawings are disciplined by the straightedge and the scale and, in their effort to reveal an intended built reality, become more nearly "photographic." Construction drawings follow accepted standards that minimize the visible expression of the unique qualities of the draftsman. Because sketches are a very direct product of the mind and hand of the person who makes them, they automatically become personally expressive, even if this is not the designer's aim. To have a personal style in sketching of course usually *is* an aim of a designer. It is an aim encouraged by the increasingly wide acceptance of the idea that the sketches by architects and designers are an art form worthy of collecting and study for their own sake.

We are also constantly made aware of sketches made by any number of famous creative people—sketches that are worth studying for the insights they grant into the mental processes of design and into the character of the people who made them as well. One hears of architects and designers, sometimes quite successful and even famous, who never make sketches of any drawings at all—people who design by giving verbal instructions to others who produce drawings or who proceed to execute work "by ear" entirely without drawings. The latter method of work can only serve for small and simple projects—the design of an object, for example. The former situation is quite common in the world of big business architecture, where teams of designers and draftsmen produce whatever a project requires on the orders of principals or partners too busy to actually draw.

Whatever the impact of such methods may be on the quality of design produced (a matter for debate that does not belong here), it is certain that we are cut off from an important line for understanding the design process, and we can assume that such non-drawing designers are themselves cut off from one of the main pleasures of that process. Of all the arts, architecture is most constrained by the reality pressures of clients' demands, legal and budget restrictions, and all the other burdens that the working designer must cope with. Drawing—at least design drawing in the conceptual and developmental phases—is largely free of these constraints. Sketches can show whatever the mind may conceive, and the vocabulary of drawing chosen to show ideas is entirely of the designer's own choosing.

Personal freedom begins with the choice of tools and materials, extends to size and scale, and includes the choice of mode (plan, section, elevation, perspective, and combinations) that will be most effective in making visible the ideas that come to mind. Such choices may vary from project to project and from time to time, but most designers gravitate toward habits that become comfortable and familiar and so move toward the development of a personal style of sketching that can become unique and special as a particular handwriting. The drawings of such masters as Alvar Aalto, Le Corbusier, and Louis Kahn are every bit as distinctive as their executed work and may, in the long run, be just as or even more influential. Access to real buildings and interiors is always limited by the realities of geography, occupancy, and available time. Access to drawings, at least in the form of reproductions in books and magazines,

Design study for a special drawing table viewed in plan. (Norman Diekman, designer)

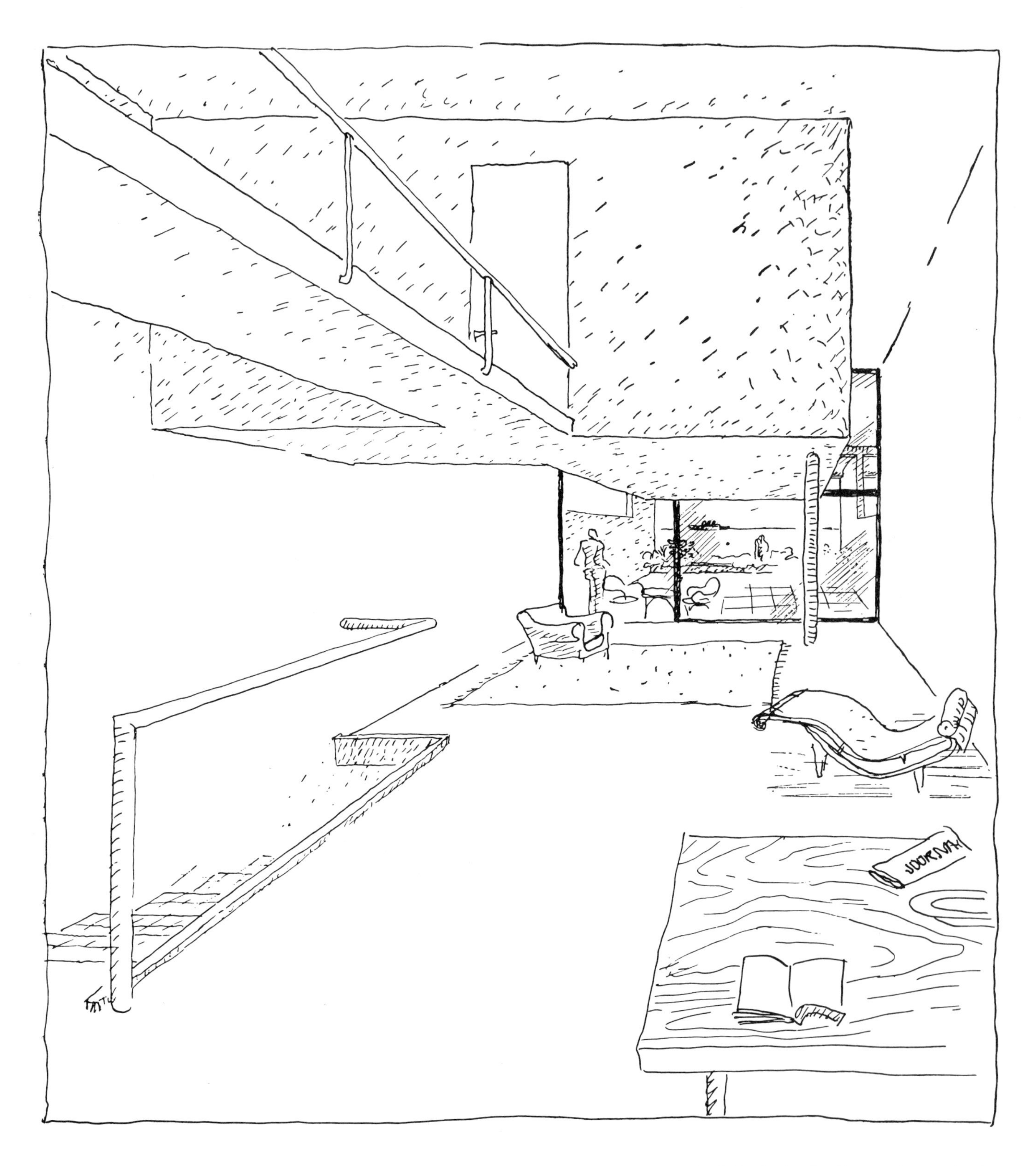

Le Corbusier habitually carried a notebook, various pens, and colored pencils. The special character of his pen-and-ink sketch is highly expressive of his unique design thinking.

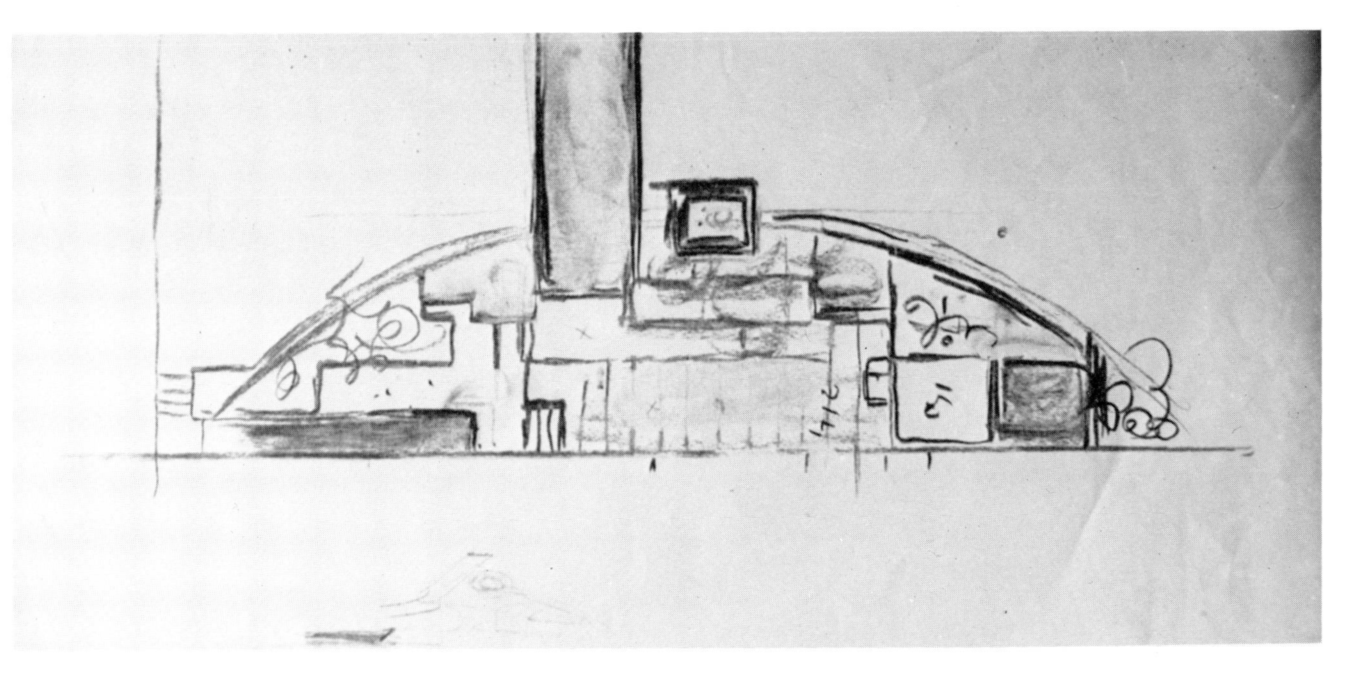

Carlo Scarpa's design study for the Exedra Garden of the Banca Popolare in Verona shows exuberance and mastery in the use of charcoal for sketching. (Photograph courtesy of Giuseppe Zambonini)

is easy and can be as lasting or as often repeated as may seem desirable.

Students of architecture and design, and working professionals in these fields in particular, can never hope to have as much direct experience of great work as they might want and need. Photographs are a weak substitute; they lack the sense of direct communication that is present in actual built works and often even more strongly present in the drawings that led to built work. The finished project tells us nothing about the *process* of design thinking that led to a completed project, while a sequence of sketches can make it possible to virtually relive such a process. For every completed work there are likely to be two or three that were never executed or were so changed in execution to become something different. One thinks of the Le Corbusier project for the Palace of the League of Nations or the Saarinen design for a Smithsonian Museum of Art—projects never built but with a lasting impact far beyond that of most actual structures.

Development of a truly personal vocabulary of sketching is not something that can happen in an instant. Students may learn from their teachers, but should also not hesitate to experiment with direct imitation of the style of one or more of the masters whose work is now available in near facsimile publication. The process of imitation does not lead to loss of individual expression; rather, since imitation is never total or totally successful, it becomes a basis on which personal style can grow and expand.

Le Corbusier must surely be one of the most imitated of masters. His limpid pen line drawings are deceptively simple, superficially easy to imitate, but actually astonishingly subtle in their unpretentious directness. We are fortunate to have access to a vast store of documentation in the now-published, many-volume sketchbooks. Carlo Scarpa's sketches tend to be more expressionistic and seem to be emotional in character—less literally informative and so more "conceptual," but still full of information, as comparison of sketches with built projects will demonstrate.

Among designers currently practicing, we find an increasing interest in all forms of drawings and in sketching in particular—along with an interest in exhibiting and publishing sketches that only a few years ago would never have been made or would perhaps have been discarded as meaningless away from the designer's drafting table. There may be some dangers hidden in the new interest in marketing and collecting architectural and design

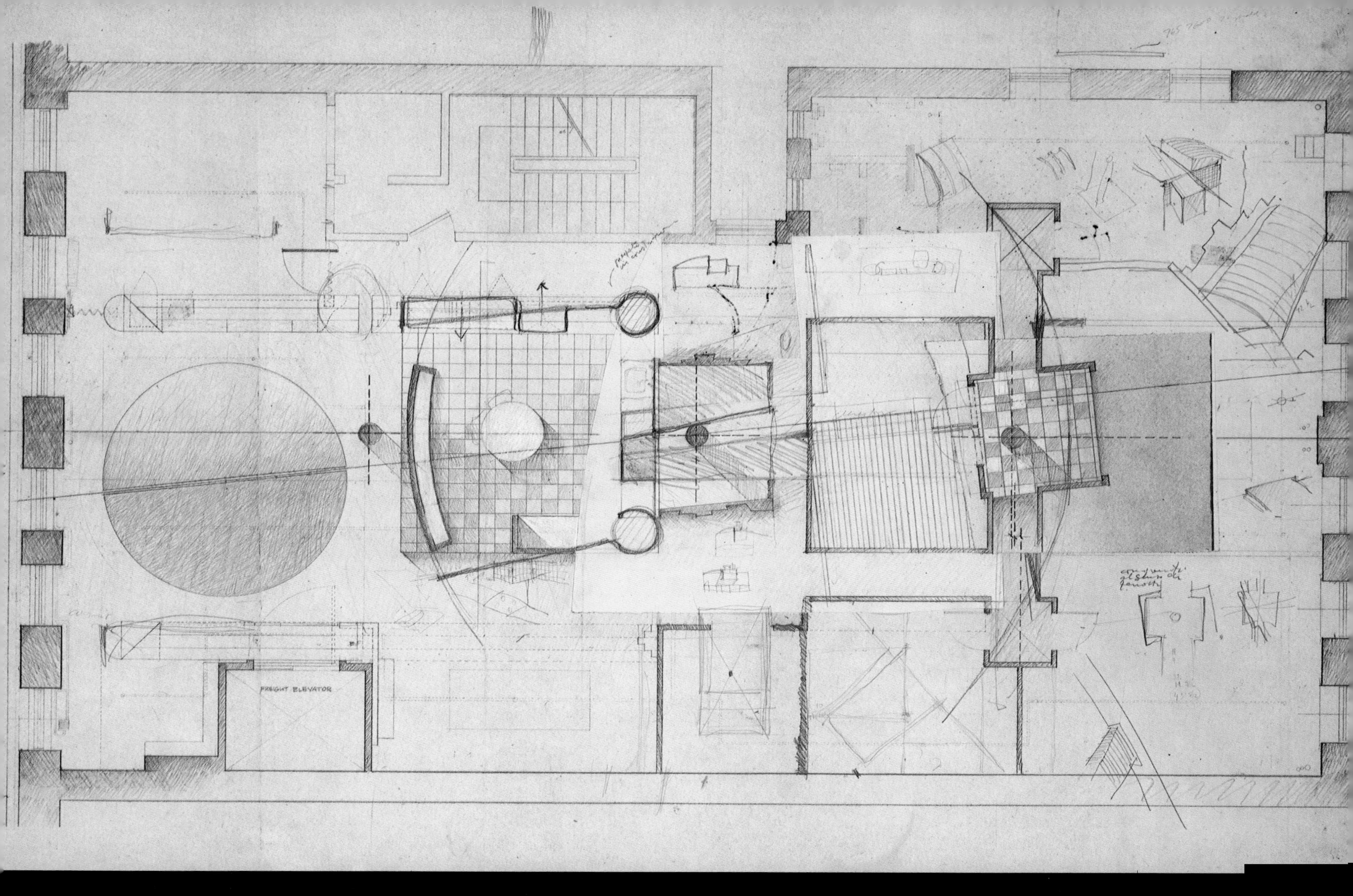
FREIGHT ELEVATOR

drawings. It may lead to a self-consciousness and preciousness where designers come to think of every sketch as a serious "work." Still, it is certainly bringing about access to material that is interesting and informative, sometimes beautiful in its own right, and always useful study material.

Thinking of the work of architects James Stirling, Carlo Scarpa, Mario Botta, or Michael Graves almost inevitably leads to recollection of drawings along with built projects. The drawings of Stirling and Graves suggest a line of descent from Le Corbusier while Scarpa's seem close in spirit to Frank Lloyd Wright; however, in each case there is an individual, personal style strong enough to make it possible to recognize the authorship of a sketch first seen without identification. All of these draftsmen seem to have grown out of the traditions of fine art expression.

In recent years interior design drawing has seemed to move away from expressive drawing toward, on the one hand, mere decoration accomplished through verbal instruction and purchase of artifacts and on the other hand to "space planning" of offices and commercial projects that suggest engineering in their mechanical production of impersonal spaces.

The Diekman project of pages 158–168 and Giuseppe Zambonini's drawings (pages 42–43) suggest other highly personal and individualistic styles in current use in the creative phases of developing projects.

Giuseppe Zambonini's color sketch for a New York loft continues a tradition extending from Palladio to Scarpa as a personal style of "drafted sketching."

Following pages: Detail of the preceding drawing. Note an overlay piece of paper on the right where a checkered floor is introduced—a use of collage suggesting the layering of "idea upon idea," which is very much a part of the designer's process.

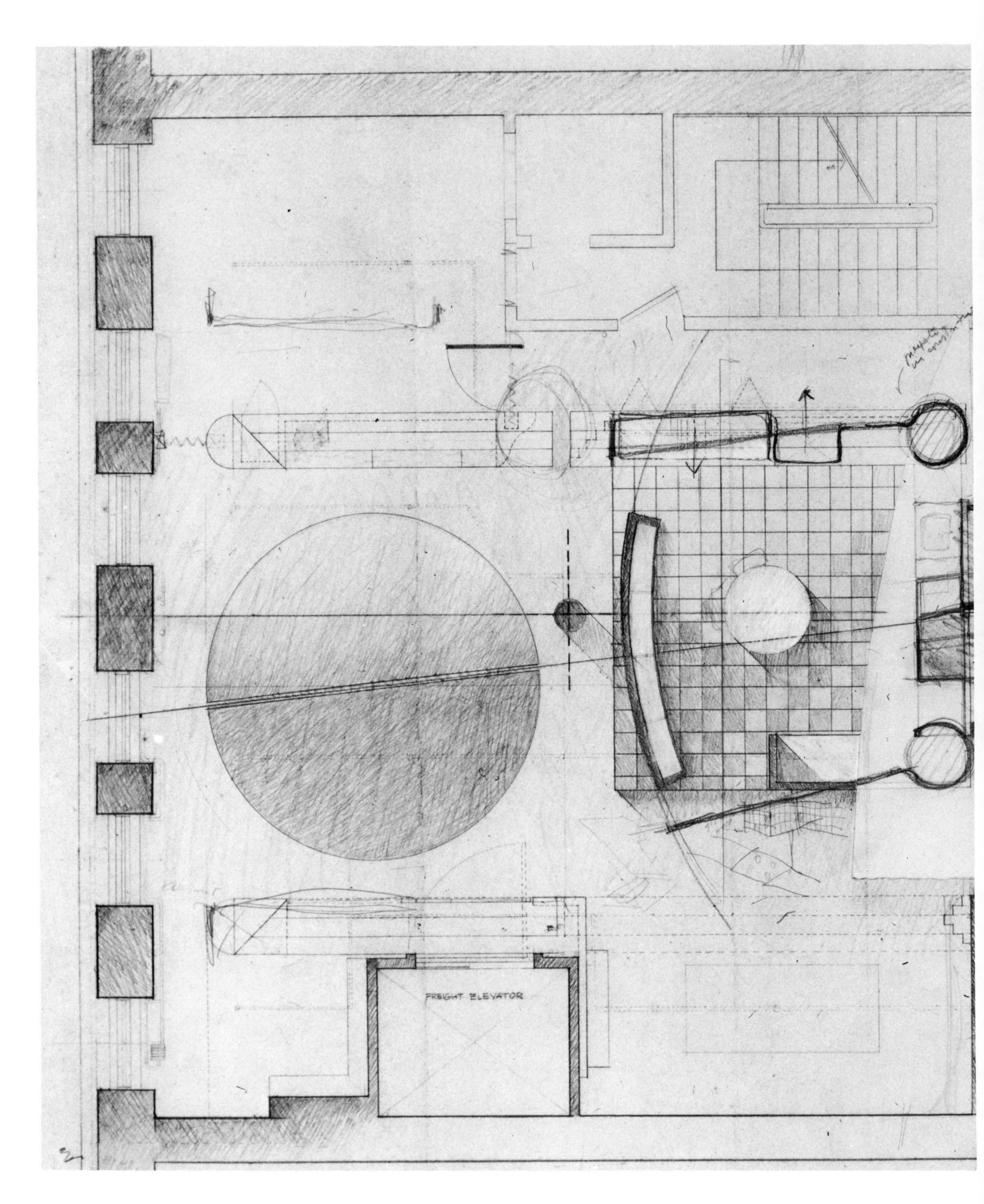
FREIGHT ELEVATOR

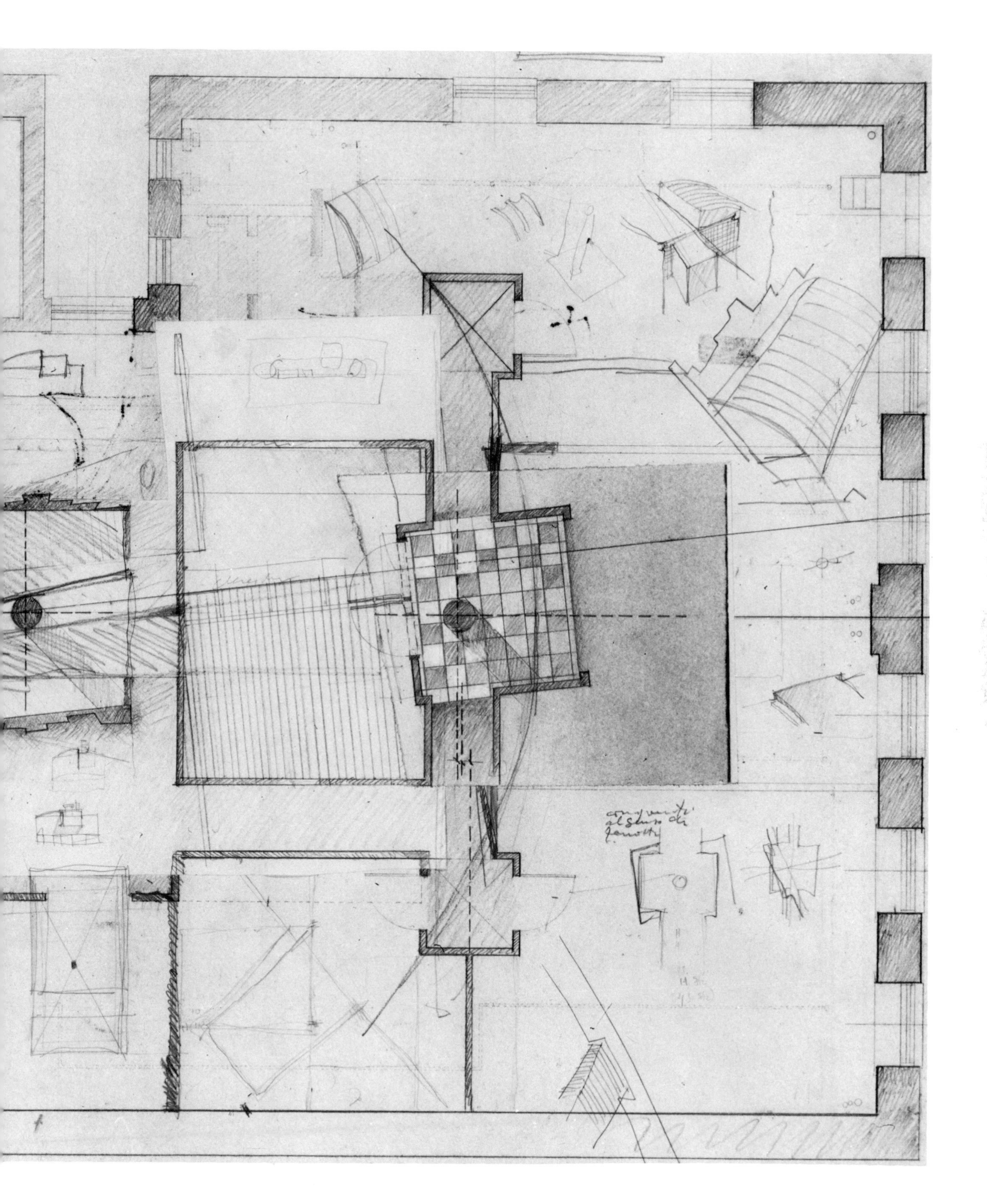

A Joseph Paul D'Urso house design—a flood of ideas with the pen seeming to function as a "brain-scanner," with the mind "walking through" the space, tracing its thoughts on yellow trace paper.

Norman Diekman's sketches of a daybed between columns. This is a refined drafting style, incorporating rapid sketch elements—a surprisingly fast and eloquent technique.

3

Concept Sketching

Any design project that is to go beyond the routine and ordinary must have a powerful, overriding idea, a central theme or, as we will call it here, a "concept." When a building, a space, a room is simply put together without thought, it may turn out to serve some utilitarian purpose and may even, with luck, be visually inoffensive, but it is hardly likely to be exciting and memorable. The buildings and spaces that stick in the memory and that turn out to have the kind of expressive character that justifies the term "a work of art" are almost without exception demonstrations of the realization of a concept which organizes every aspect of the project in relation to a central idea.

In a completed project, the original conceptual idea may not be instantly evident to any viewer. It may be abstract and subtle but still felt as a kind of purposeful quality that holds together the many details of which buildings and their interiors are made up. Critics of architecture and design students find themselves almost detectives in trying to search out and describe the concept that motivates a successful piece of work. For the designer going through the process of developing a new design, the finding of a strong and appropriate concept is a key to lifting a project out of the ordinary and making of it something exciting and important.

This process might be called, in ordinary conversation, "trying to find an idea." It is a necessary basic step in any serious creative work, whether it be writing, music, painting, or sculpture. In some fields the "idea" can always be expressed in words, but design ideas, although sometimes easy to verbalize, are often almost totally visual. Modern education puts so much emphasis on verbal skills that it is not always easy to accept the notion of a concept that cannot be described, but design concepts are often, even usually, of this sort. We all tend to equate thinking with words, but for the designer, thinking about form and space can be done best if words are put aside. This is what leads to the vital importance of concept sketching.

Exactly how a design concept develops in the mind is a matter still being explored by psychologists studying what is often called "creativity." However a design concept comes about, it is a universal designer's experience that, by thinking about a design problem and mulling over the requirements to be satisfied within the limitations that exist, ideas come to mind that suggest a route to problem solutions. Such ideas are not usually primarily verbal; rather, they take the form of images, but images not very clearly or completely formed. They are often, in fact, not images of specific "things," but of more abstract forms and relationships. They might be called "diagrammatic" ideas. Given some such ideas, the designer needs to institute a process of review and self-criticism aimed at evaluating, choosing, and developing an idea into something of a more specific nature that can, ultimately, be turned into a constructed reality.

Human memory presents problems in trying to hold such conceptual ideas, in presenting alternatives for comparison, and in going back to an earlier idea that may have been put aside. All of these problems—common experiences of the design process—lead to the inevitable conclusion that developing a concept calls for drawing and, in early creatives phases, sketching. Almost by definition, sketching is quick.

First design concepts are quickly expressed in felt-tip pen and Prismacolor pencil on cream tracing paper. (Norman Diekman, designer)

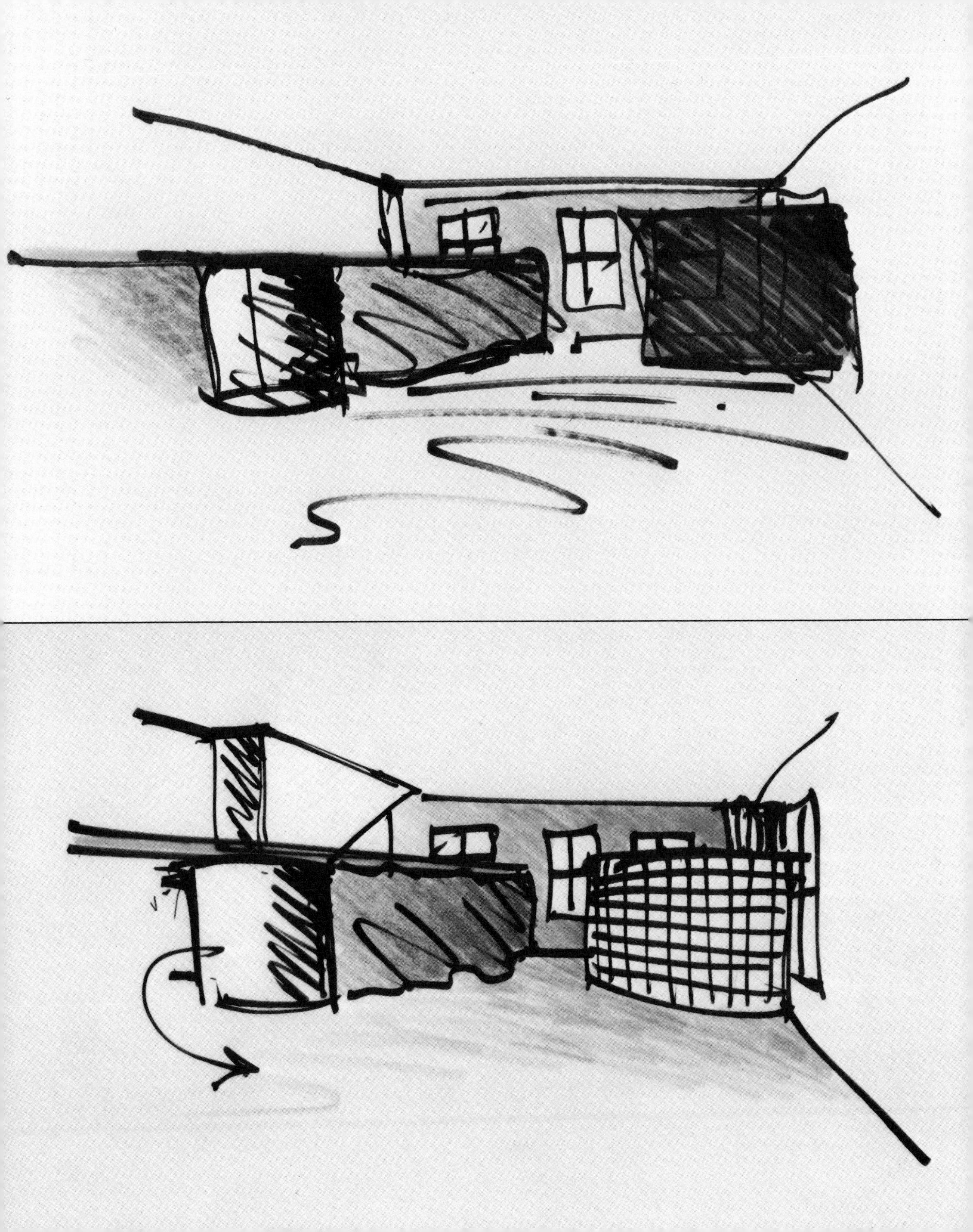

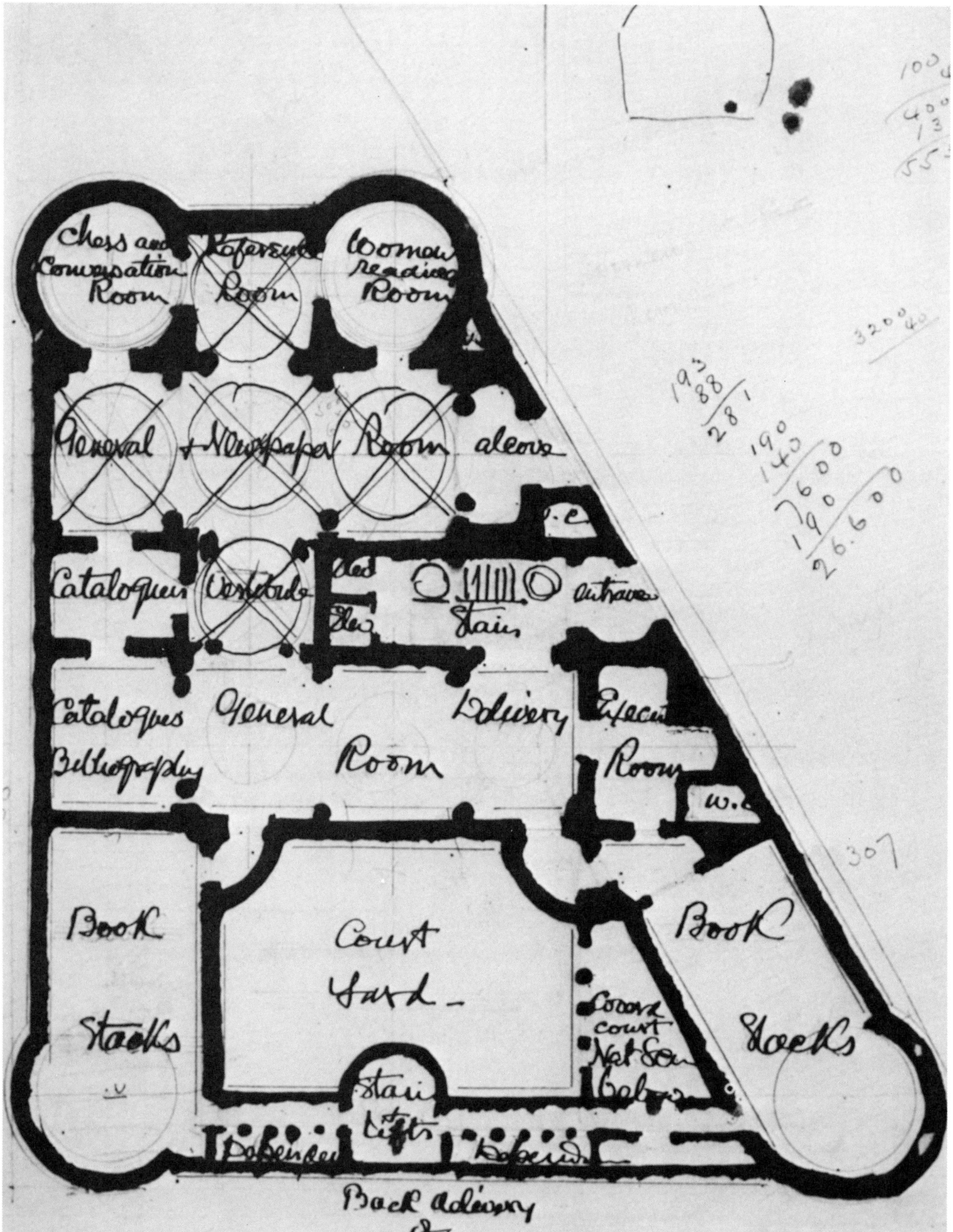

Chess and Conversation Room

Reference Room

Woman reading Room

General + Newspaper Room alcove

W.C.

Catalogues Vestibule

Elev

Stairs

entrance

Catalogues Bibliography

General Delivery Room

Executive Room

W.C.

Book Stacks

Court Yard

Book Stacks

Covered court

Stair Lifts

Back delivery

193
88
281

190
140

7600
1900
26600

3200
40

307

It commits ideas to paper with enough rapidity to keep up with, or at least not fall too far behind, the process of thought. Sketching can also be drawing that is "rough," not overly specific, and even vague. In the development of a concept, such lack of specificity can be very helpful in avoiding the inhibiting nature of making a more careful and finished drawing. The commitment of time and effort involved in a careful drawing leads to hesitation about even beginning until ideas are fully formed and, once something is on paper, tends to make change and development less attractive than they need to be in early creative stages.

Sketching is a matter of putting down on paper, as quickly and easily as possible, whatever conceptual ideas may come to mind, however unformed or abstract they may be. Often done in a moment, the sketch is suddenly *there*—a reality that can be looked at, discarded or put aside, or evaluated and developed. Alternatives can be spread out for comparison, and discarded ideas can be brought back for reconsideration or incorporation into the next stages of progress. Generally speaking, concept sketches are intended only for the eyes of the designer and, possibly, a trusted associate or critic. They need not be fully explainable in words, although in order to have value they must be full of meaning. The meaning can be of a visual sort, however, that will only take on the kinds of meaning that can be converted into words through further development.

Concept sketches can appear on almost any material; the proverbial back of an envelope is not unusual, while 3 × 5 index cards, always at hand in a pocket, are routine practice with some designers. Short rolls of yellow trace are the most usual material at the drawing board, while soft pencil is most often the medium. Black ink and pen are also common, although felt-tip pens are tending to take over because of their undeniable convenience. Charcoal is a classic medium, satisfying because it enables one to put down a full range of gray tones and to produce erasures and whites easily with a (kneaded) charcoal eraser. Charcoal is messy and produces a sketch that is easy to smear unless handled with care or laboriously sprayed with fixative.

Concept sketches can put down ideas in any of the familiar formats of design drawing: plan, elevation, perspective, isometric or axonometric, section or sectional perspective, or almost any combination of these forms. In fact, a concept sketch may not even follow any of these forms. It might be a diagram of movement through space or even an indication of sequential experience in units of time. Since the concept sketch speaks only to the designer, any visual language is acceptable as long as it has meaning to the person using it. However wide this range of possibilities, probably the vast majority of concept sketches are plans. Carlo Scarpa's plan (pages 52–53) is a fine example. The habit of starting with the plan and thinking in plan is so firmly ingrained in the education and practice of architects and interior designers that this tends to seem the natural starting point.

In Michael Kalil's concept sketch (pages 54–57) we see in plan the germ of a guiding idea for a residential project. We can see at once that the elements of the project are to be organized by and tied together with a lengthwise "spine," a central band to which the parts relate as the parts of a vertebrate creature relate to the backbone. The drawing does not tell us, and so it is only known to the designer (unless he tells us) that this central spine is to be a channel of water that will dominate the project conceptually, suggesting the way in which fountains and running water dominate the courts of the Alhambra. The water spine leads at one end to a round element that turns out to be, appropriately, a shower! On pages 56–57 we find the same designer developing the project in sketches, still conceptual rather than illustrative, in perspective.

Conceptual sketching is most often part of the early development of a design project, but it is not always confined to this phase of a project. Changes and revisions that come later, even while a project is actually in the construction phase, can involve concept also, at least in details. The Zambonini sketches on pages 58–59 were developed on a job in progress, with the sketching taking place within the actual space under construction.

Concept sketches are not always and inevitably abstract and general in nature. They can also be quite specific in situations where the concept itself is specified and developed from the first. The sketch by Norman Diekman on page 60 shows a conceptual proposal for the entrance to a display of art fabrics at a local museum. The Sheila Hicks fabric sculpture illustrated on page 61 was the inspiration for a precise realization of the concept drawing. Concepts can move in stages from existence in the designer's mind to sketch expression in space to actual realization.

Bold strokes block out a library plan by H. H. Richardson. (Courtesy Houghton Library, Harvard University, Cambridge, Massachusetts)

Carlo Scarpa combines drafting and sketching in an encompassing technique covering the entire surface of the paper. This drawing, a plan for a 1962 Venice Biennale Pavilion, may have been made over months of the project's development. (Courtesy Giuseppe Zambonini)

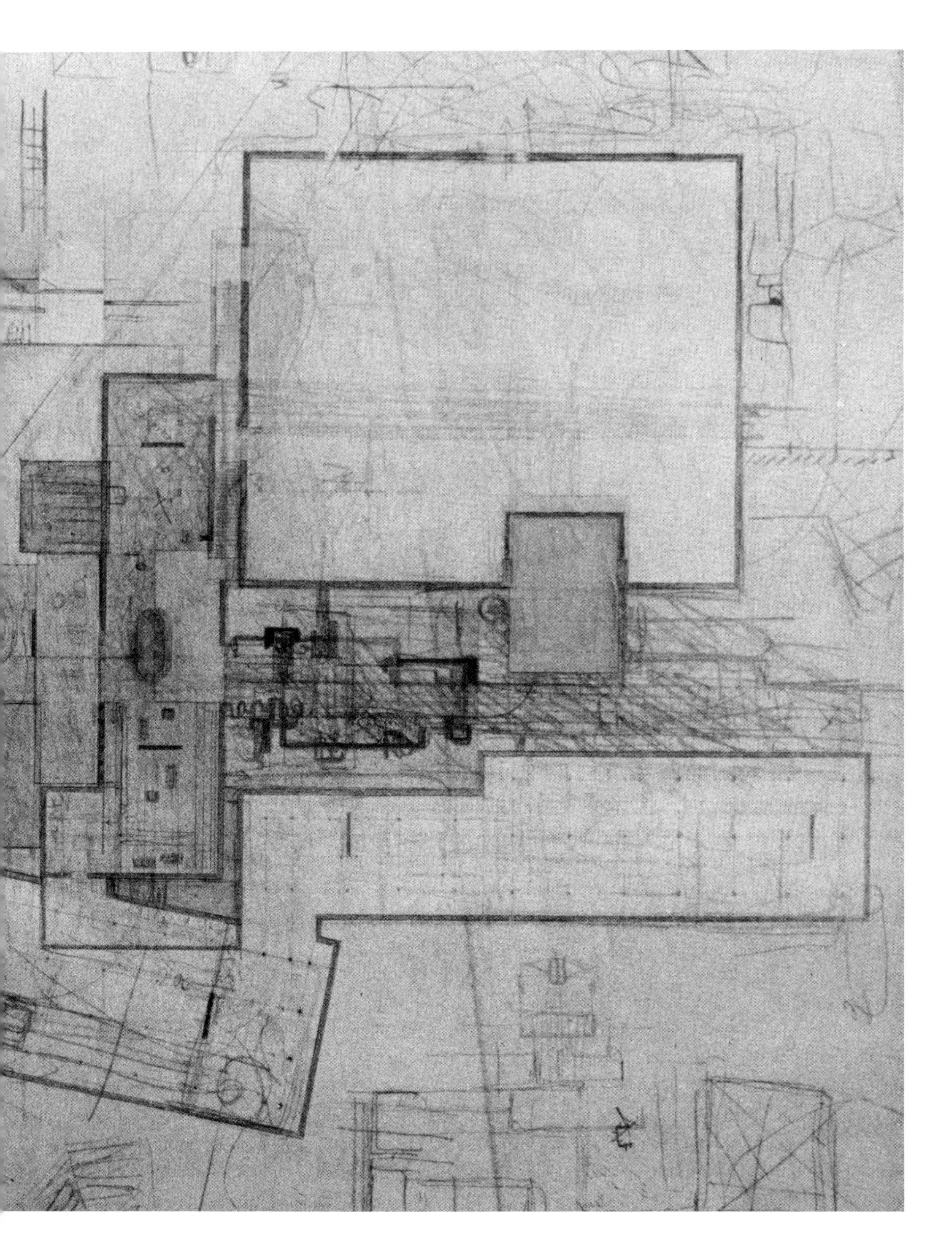

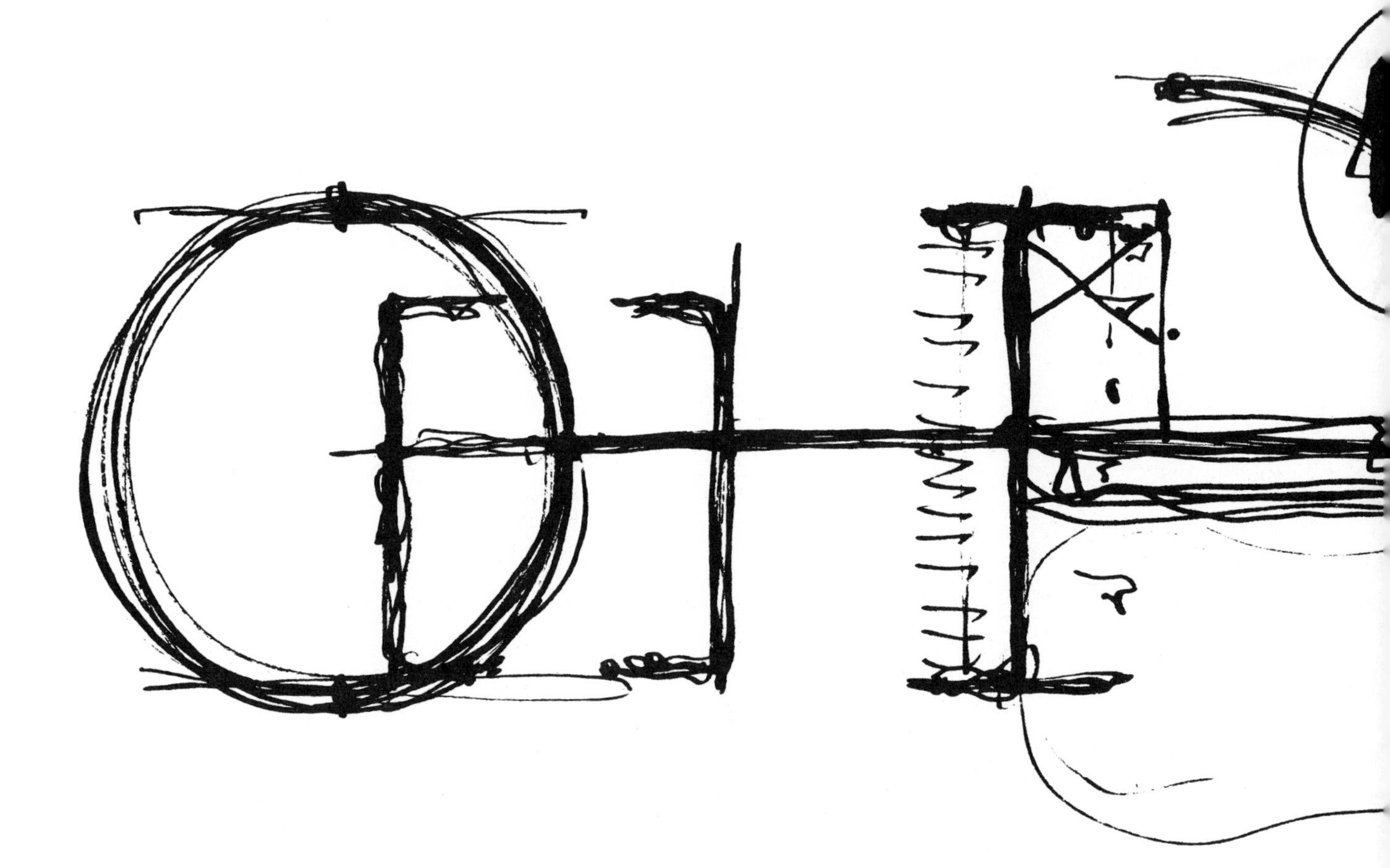

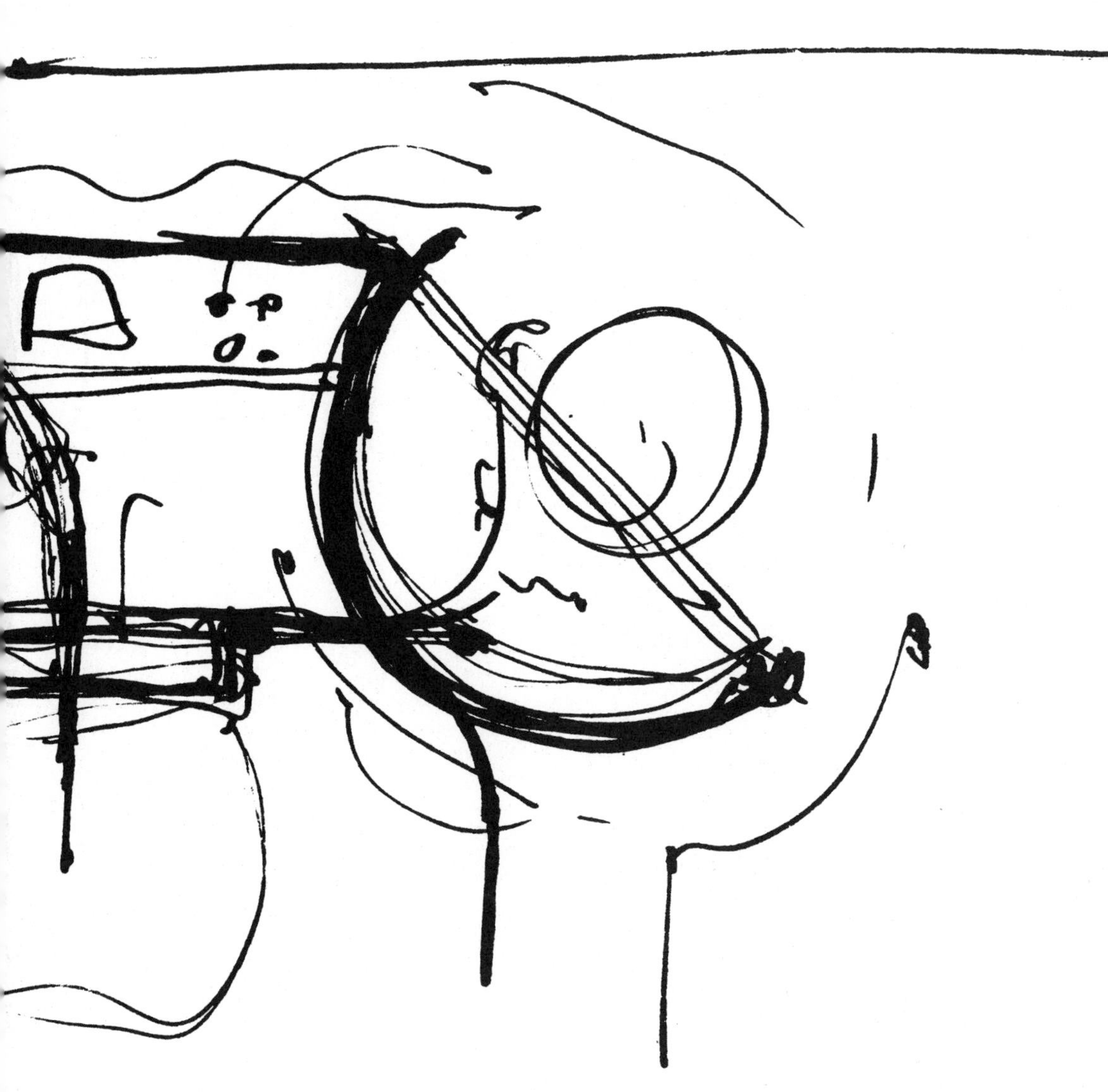

The exuberant thinking of Michael Kalil in plan and perspective sketches dealing with the theme of water flow in relation to a kitchen and bath grouping.

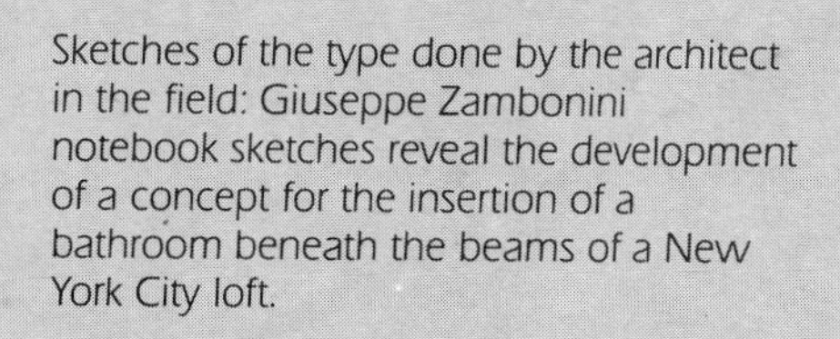

Sketches of the type done by the architect in the field: Giuseppe Zambonini notebook sketches reveal the development of a concept for the insertion of a bathroom beneath the beams of a New York City loft.

The Sheila Hicks work shown above provided the inspiration for incorporation into the sketch at left showing the sculpture as a key motif at the entrance to an exhibit area. (Norman Diekman, designer)

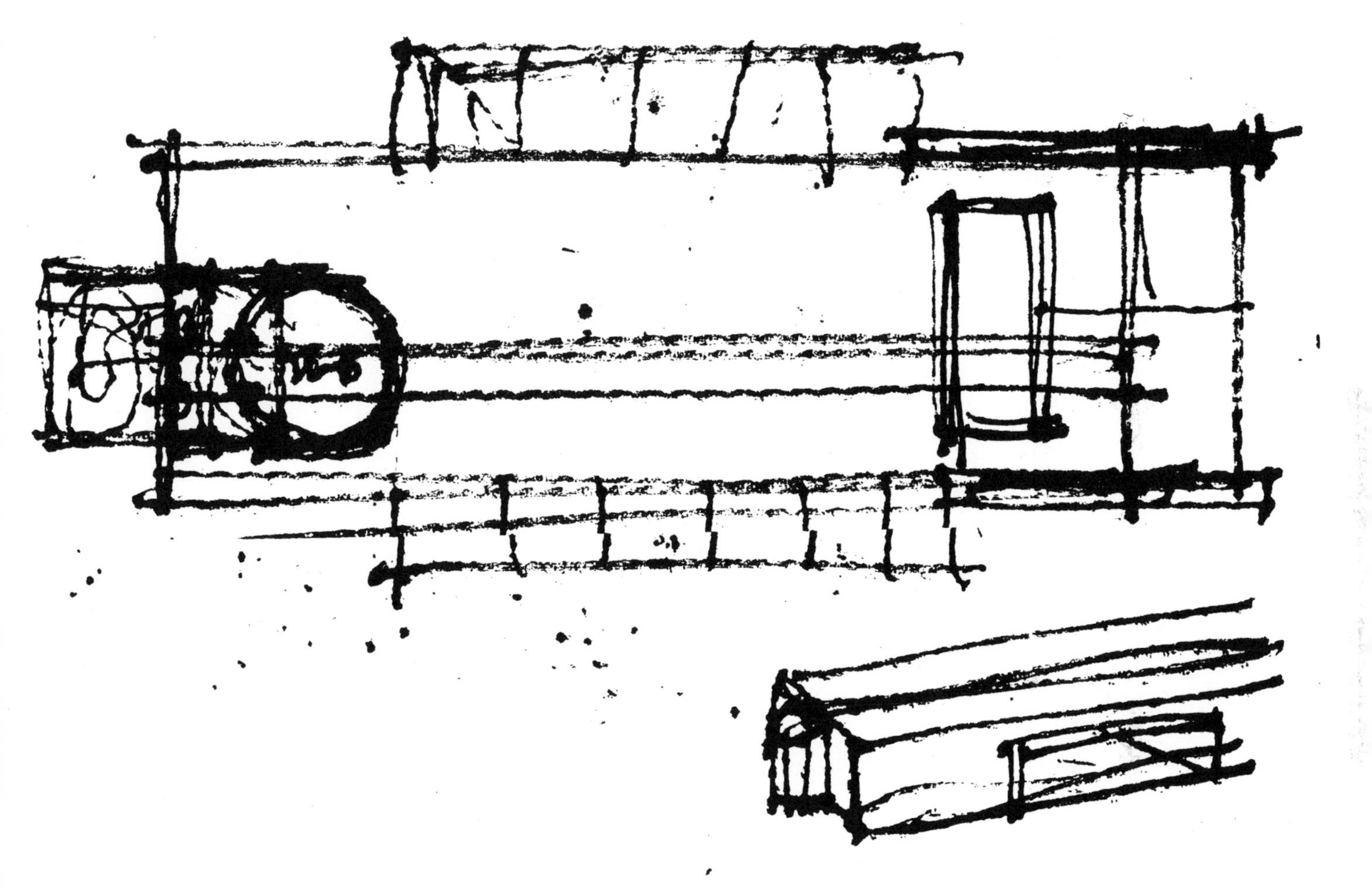

The essence of concept sketching is capturing random ideas as they surface in early phases of design study. This sheet (left) exposes such a flow of ideas: The table forms that surface here are the beginnings of the developed table drawing illustrated at the beginning of Chapter 2.

A first idea plan sketch for a design studio is shown above. A connecting service spine links kitchen and bath at opposite ends. Skylit, greenhouse spaces are indicated by the bands of squares above and below. (Norman Diekman, designer)

4

Design Process

Between the development of design concepts and readiness for presentation to a client, there intervenes the main body of design work—the process in which concepts are filled out in detail and with specificity that bridges the distance from first idea to developed design. This process is a somewhat private dialogue that takes place in the mind of the designer and, most important of all, on paper. The process drawings are sketches—often dozens, even hundreds of sketches. Such sketches are not directed at an audience, but are simply a means for furthering design thinking by making visible the designer's thoughts. Colleagues who work together closely may find such sketches a useful aid in collaboration, but as often as not the process sketch may be mysterious or confusing to anyone except the person who has made it.

An effort to understand design thinking in general, or the design thinking of a particular designer, can be greatly aided by a review of process sketches, laid out in sequence. Each gives a glimpse of a stage of thought, often with sketch changes and overlays acting almost like a moving picture following steps of design thinking as they take place in a time sequence. The viewer must, as often as not, make some creative effort to understand what is taking place, but this is an effort that is in itself an excellent way of studying design. The beginner's fantasy that the skillful designer arrives at a complete "solution" in one stroke gives way to a realization that all design involves a step-by-step effort in which self-criticism leads to a flow of changes and improvements until resolution of problems finally leads to the end product that can be seriously considered for execution.

Process sketches are generally done with no particular thought for aesthetic impact, yet often they are quite beautiful—sometimes in the manner of a realistic, impressionistic drawing, sometimes in a more abstract way. Plan sketches, in particular, are almost inevitably abstract, but there seems to be validity in the idea, developed in the Paris Beaux Arts tradition, that sound planning will create beautiful abstract pattern. If this is true, a plan that looks ugly represents a scheme that will not work well. Striving for aesthetically pleasing abstract imagery in plan is also a way of striving for practical excellence in the built project.

To illustrate this process, four examples are shown here. Each is a different kind of project, and three different designers are represented. In each case, following the sketches laid out in sequence is a way of following the thinking of the designer through the crucial developmental stages of the project in question.

A House in the Hudson River Valley

Harry Wenning, AIA, architect
Norman Diekman, interior designer

This is an architect-designed house, still in the planning stage when the interior designer was retained. There was still considerable flexibility in planning decisions that could be incorporated into the architect's construction drawings. The plan sketches of pages 65–71 deal with the key first-floor areas, entrance, living and dining spaces, and the piano alcove that was a special requirement of the music-loving client. In the detailed sketch (page 67, bottom), a corner area is under study; the forms of the double pitch roof as they affect the interior are the issues being worked over.

Layer upon layer of sketched ideas is the essence of the design process.

A quick overlay plan sketch lets us follow the development of planning ideas in relation to the client's special needs. The large plan of pages 68–69 was developed as a tracing paper overlay over the architect's construction plan. In it, arrows appear suggesting directions of movement at the entrance and into the living spaces. Other arrows are reminders of the directions of window views—for example, views from and over the piano outward—which are a special feature of the house, exploited as fully as possible in the interior planning. A second version of the living area plan appears in the sketch plan at right.

The kitchen and bath sketches of pages 70–72 were made during a meeting with the client. The design ideas and drawings all developed as conversation about the project was taking place.

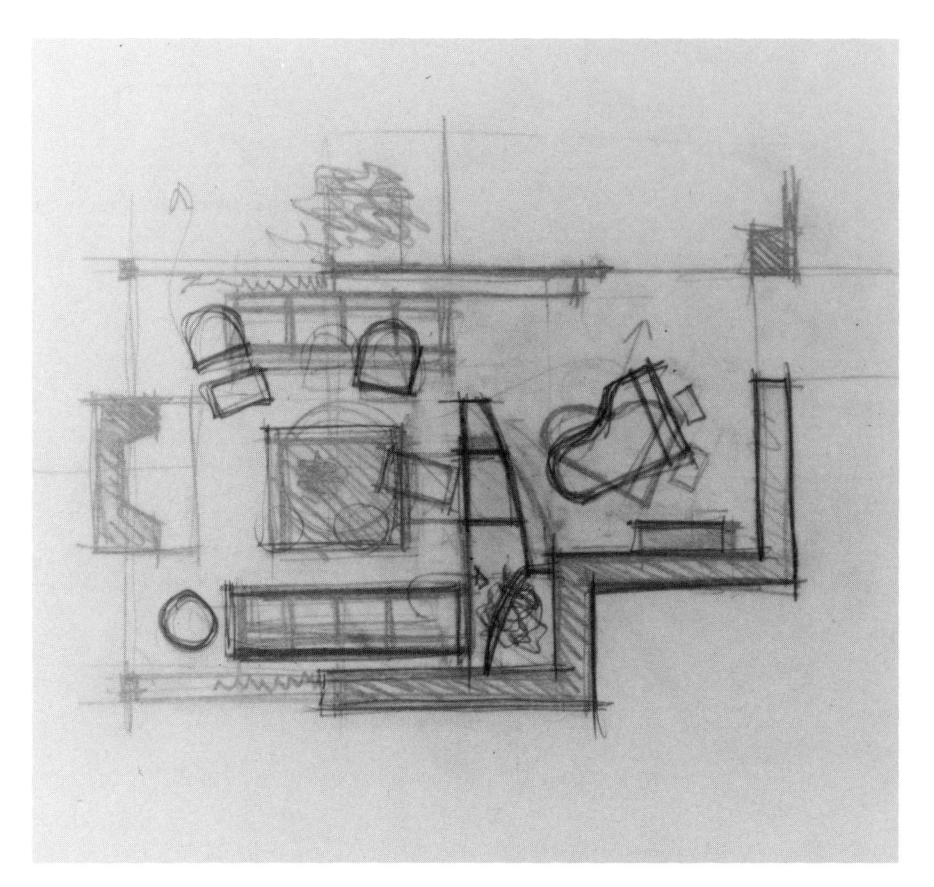

Plan sketching on cream tracing paper (above) allows movement of architectural elements and furniture before fixing final design decisions. (All sketches on pages 65–75 by Norman Diekman, designer)

In the plan at the top of page 67, a no. 314 soft-pencil sketch on cream tracing paper explores ideas for seating around a fireplace. The sketch below translates the same grouping into perspective.

Following pages show further development of the previous sketches with extension into the adjacent entry-hall area and onto the outdoor paved area.

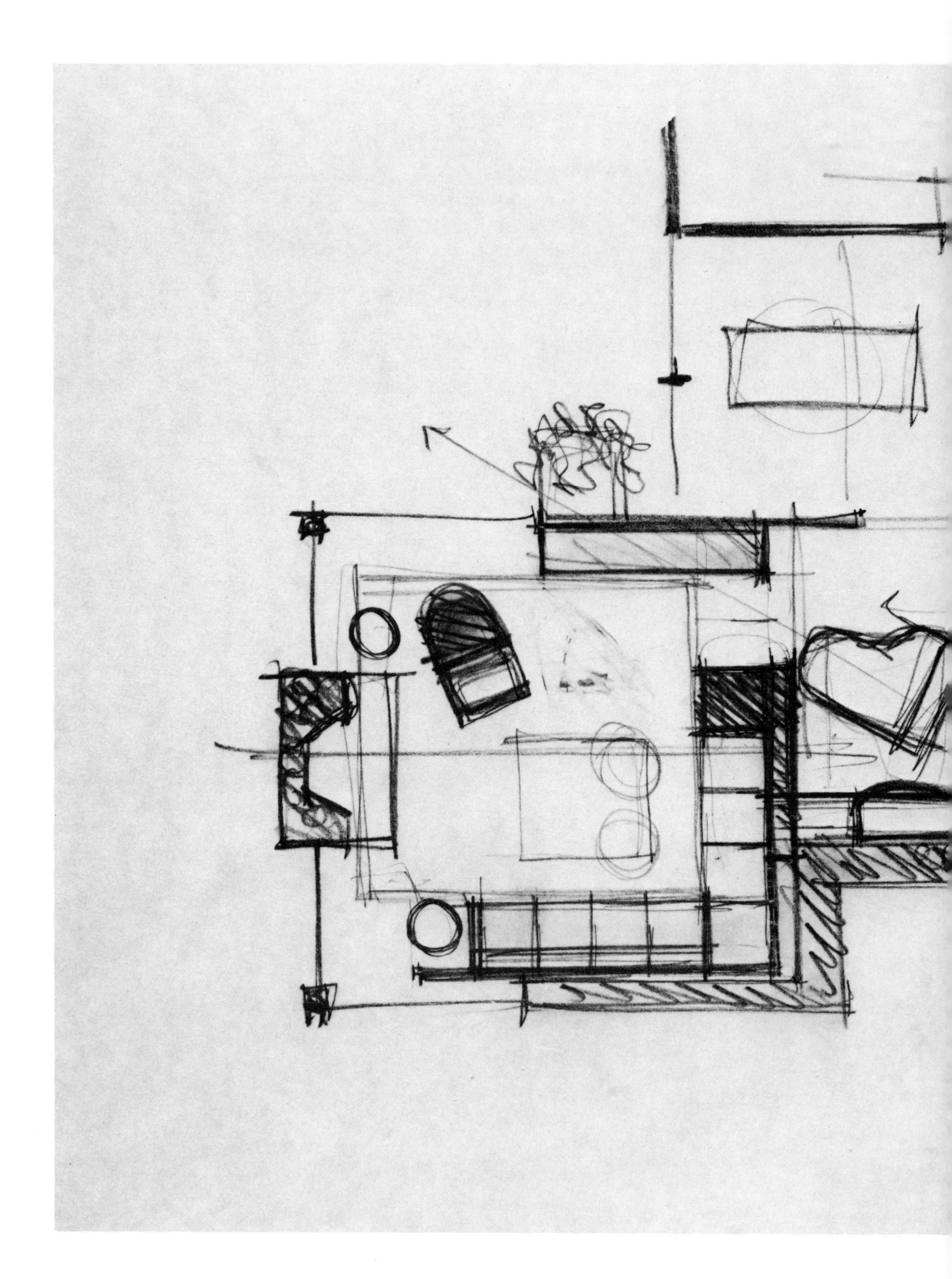

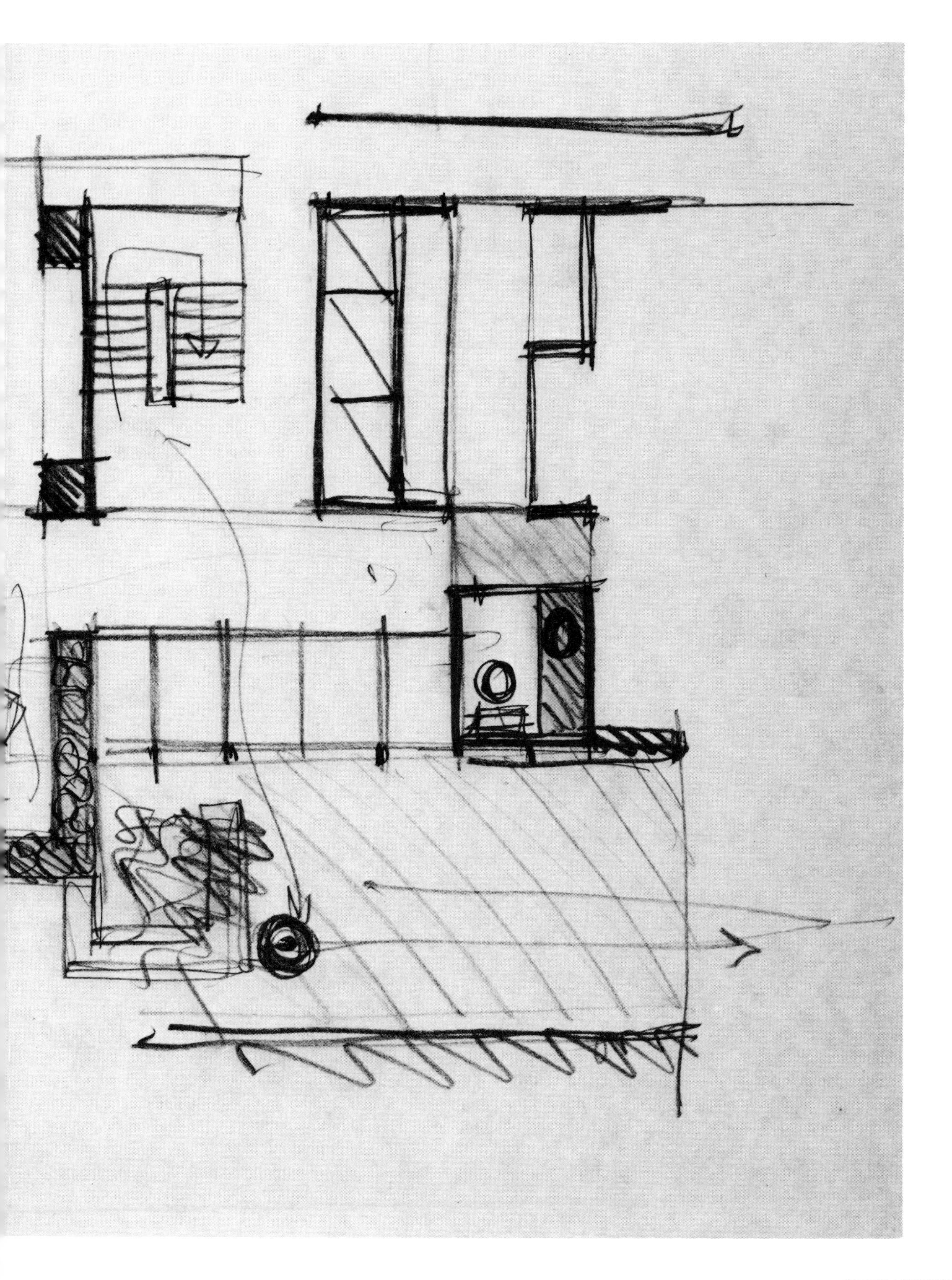

The previous plan is now developed into a more precise rendered sketch with colored pencils on ozalid paper used to show architectural materials combined with furniture possibilities. This is a transitional step between design sketch and a final presentation plan.

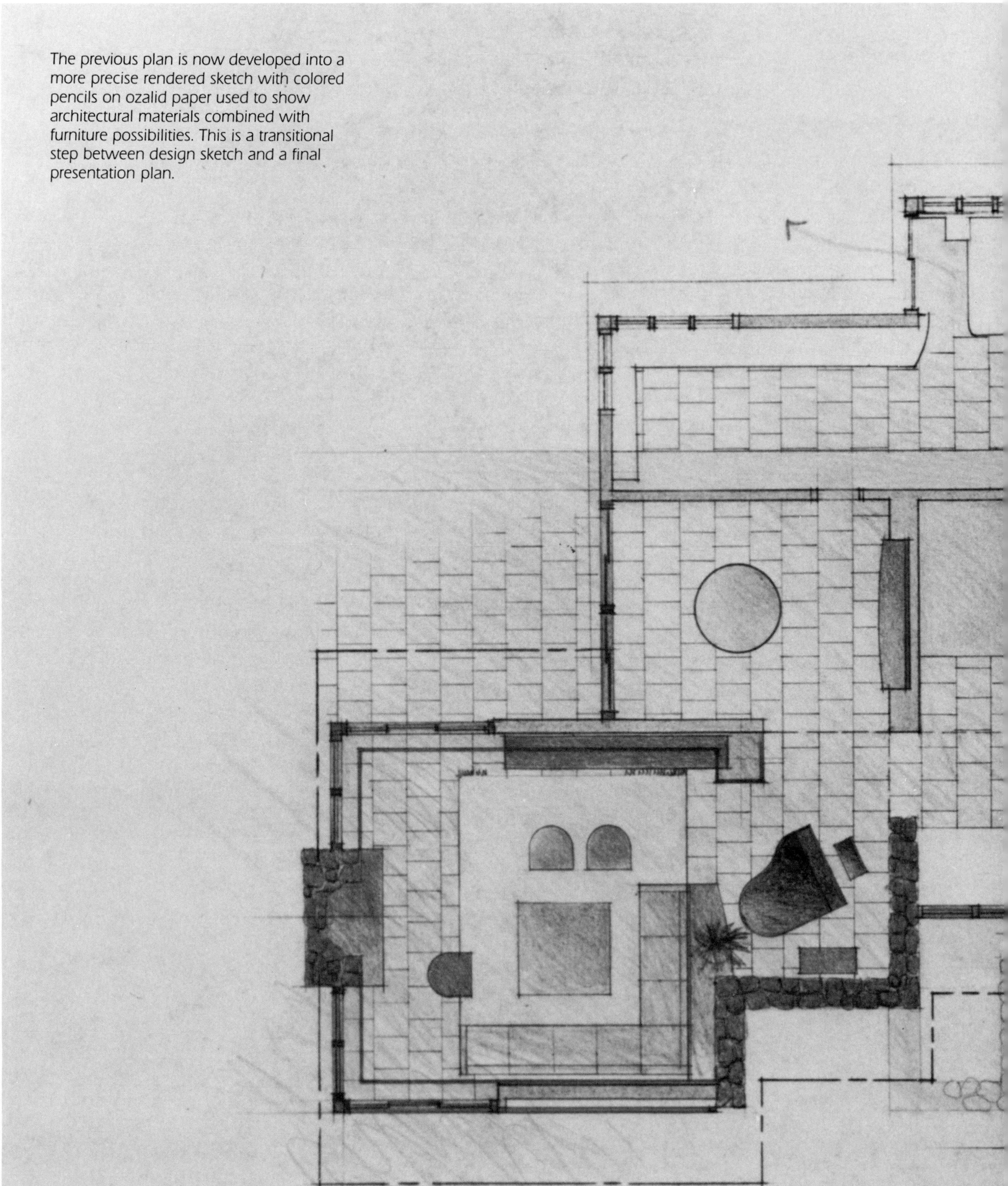

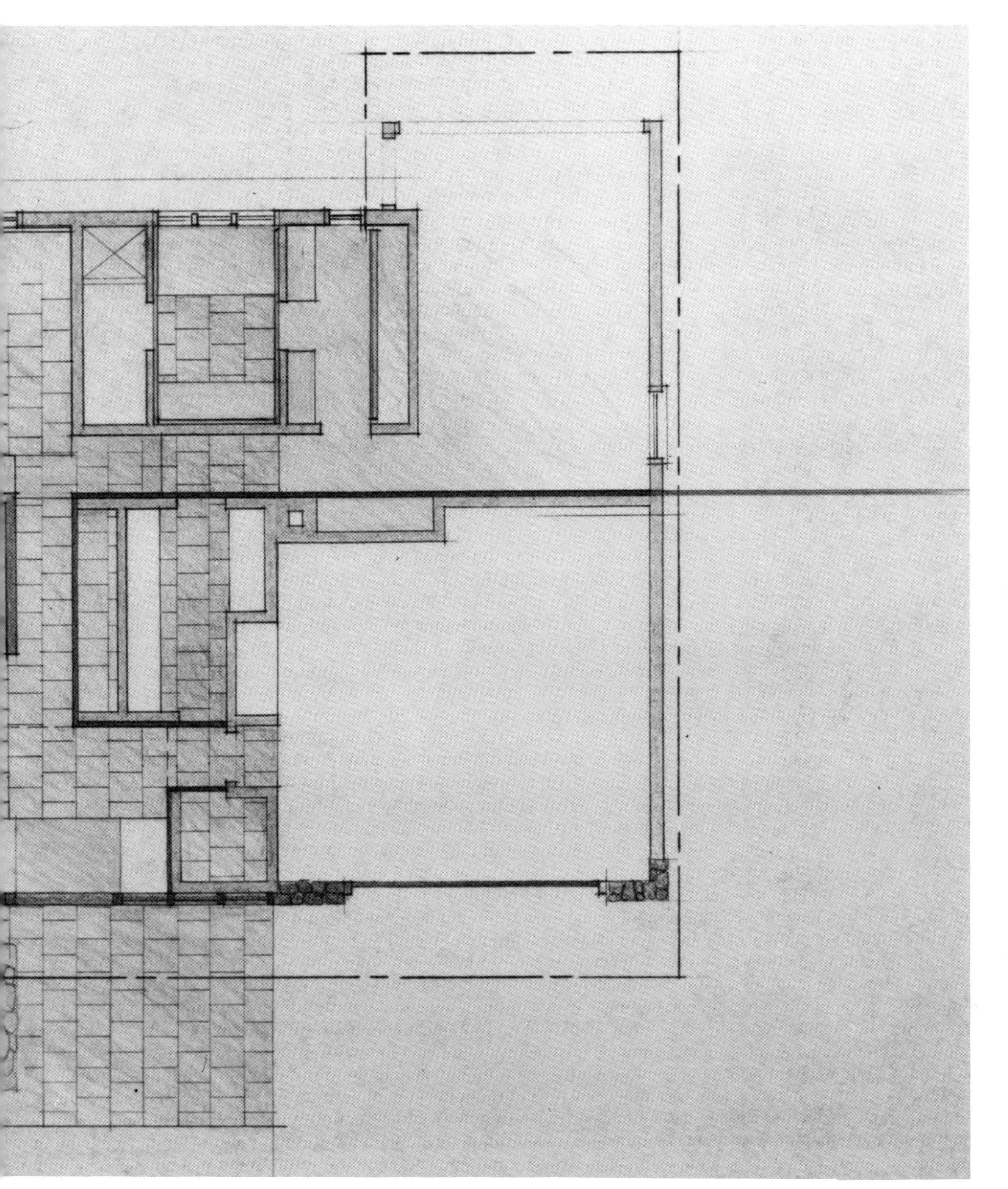

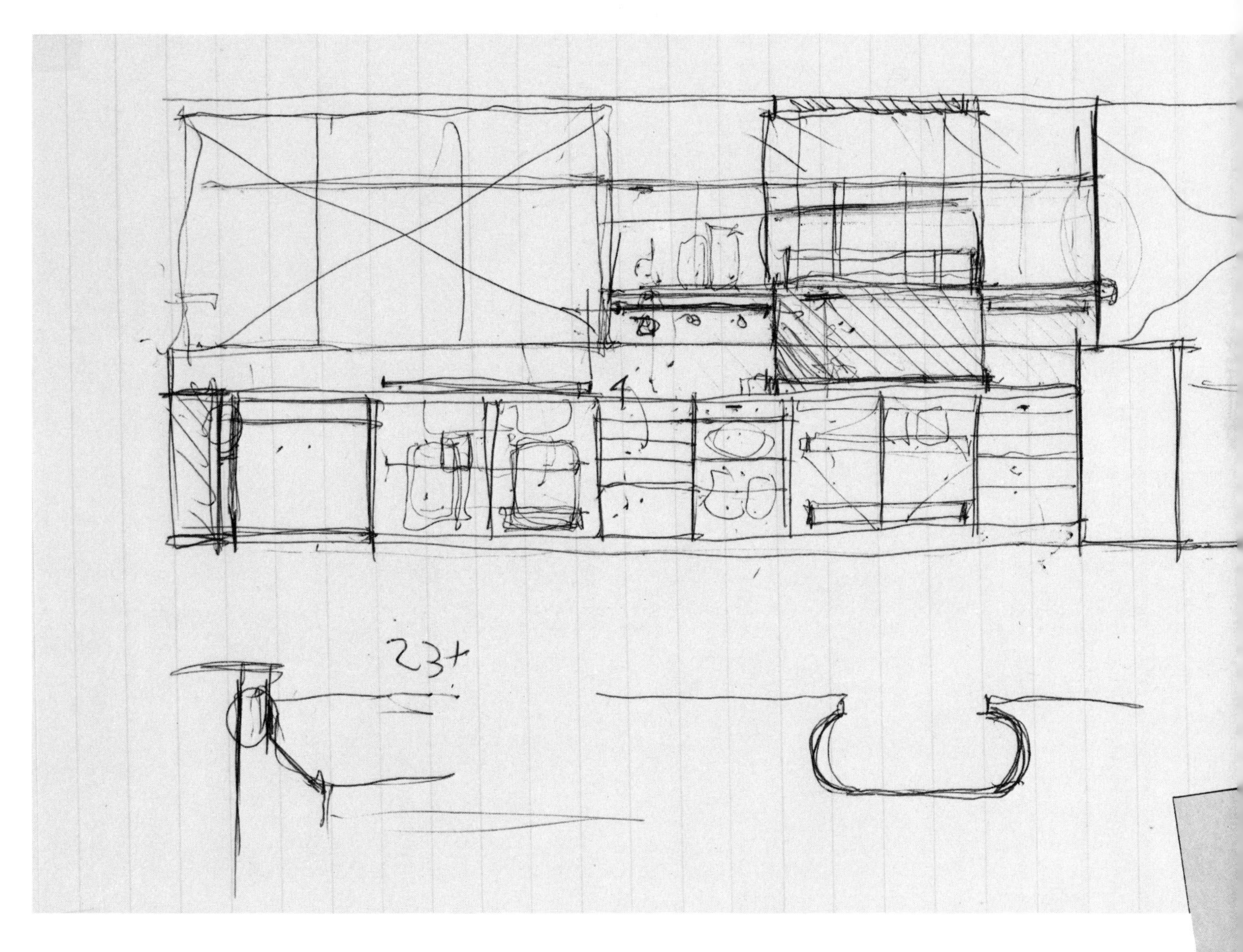

Sketches show the developing kitchen design made during an on-site meeting with the client. The drawing is on a ruled pad, drawn with a Faber Castell Uni-Ball pen. The practical designer is always equipped with some suitable pens and pencils, ready to illustrate any point of discussion with an appropriate sketch.

Sketch of kitchen detail resolved upon returning to design studio. No. 314 soft pencil and Prismacolor on cream tracing paper.

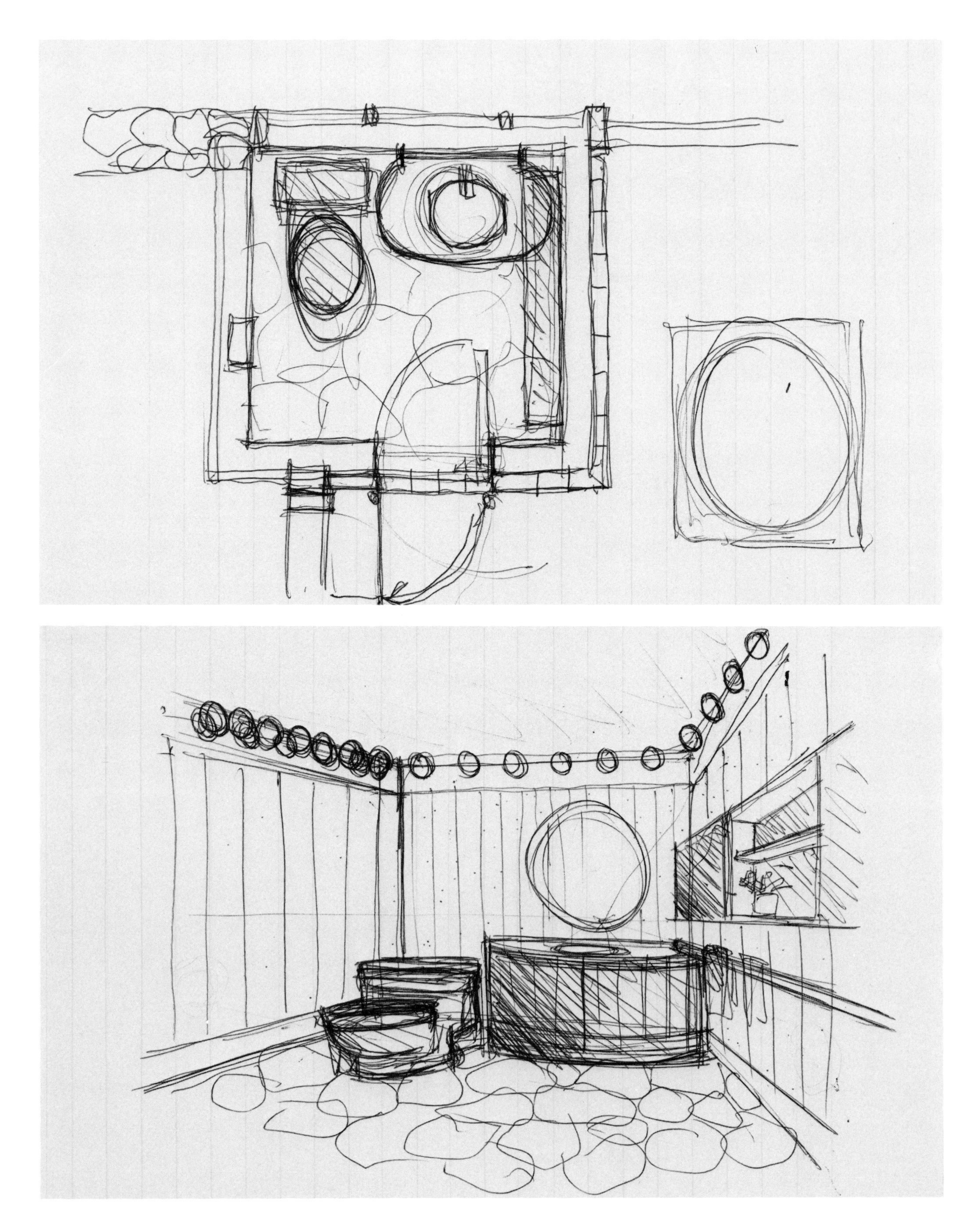

More sketches made during the meeting. Here the subject is the lavatory off the entrance hall. The fine pen line, reminiscent of Le Corbusier's often-illustrated technique, allows the capture of spontaneous ideas for later refinement at the studio.

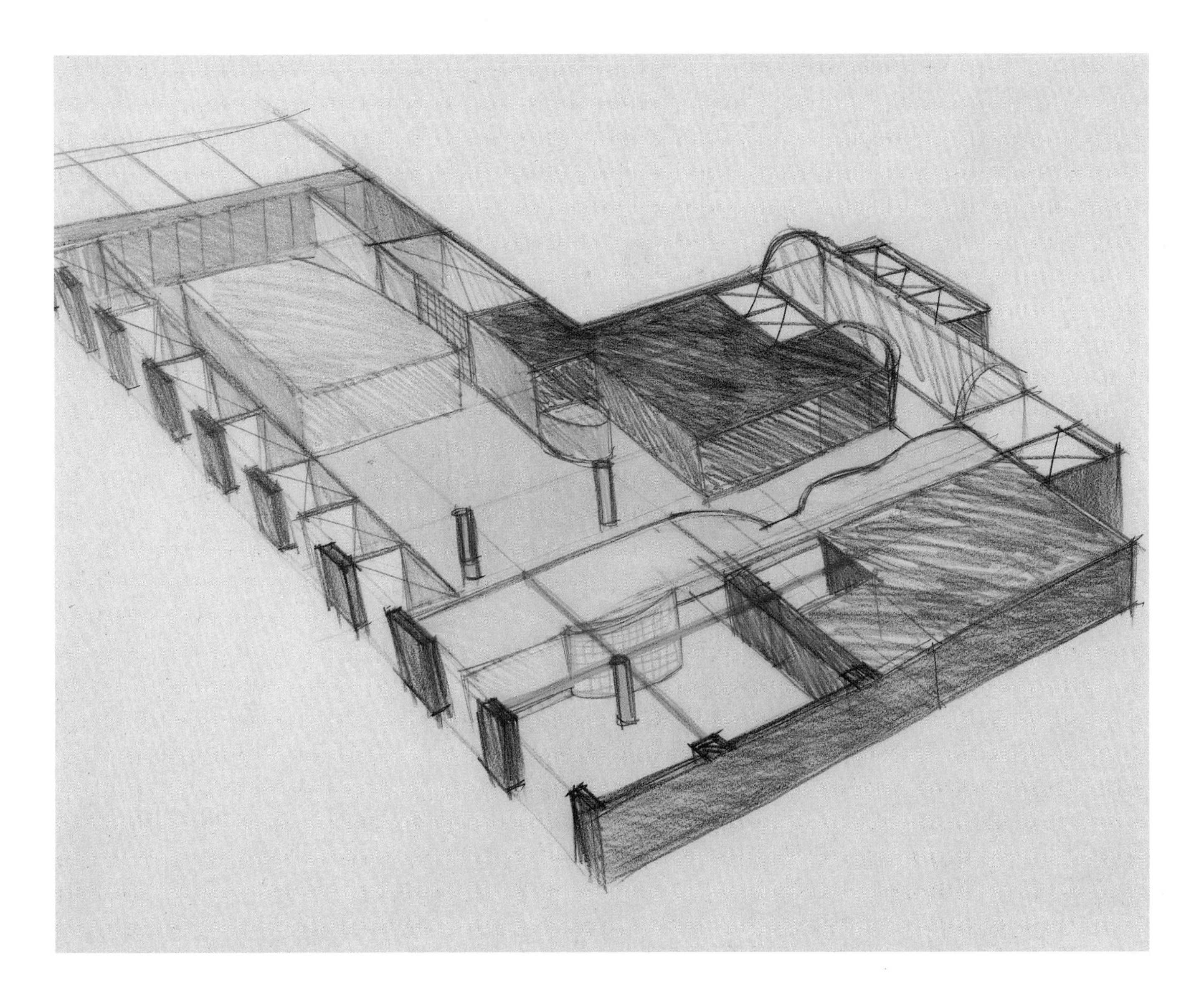

Offices for Brickel Associates Inc., New York

Norman Diekman, interior designer

An office space for a major manufacturer and distributor of modern furniture is seen here in development. The space is in a typical older high-rise office building. Without requiring any detailed description, it is possible to follow the sequential steps from developed concept to design process plan into a bird's-eye perspective that moves toward the kind of drawing that will be developed for client presentation, a drawing which shows the space in a model-like fashion that makes spatial relationships clear and that gives a sense of the height dimension in relation to plan layout.

First concept sketches for another project by Norman Diekman (no. 314 pencil on cream trace) capture basic ideas for a wood-paneled executive office. The entire project as seen through the bird's-eye perspective resembles a scale model. The immediate foreground space (closest to the viewer) was later studied in detail, leading to the presentation sketch of the following pages.

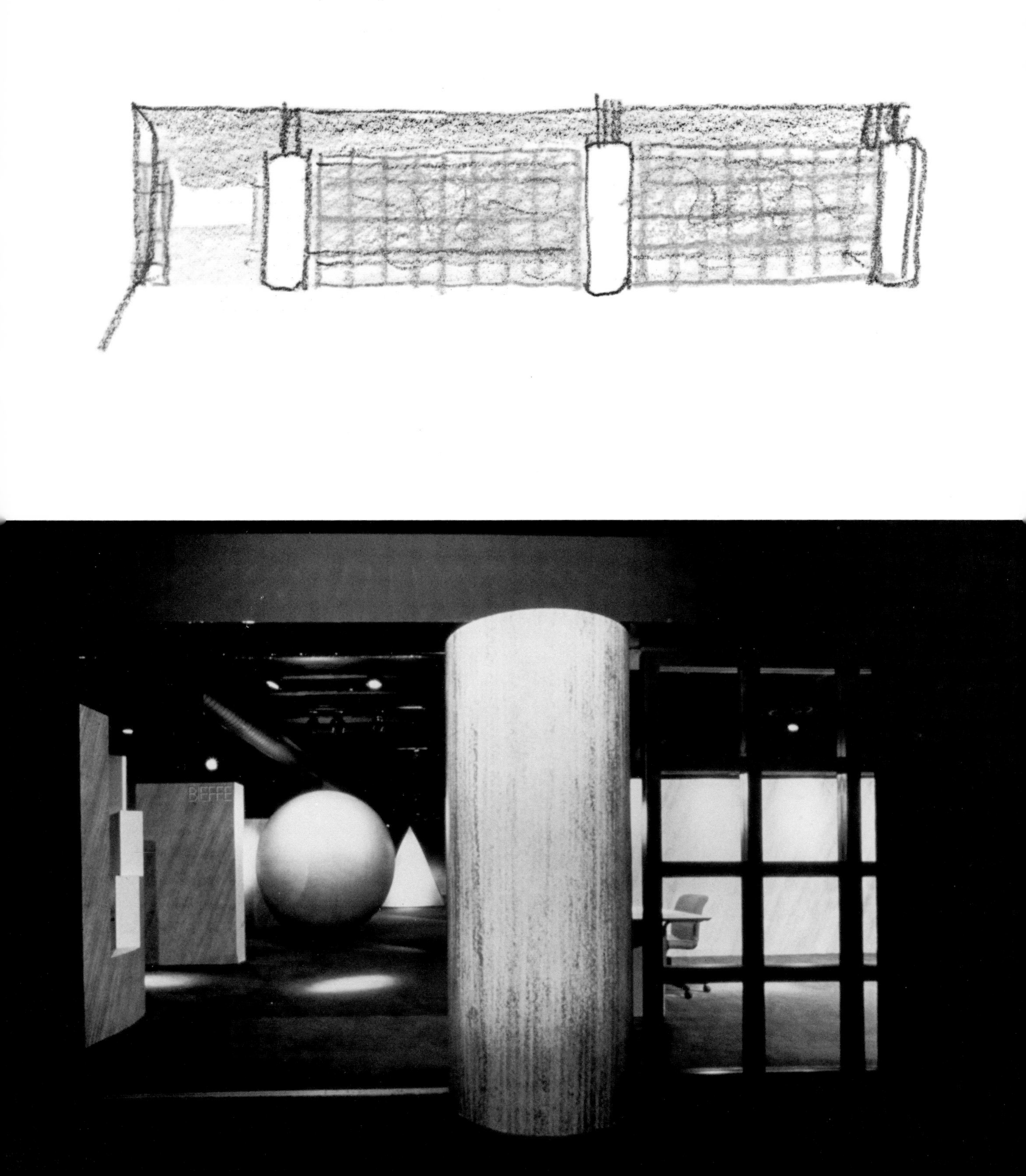
BIEFFE

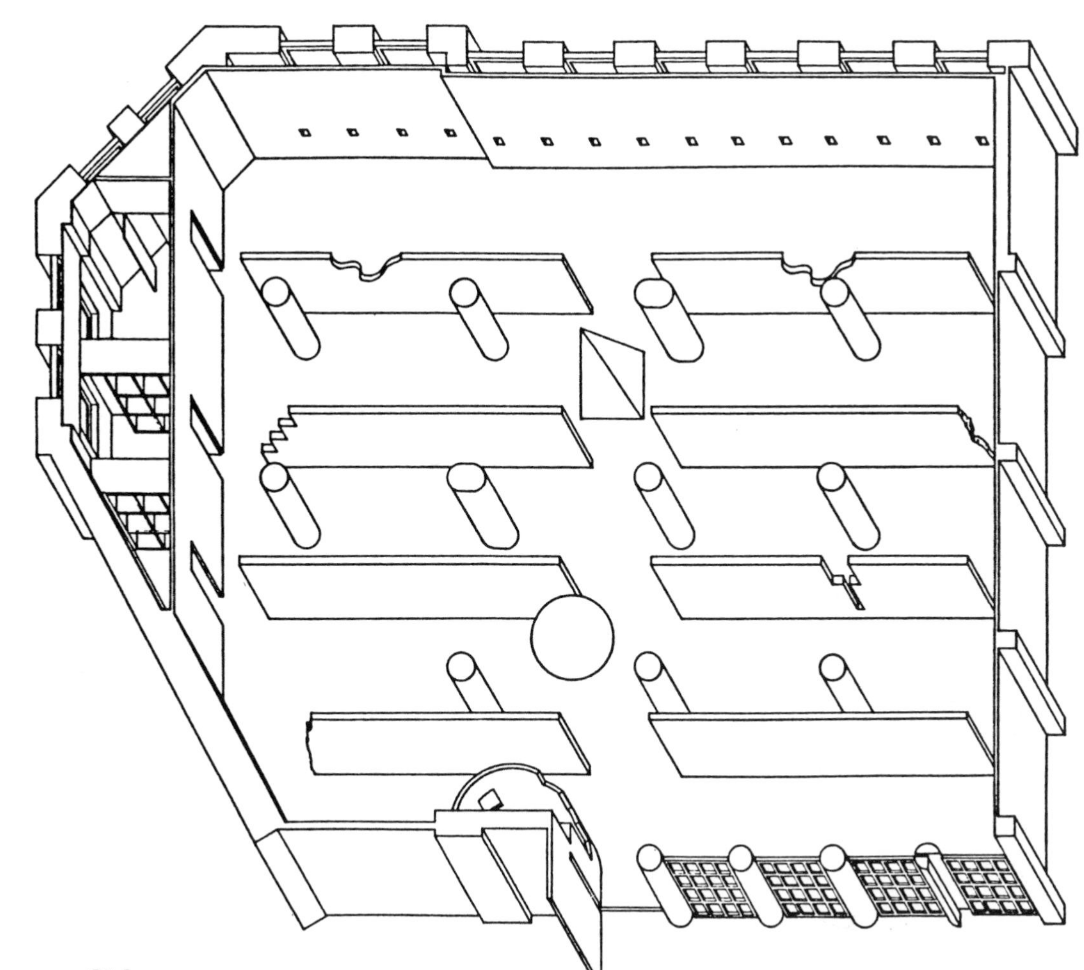

Italcenter Showroom, Chicago

Vignelli Associates, interior designers

This showroom in the Chicago Merchandise Mart was planned as a kind of stage set for display of furniture products from the nine Italian manufacturing firms that make up *Italcenter*, a U.S. distributing consortium. The nine firms required nine loosely defined areas as individual "turf" plus a larger common area for shared use. The location of existing columns suggests a basis for space division, but additional defining elements are clearly called for. So much subdivision also hints at a need for some thematic elements to unify what might otherwise have turned into a disorganized collection of small booths.

The Vignelli concept for dealing with these issues surfaces at once in an early rough sketch (overleaf). The ceiling and perimeter walls are to be dark and recessive. Division is accomplished through a series of parallel wall planes with a central access passage. Unity comes from large, abstract geometric forms (something of a Vignelli trademark) that can be spatially dominant without detracting from the furniture products on display. It is normal Vignelli practice to work on interior design projects in model form, but here sketches, particularly many successive elevation sketches, helped to move the original concept forward. The ideal scale for the geometric solids was a pivotal issue. How large should they be to dominate without becoming absurdly overbearing?

In the scale elevation sketch (pages 84–85), the total width of the space is visible with the dark ceiling and background and the existing columns clearly indicated. The sphere is placed off center and sized to match the height of the screen walls. The walls are now shown with "notches" of curved form cut out—one of the variants in the basically geometric

A Massimo Vignelli sketch for the Ital showroom (opposite page, top) presents in conceptual form a design idea which, in realization, turns out to be almost impossible to photograph (opposite page, bottom). Because of sketching, this concept, visible in both sketch and axonometric form (above), remains very strong in actual experience.

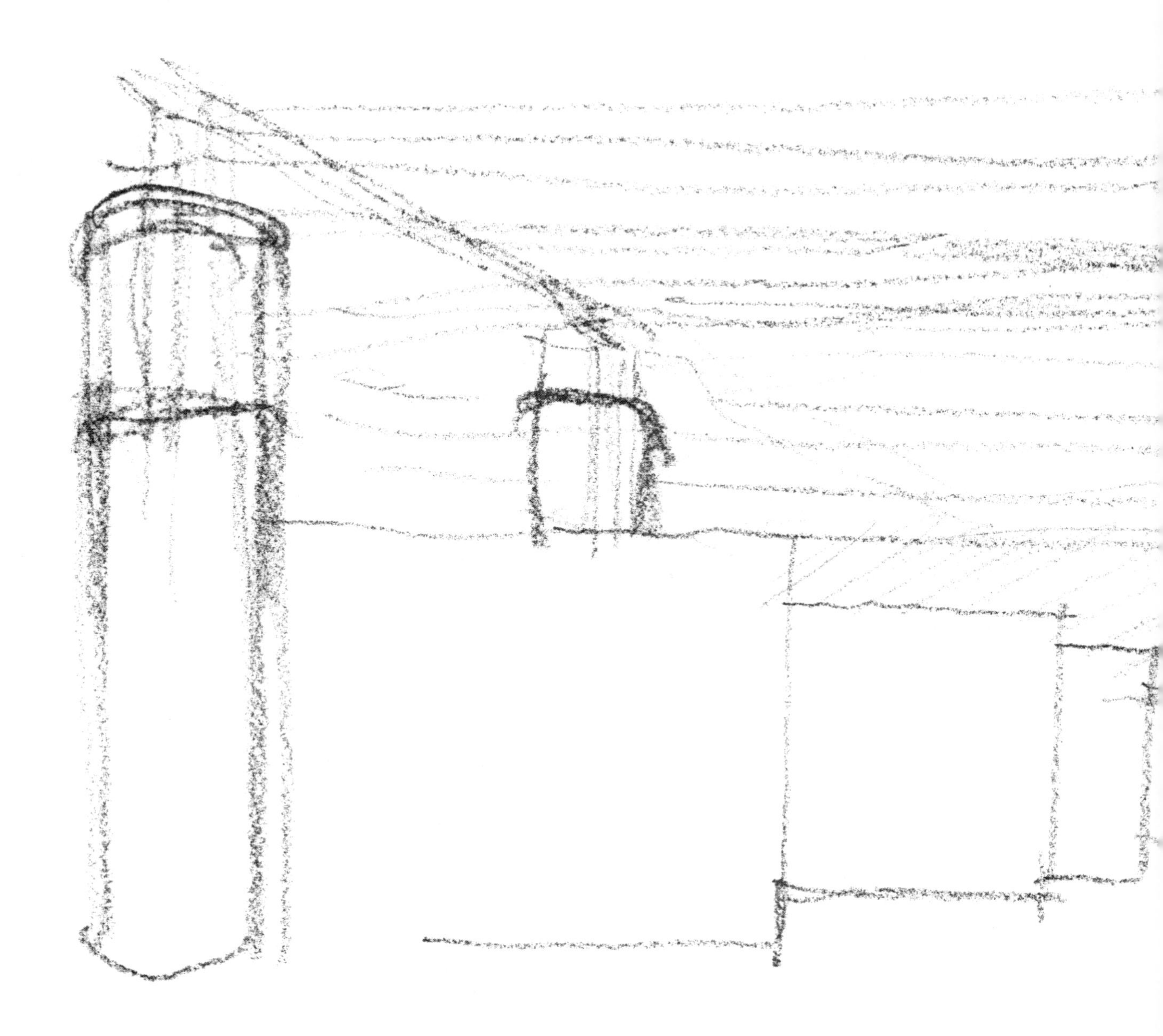

First concept sketch by Massimo Vignelli
for the Ital Chicago showroom.

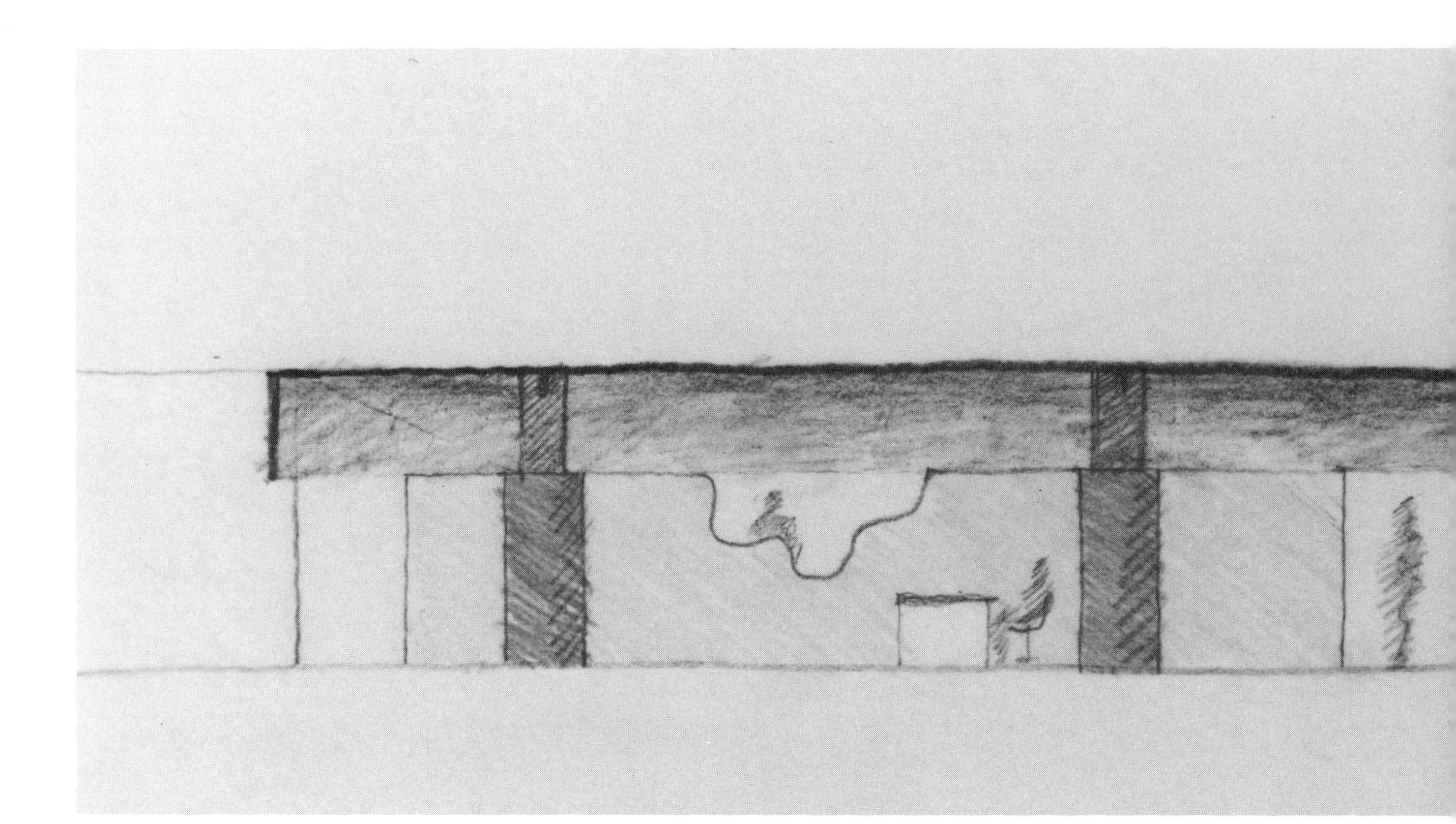

Elevation study in which the "scribble" pencil tone appears to be suggesting an idea for an artist to paint a texture that matched Vignelli's sketch

concept, destined to give the space a whimsical element of surprise. These ideas were studied in an extensive series of ribbon elevation sketches (overleaf) in which a wide range of variations on the basic conceptual themes appear. In some schemes the solids turn into actual architectural elements in giant scale. In others, the modulations of the screen walls are explored. These latter are actually, in addition to being visual play, rather subtle "in-joke" references to the work of several current "stars" of the avant garde architectural scene. The curved notch refers to a Tigerman project; the giant stepped ending (line three, left on the color page) is from an Arquitectonica project; and the "chewed away" corner "quotes" one of the more startling features of a SITE Best Products building. In the end, the more explicit architectural forms give way to the simpler geometric solids, a sphere and a pyramid.

The sketches shown here were made on white tracing paper; colored pencil was used as the medium for color study. The pencil scribble, originally simply a sketch technique for laying in tones, turns out to have value as a suitably vague background texture, which is taken up for use in the real spaces and enlarged up from scale to full size to give to the realized walls the character of a sketch converted into three-dimensional reality.

Still another sketch (page 80) explores the approach to the entrance area with its large-scale, gate-like glazed grid fitted between column forms. Facing a corridor, this facade is never seen as an elevation and is hard to photograph in any view that sets out its reality as the sketch does. In fact, the entire space is difficult to suggest with photography since it is a sequence of small spatial units that must be walked through one at a time, building up a mental impression through movement in time and space. The sketches present the whole design in a form that can be seen all at once and understood in an overall conceptual fashion. Experience of the built space, in contrast, has a certain quality of mystery and of "mystique" that is its special quality, giving complexity and significance to what might be expected to be rather banal.

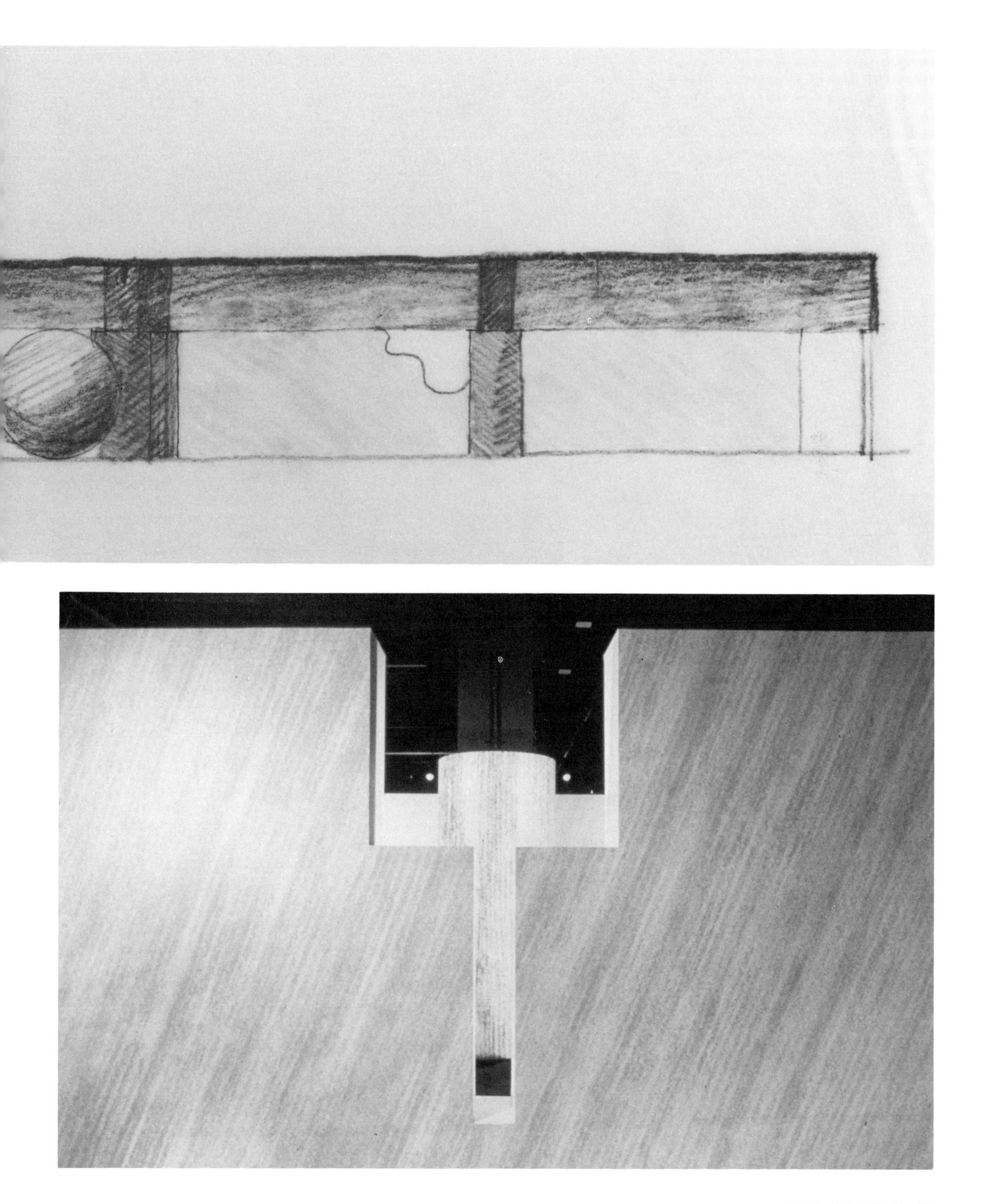

Elevation studies presenting the successive parallel screen walls that divide the Ital space into a series of "slices," as shown on axonometric (see page 81).

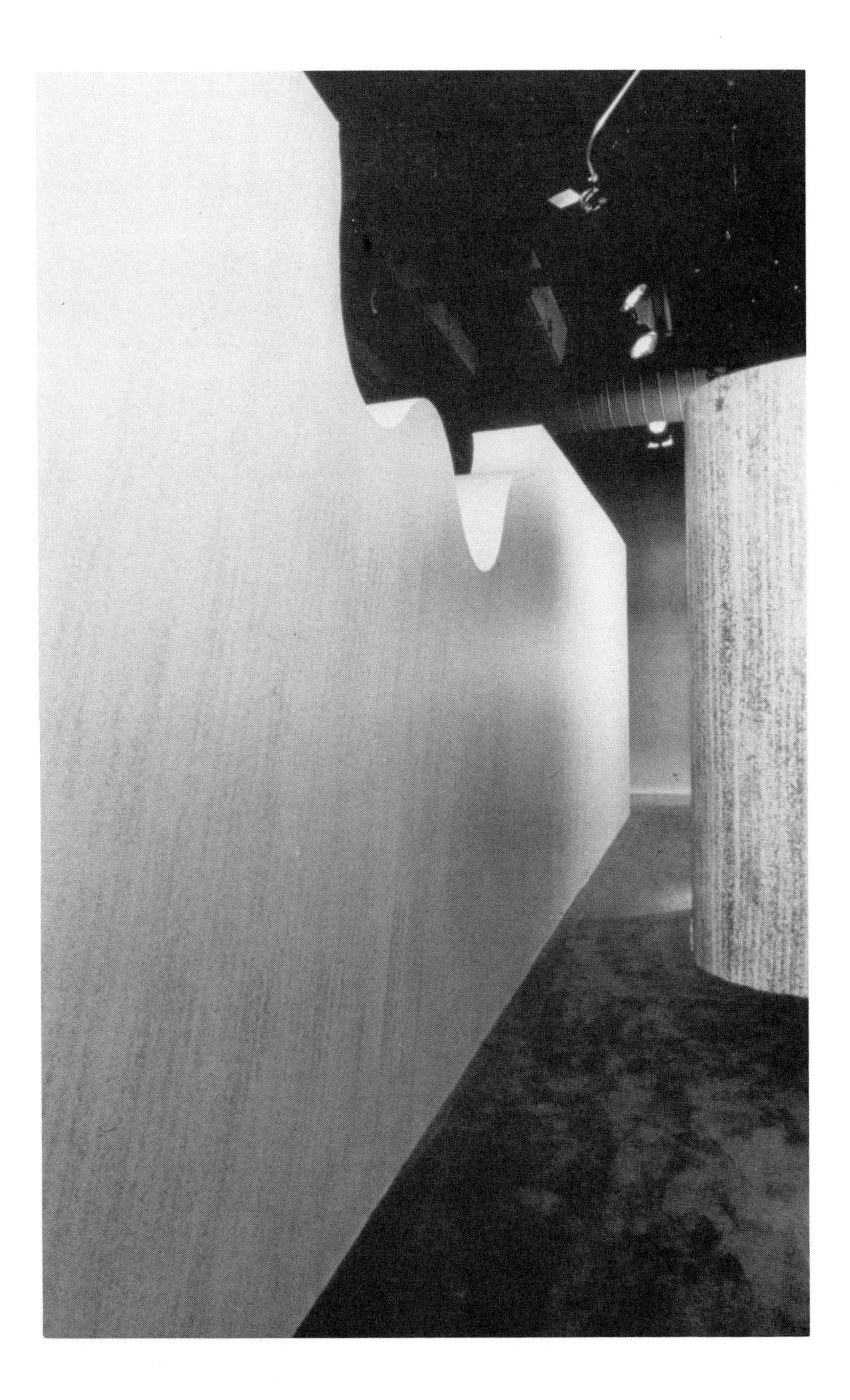

The photograph indicates the close integration of sketch and finished walls.

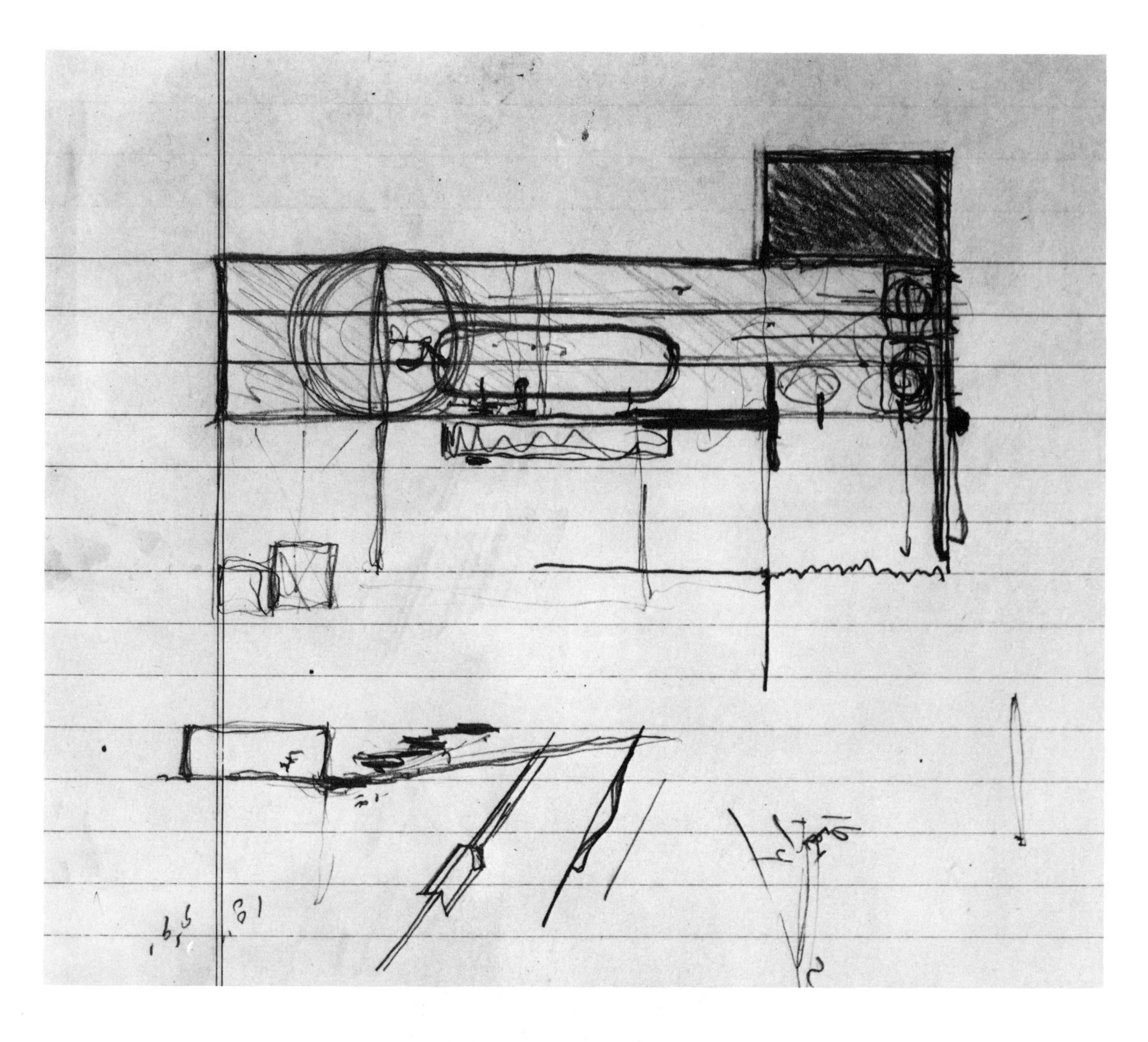

A Michael Kalil plan sketch—a first idea for a long, narrow bath. At left, indication of a mirrored wall appears in "shorthand" indication of reflections.

Pen-and-ink drawing (right) on a lined yellow pad begins development of the space in perspective. The unusual pedestal washbasins make their appearance and are seen reflected in the mirror wall where the reduction of detail shown makes the idea of reflection apparent.

Bathroom in a condominium apartment, New York

Michael Kalil, interior designer

This long, narrow space in a city high-rise apartment building was developed as an unusual, luxurious bathroom. Much of the design development came from direct, on-site experience with the actual space. This design study was oriented toward making the space a rich, visual experience quite unlike the standard, cramped bathroom of a typical city apartment. The study of page 89 shows the effect of one fully mirrored wall. In the tub-shower study (page 93) it is possible to see the designer's approach to space division: Furniture and bathroom fixtures are all fused into an overall "high-tech" concept that will make this space unique.

One can also watch the progress of design thinking in the sketches that trace the development of the sink–washbasin cluster (pages 90–91) and of the shower space, seen in perspective sketch first and finally in a sketch working drawing ready for transfer to actual construction drawings.

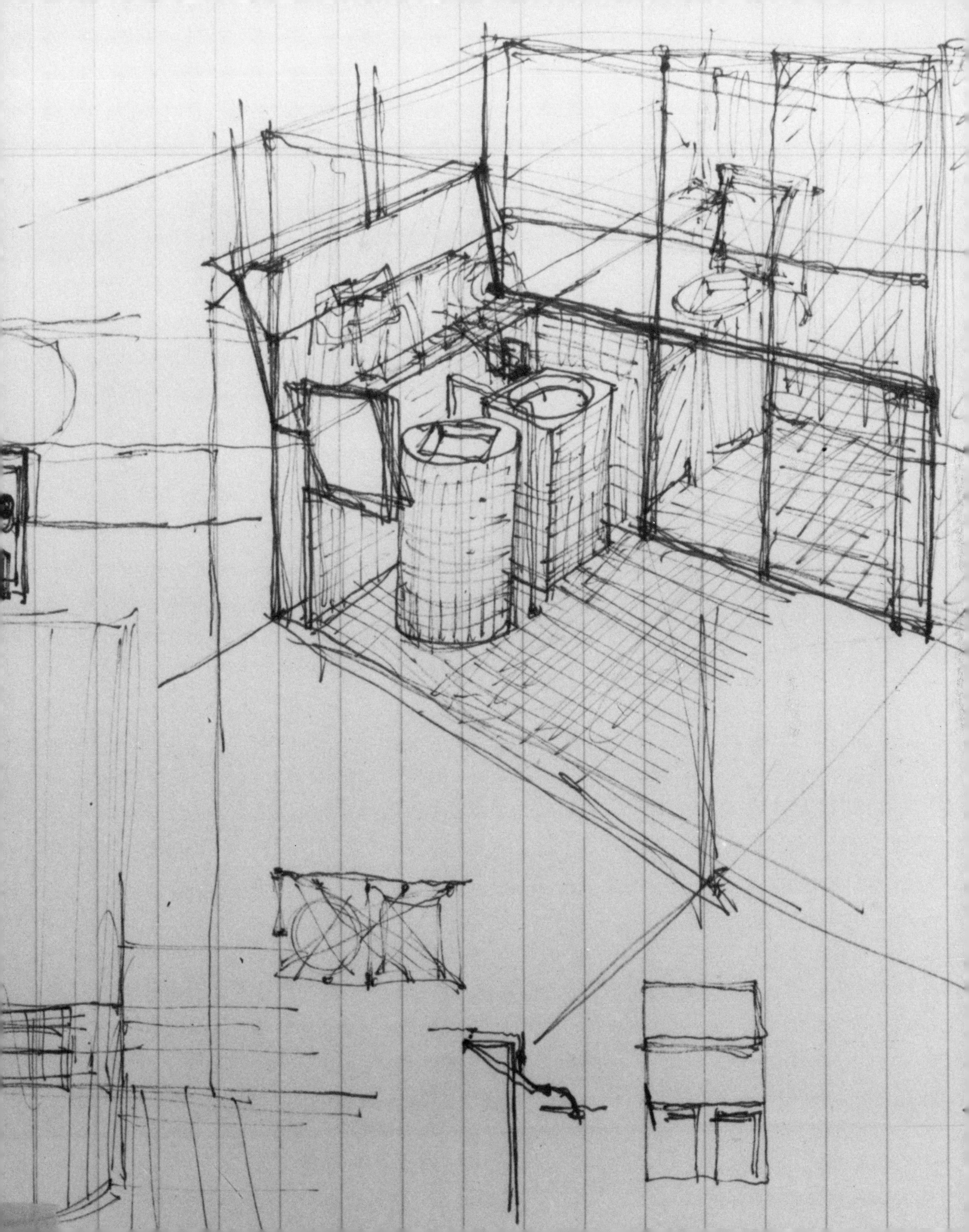

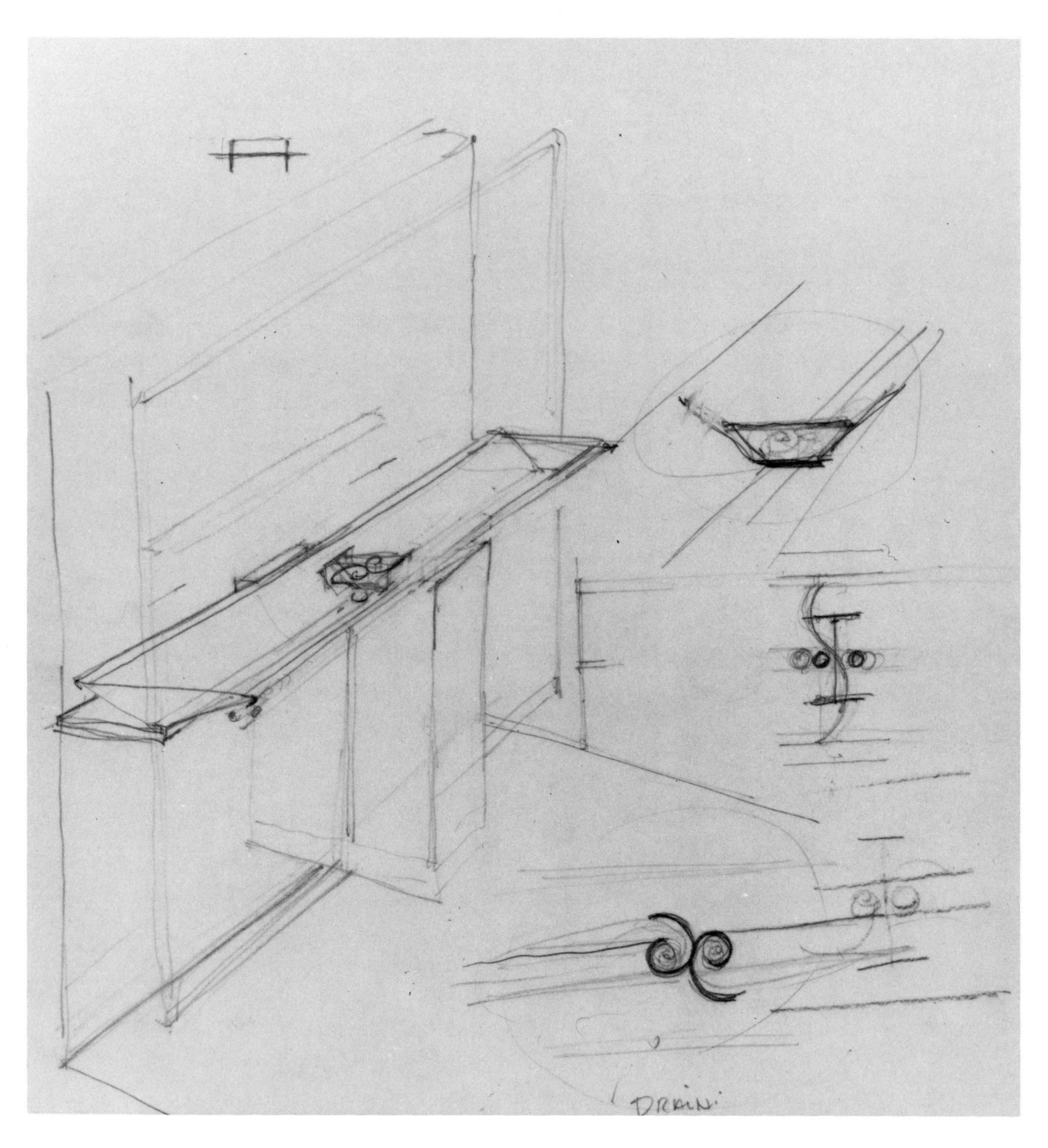

A studio sketch on cream tracing paper. The detail theme of water flow from a spiral element appears in the pattern at the lower right and in several variations on the element at the center of the trough-like basin.

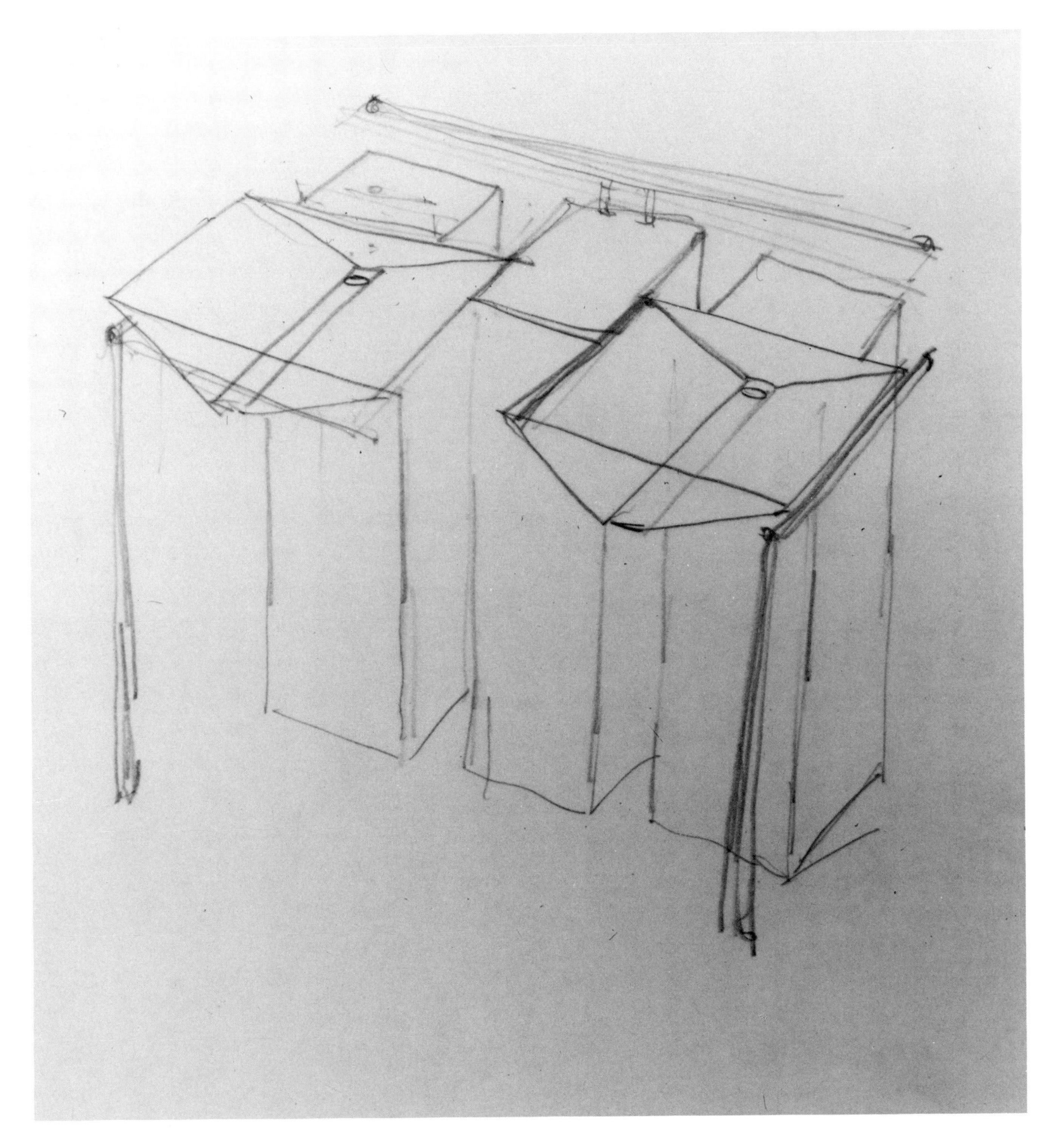

Still another washbasin study, here with twin trough-form basins. Sketch done with Eagle 314 Draughting pencil on cream trace.

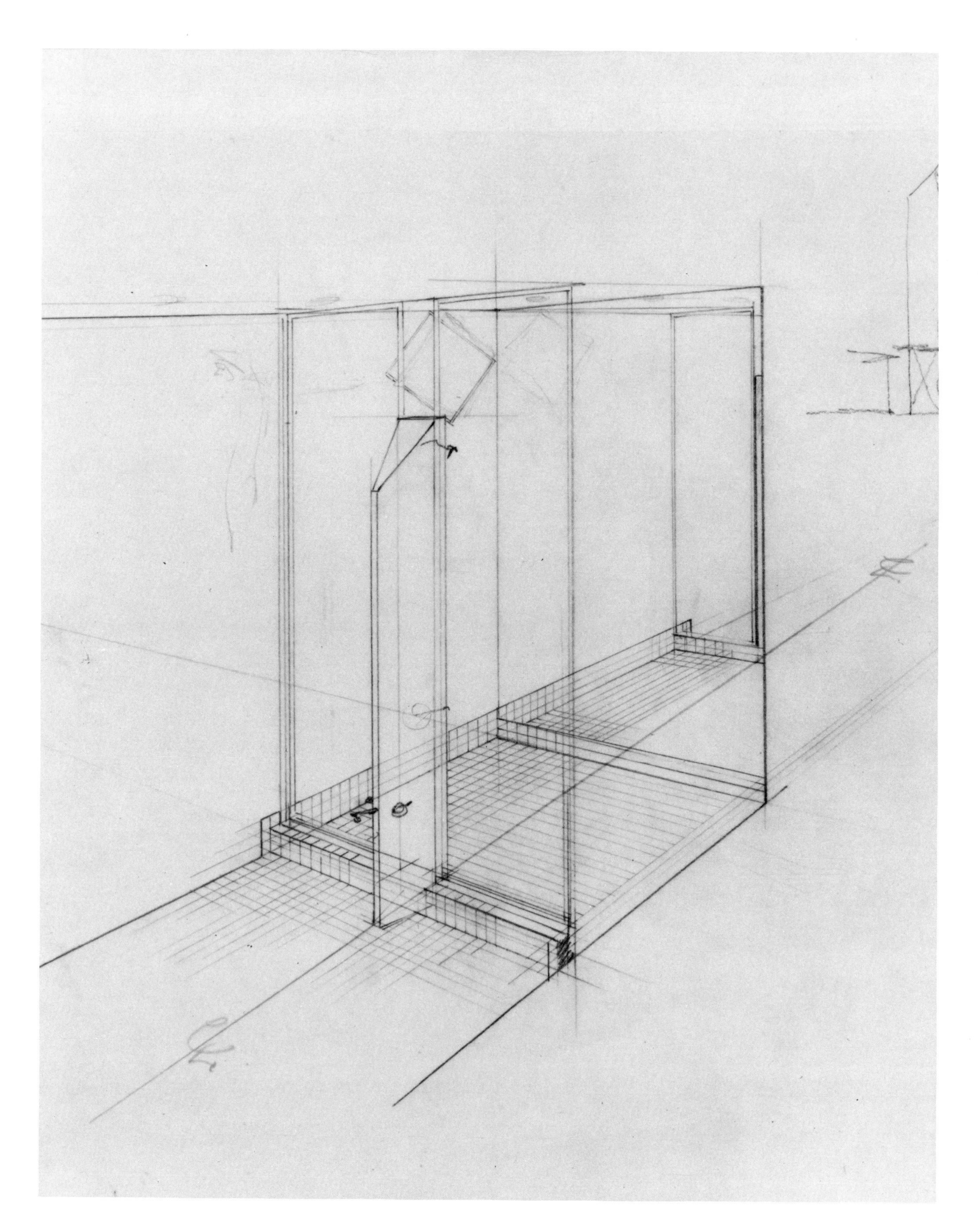

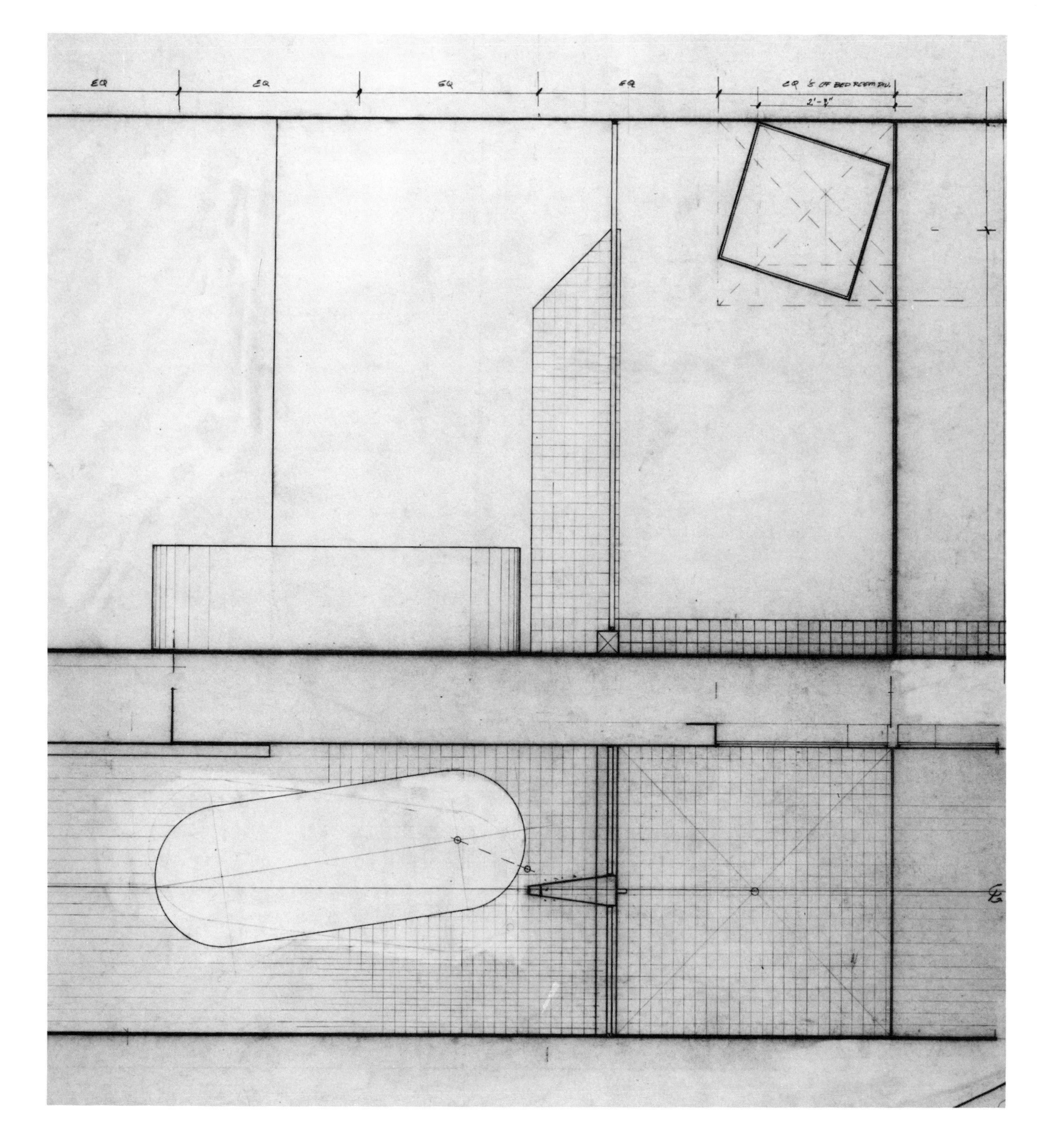

The shower enclosure in perspective and tub and shower in plan and elevation, drafted now with sharpened No. 2H pencil on Clearprint white tracing paper. A transitional step from sketch to working drawing.

5

Presentation Sketching

The term "presentation" is a curious one, suggesting the giving of some sort of ceremonial gift. It has worked its way into the design world, probably coming from Madison Avenue where advertising firms make presentations to show proposed campaigns and to secure clients. Wherever the word came from, "presentation" is now in general use to describe the way a design proposal is shown to a client to give information and to gain (the designer hopes) approval. Presentations for large projects may involve elaborate renderings, models, even film or taped TV techniques to make it easy for a group to understand and appreciate the proposal.

To speak of a presentation sketch may seem something of a contradiction, but sketches are, in practice, a very useful presentation device. In the case of smaller projects such as a residential interior, shop, or showroom, elaborate rendering seems out of place. It is also costly and takes time. A sketch is by its nature quick, and it is likely to be produced as a part of the design process in any case. There is also something intimate and direct about sketches: They can seem true "works of art" coming directly from the hand of the designer and they tend to draw the client (and any other viewer) into the designer's thinking process. It is easier to *dislike* a cold and formal rendering than a simple sketch that speaks directly of the designer's intentions.

Any sketch *can* be used in a presentation, however, concept and developmental sketches are sometimes abstract to a degree that is meaningful only to the designer and, perhaps, colleagues.

When sketches are intended for presentation, somewhat more "finish" and clarity are usually in order so that the meaning will come through with only limited verbal explanation. Sketches may be sheets of a pad or booklet or loose sheets of tracing paper, or they may be stretched and mounted on board. The latter treatment is some protection against wrinkling, folding, and the slight confusion that can go with unrolling and spreading out sheets—possibly on a desk or table where there is no clear background space. Too much care with mounting and matting can rob a sketch presentation of its informality, but there is no particular merit in showing material that is messy and disorganized.

Presentation sketches are also particularly well suited to reproduction in print—in brochures, magazines, or newspapers. A complex and elaborate drawing, especially one in full color, often does not reproduce well when reduced and subjected to the coarse halftone screen of much printing. The simplification and smaller size usually characteristic of a sketch are likely to survive printing processes better and also serve to convey the sense of direct communication from the designer. The pen-and-ink sketch from the office of Mitchell and Giurgola (page 95) showing the design proposal for the AIA Headquarters building in Washington, D.C., is a good example. Its simplicity reproduces well while conveying a feeling of freshness and close communication from the designers.

The most direct use of sketching for client communication occurs when the sketches are made in the client's actual presence as an accompaniment and support to conversation. Backs of envelopes or menus are the traditional materials, a pen and black ink the usual medium (now most often replaced by a felt-tip marker pen). Many famous figures of the eclectic era are said to have been masters of this means of holding a client's attention while communicating ideas in a way that demonstrates skill and mastery of a sort that can be extremely impressive to laymen. Frank Lloyd Wright, Eliel Saarinen, and Bertram Goodhue were all said to have been masters of this way of spellbinding an individual client, a committee, or a board of directors. Goodhue could even draw with either hand! In the modern world of corporate clients and large design firms, the skill of sketching while talking tends to be forgotten, but the recent revival of interest in drawing is bringing it back. There is no question that the typical client is impressed and often charmed to actually be present as creative design develops along with conversation. Such presentation sketches also become their own conference notes; with modern duplication techniques, they can easily be reproduced for client, office file, and (should the possibility arise) publication.

A variant on this situation can arise when communication with a client must take place by mail. Thumbnail sketches added to a letter form a kind of presentation that is at the same time informal and direct but also useful in ensuring that a "meeting of minds" is present as to how a project should proceed. The well-known letters of Le Corbusier to a "Madame M." are an example of the way in which sketches can be used almost as a moving-picture view of how a project will develop.

The sketch and photographs of pages 100–101 illustrate another situation. The client here, an advertising

A drawing by Romaldo Giurgola in which a refined use of pen-and-ink technique succeeds in suggesting the relationship of outdoor daylight and interior lighting. Proposal for American Institute of Architects Headquarters Building, Washington, D.C. (Courtesy of Mitchell/ Giurgola, architects)

agency, had commissioned the design of a model bathroom to be built and to appear illustrated in design magazines. The sketch had the multiple purposes of showing the design to the art director for approval and acting as a guide to the photographer selected to make the photographs for use in the advertisement. The comparison of sketch and photo is an interesting demonstration of how closely drawing can simulate reality, even though the photographer must, in the end, make adjustments to deal with the limitations of the camera and the specifics of the built reality.

The presentation sketch is most often a perspective. The ability to draw freely in perspective is developed through familiarity with the two divergent ways of perspective drawing—freehand sketching "by eye" from observed reality and the making of accurate mechanical perspectives. Each way of working supports and aids the other, different as they are in approach. Drawing from observed reality leads to an ability to put onto paper a reality that exists only in the mind, in imagination. Ease with mechanical perspective makes it easy to convert a concept, thought of in plan and elevation, into a perspective with enough mechanical correctness to have a visual quality of believability. It is often helpful to make a quick, entirely freehand "revolved plan" perspective layout, complete with horizon and vanishing points at thumbnail scale, as a basis for starting a free sketch that will still have considerable accuracy in terms of proportions and placement of elements. With practice, it can take no more than a few moments to do this in preparation for making an otherwise free perspective sketch.

At other times, it is worthwhile to make a more complete constructed perspective layout as an underlay sheet over which to sketch. A fairly "tight" mechanical drawing of this kind can establish the geometry over which a freer sketch can be drawn with confidence that the view resulting will be consistent and convincing in perspective terms and also "true to life" in its accuracy as to the designed space that it shows. The informality and softness of freehand lines will often convert a hard and mechanical drawing into something much more personal and therefore more acceptable.

The plans and perspectives of pages 102–105 are examples of this way of working. They were produced to illustrate a booklet introducing new offices before occupancy. The two plans illustrate two alternative layouts for a typical "manager's office" with wood furniture shown in one, metal in the other. The perspective of page 103 illustrates the wood furnished version. The perspective of page 104 shows a partner's office, a somewhat larger space from the same project. Although these drawings are all quite precise in character, they are all in freehand ink line (drawn with a technical pen), as can be seen on close examination. The very slight waver of the line gives an effect of "sketchiness" that helps to relieve any feeling of hardness or coldness. Notice the way the large windows are filled in with drawn architectural elements, somewhat conventionalized, but still giving the sense of view from a high floor that is an important element in making these spaces seem attractive. Each of these drawings was produced by first making an accurate, drafted drawing in pencil as a base sheet. Vellum tracing paper (for its good transparency) was then laid over the layout. The final drawing was made freehand, but with great care to keep the line quality consistent and *almost* mechanical in its precision. Details of plants, books, and small objects help to give a sense of realism and a quality of "charm" that help the future users of these offices to identify with them as their own.

The presentation plan of pages 106–107 shows a similar space in plan with color tints added, suggesting the realistic color of the pieces of furniture and other objects in the space. A drafted plan was used as an underlay here also, but the final drawing is on cream tracing paper. The basic drawing has been made freehand with a thin, brown line. Color tints are then added with markers, defining the objects. Choice of marker color is impor-

Pentel markers and Prismacolor pencil used for an exuberant sketch of a design studio. (Norman Diekman, designer)

tant in making this technique a success. Most sets and collections of markers include too many harsh, bright colors. A collection of subtle, near-neutral tones is most useful, and excellent ranges of color are available in a number of marker brands. It is wise to do a trial of colors alone on scrap tracing paper to ensure that an attractive color harmony has been found before adding color to the final drawing.

Although plans and perspectives are the most common sketch presentation drawings, elevations also can be useful and give exact information about height (and other) dimensions which can be useful later when construction drawings are to be made. The elevation drawings of page 108 show a small display pavilion or kiosk in two elevations. Both are roughly drafted in pencil line on yellow trace; one, in which the panel of displayed material appears at an oblique angle, has had a few scribble tones added to give a sense of roundness to the tubular, column-like supports.

The same display is illustrated in the perspective sketch on page 109. This is a very rough and quick "idea" sketch made in a moment or two before the elevations were worked out. It was done with a coarse black felt-tip marker, with scribble tones added with colored pencil. The white tone of the back wall is white colored pencil scribble on the *back* of the yellow tracing paper.

In this situation, as is often the case, the designer's concept or idea sketches, originally made as an aid to developing the design, can serve as an informal presentation to a client. The directness and even roughness of such drawings, which might not be appropriate for an elaborate presentation of a major project to a committee or board, can be exactly right in support of verbal discussion of ideas for a developing project where the client is involved in development of details and already disposed toward accepting the designer's proposals.

Selection of sketch presentation techniques appropriate for a particular stage of a design project's development can be a great aid to communication with a client—an aid to gaining understanding and acceptance of design ideas and to creating a sense of participation on the part of the client which is often of great help in moving a project forward in a way that turns out to be satisfactory to everyone involved.

Two small pen-and-ink sketches made on a coffee shop place mat capture daydreams of a house overlooking the ocean. (Norman Diekman, designer)

Full color used for a presentation sketch leading to a constructed room photographed for use in an advertising campaign. (Norman Diekman and William Machado, designers; photograph by Tom Yee; courtesy of American Standard, Inc.)

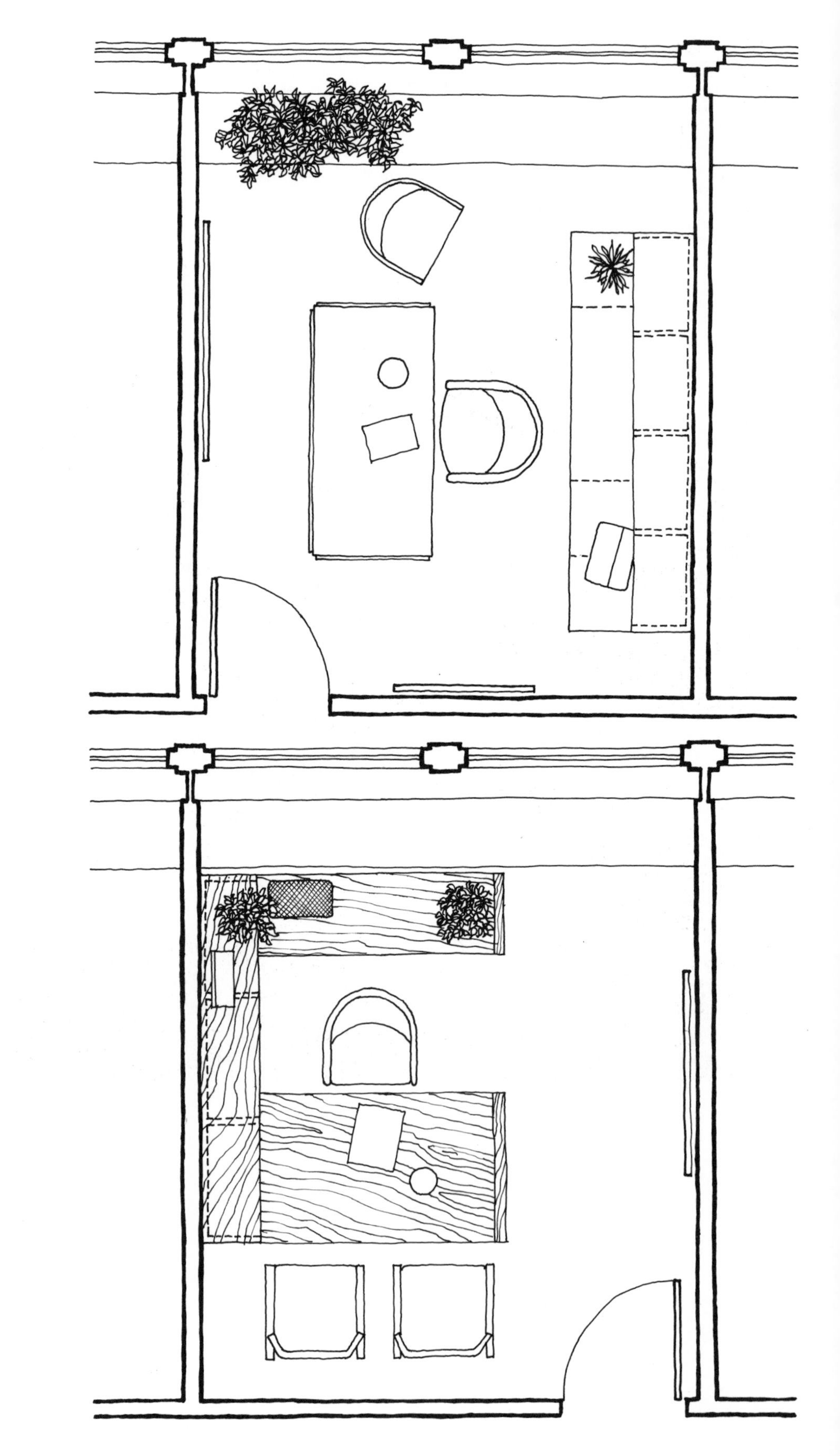

Floor plan sketches using a freehand pen-and-ink line in a way that suggests clarity which aids the client's understanding. The perspective page (above), with the same technique, provides a realistic image of the proposed office types.

An ink-line perspective similar to that of the preceding page, but presented here as a negative. The white line on black makes for an unusual impact suggesting power and drama. The viewer tends to see such a drawing as a night scene, probably because of the black outdoor sky and the ceiling light fixtures which show up as bright disks against a dark background.

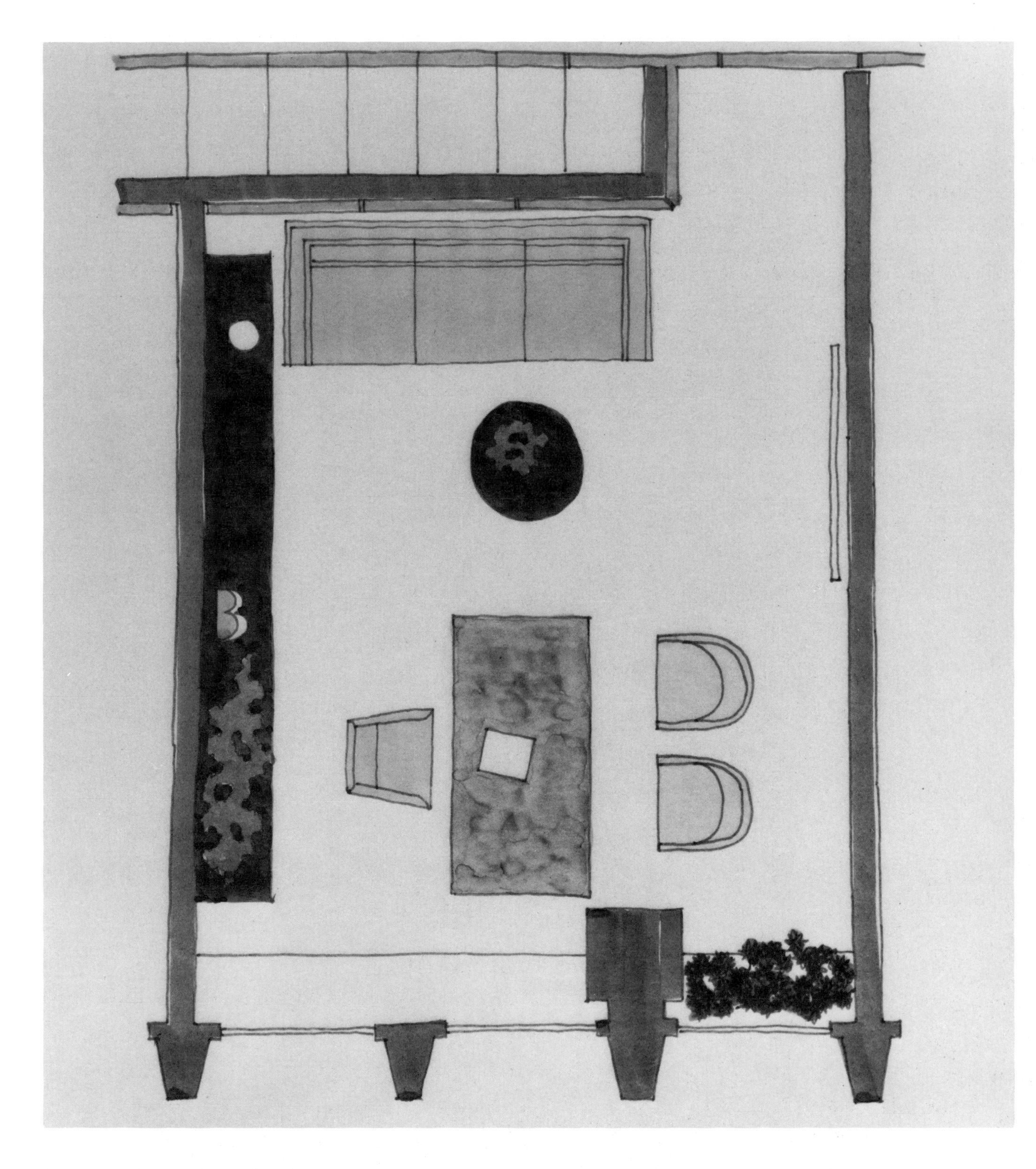

Plans show alternate layouts for private offices from a large office planning project. Felt-tip pen is the drawing medium with addition of some areas of color tone applied with broad markers. (Norman Diekman, designer)

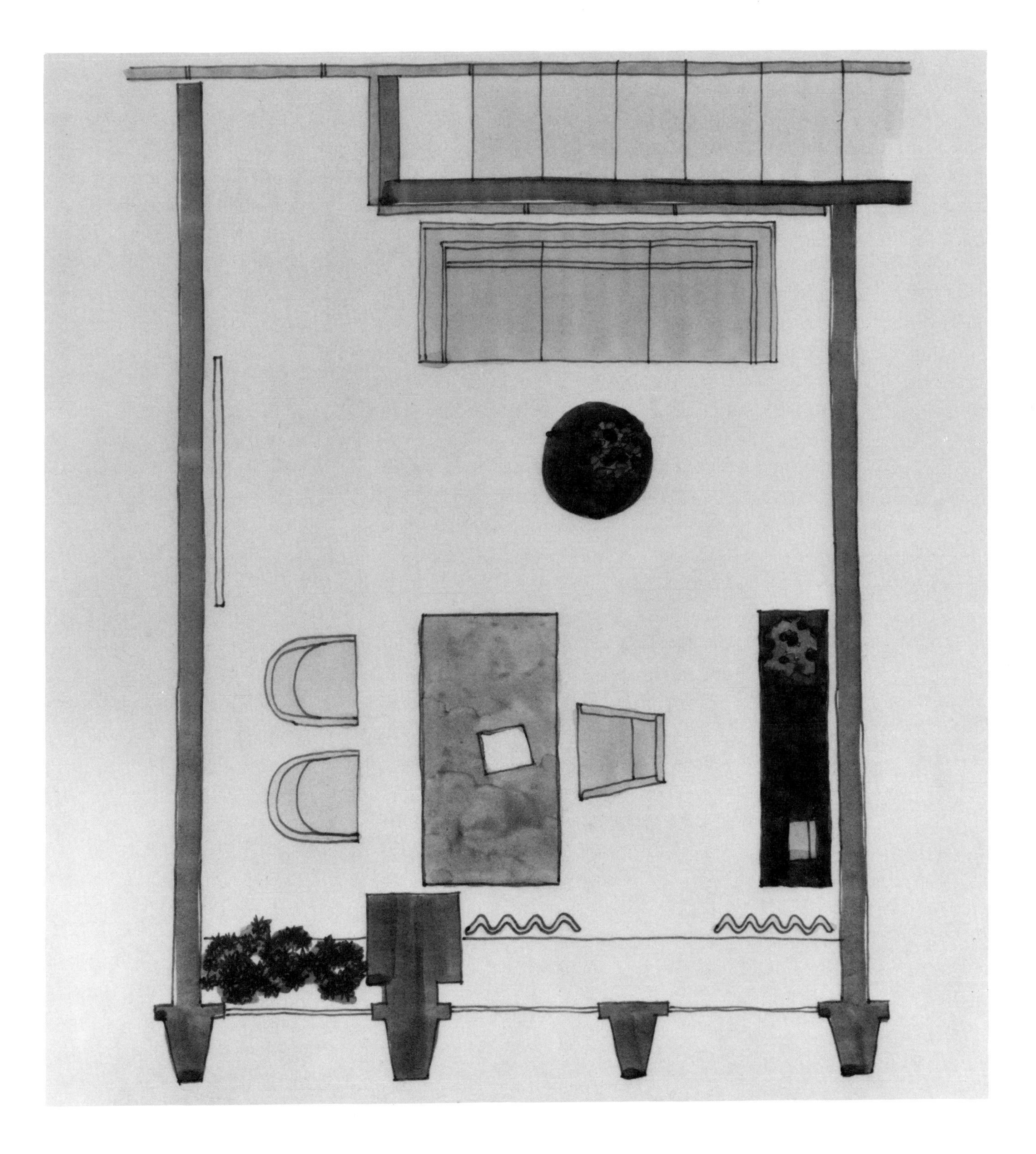

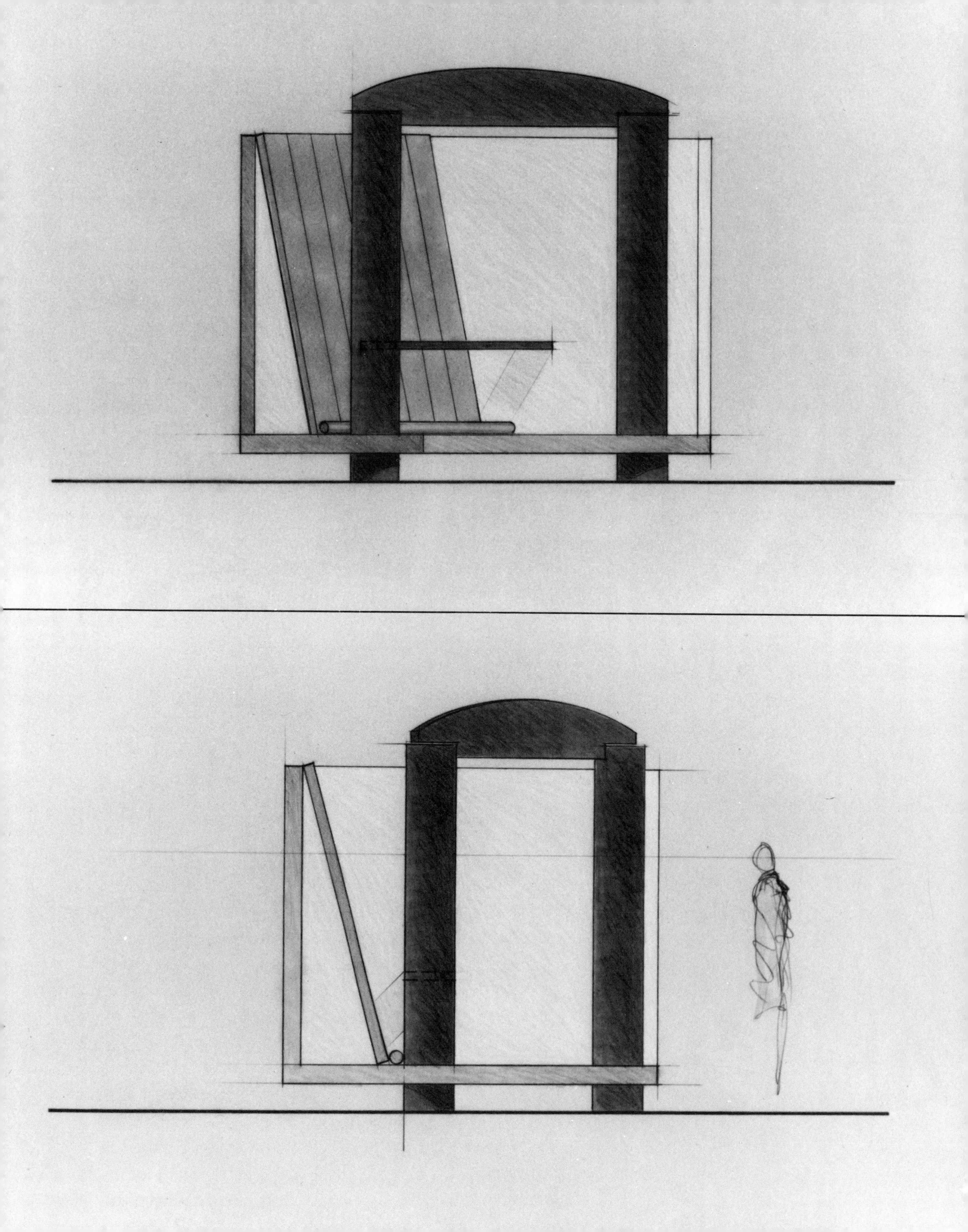

Elevation studies for an exhibition pavilion using a "drafted sketch" technique to establish an accurate study of scale and proportion based on the first idea sketch shown above. (Norman Diekman, designer for Tarkett Flooring)

Sketches using bold, quick strokes. Above: A large room is suggested with a free technique suggesting brushstrokes. (Norman Diekman, designer) At right: A smaller, private room is drawn with more precision. (William Machado and Norman Diekman, designers) In each case the choice of technique aids in capturing the spirit of the proposed space.

6

Sketching Furniture and Details

Although many interior design projects (including some very large ones) are developed in terms of large concepts of space and color, details can be very important, as they give a project special character at a more intimate scale. It is all too easy to rely on "standard" details and available products. This practice can save time and effort, but it tends to make projects too similar to one another and denies the designer some of the most interesting opportunities to work out ideas that make a particular space unique, memorable, and personally involving for the user/occupant.

One cannot think of the interiors designed by Victor Horta, Josef Hoffmann, or Frank Lloyd Wright without thinking of the fascinating, highly personal (sometimes eccentric) details of built-in fittings, light fixtures, and furniture that were developed for particular interiors. Wright's furniture is sometimes spoken of rather unkindly (it is actually both more attractive and more practical than it may seem in photographs), but it is certainly true that his interiors would be far less interesting if they had simply been furnished with the standard products available from manufacturers at the time. Wright even designed china and linens for hotel and restaurant projects, and in some cases, even costumes for the wives of residential clients.

The role of sketching in the development of details is not always obvious. We tend to think of the sketch as a means for developing conceptual, large-scale ideas and to leave detailing for later consideration—perhaps as part of the construction drawing phase of project development. Unfortunately, that later phase often suffers from time pressure and may be, all or in part, in the hands of technical people whose concern for design is sometimes secondary. If the designer wants to make unique and interesting details part of an interior project, thinking about those details and their development in sketch form, should move forward with overall design concepts from the very beginning of a project.

Surprisingly, it often can turn out that an interesting detail, developed early in a project's conceptualization, can become a thematic key to the whole development of a space. Certain aspects of interior architecture seem to invite interesting detailing. A major entrance, a focal window, a fireplace, a stairway are all obvious opportunities to do something that will be more than routine. Furniture has similar possibilities. Built-in units, so often treated as mere utilitarian elements detailed in routine ways, can be developed into thematic or focal elements. Movable furniture can take on a life of its own, possibly being manufactured and distributed so as to have more currency than the project that led to its creation. Many famous furniture designs originated as details of a particular project and many have outlasted the project that brought them into being. One thinks of Mies van der Rohe's Barcelona chair, still in production and widely used many years after the Barcelona Pavilion (a temporary, exhibition structure) was demolished.

Most designers hesitate, probably

A Giuseppe Zambonini study for a loft space. The drafted sketch technique shows built-in furniture and architectural space fully integrated.

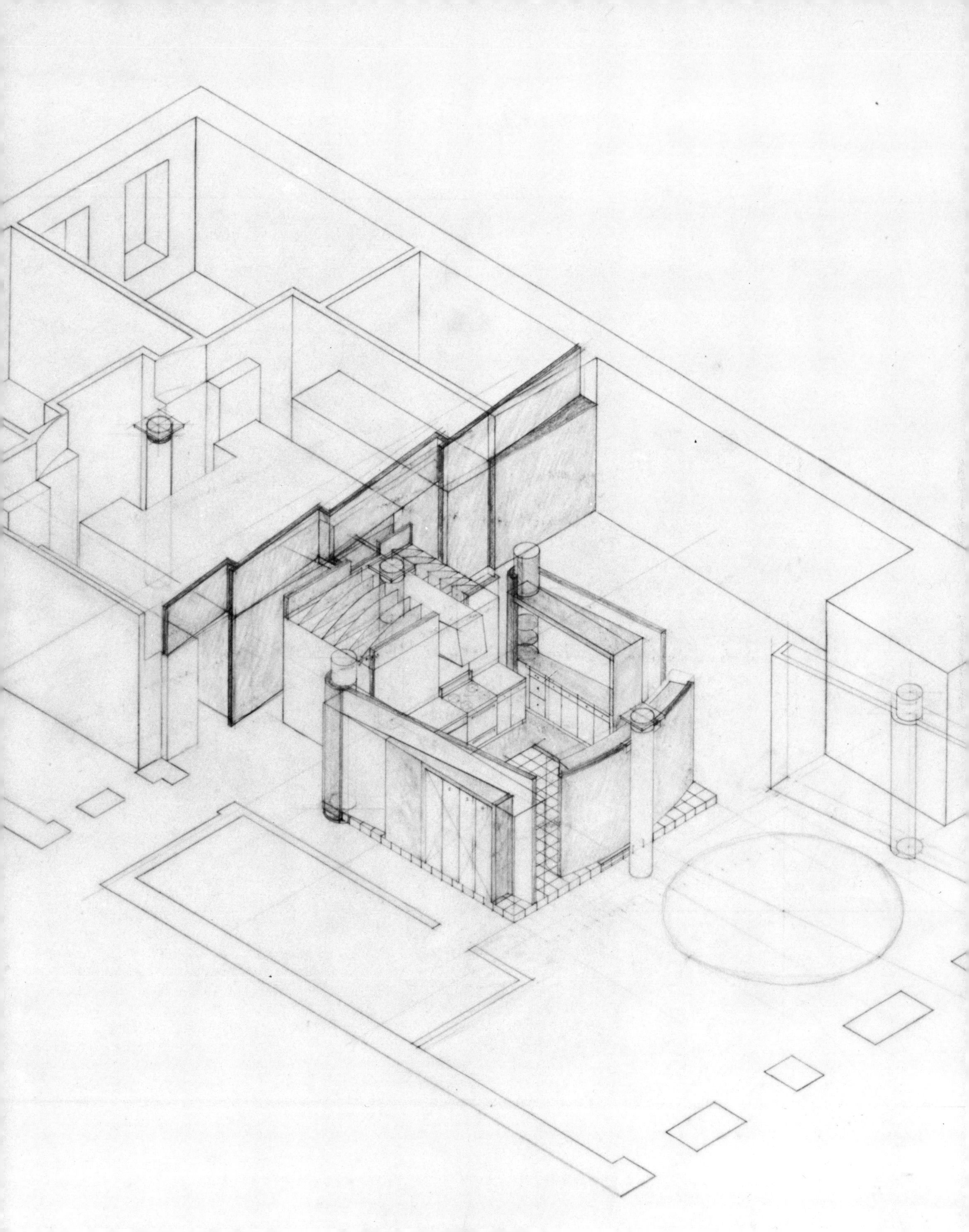

wisely, to develop highly special movable furniture for individual projects. Tables, desks, and storage units do not present great problems, but seating, with its special relationship to bodily comfort, must be designed with great care and, if at all possible, with provision for a stage of experimental prototyping to check out matters of scale, comfort, and structural solidity before actually producing final versions of totally original designs.

As with all other design sketching, detail sketching moves from the conceptual through stages of increasing specificity to a sketch that is close to being a construction detail and is a basis for the making of final, dimensioned working drawings. Not every detail needs to go through many stages; sometimes a rough idea sketch can convert directly to a working drawing. In some cases, craftsmen can work directly from a rough sketch (perhaps with the addition of some verbal instruction) to finished detail. Working directly from a rough sketch was common when skilled craftsmen with long experience were the norm of such trades as cabinet making and upholstery. A few craftsmen with such skills are still to be found, but details that are to be produced by production shops and normal construction workers must now usually be spelled out very specifically, often at full size, in order to have some assurance that the finished work will match the design intention.

The sketches illustrated here represent a variety of situations in which details have a vital role in an interior project.

In the axonometric by Giuseppe Zambonini (page 113) we see a marriage of architecture and interior design through the development of detail. A kitchen and related storage units located within a larger space are developed with highly personal form and detail to become almost a building within a larger building. The sketch, with its model-like overview from above, makes the complexity and subtlety of the design ideas understandable in a way that could hardly be managed through plans, elevations, and perspectives. The built project will never be seen in this way, but the sketch establishes the controlling ideas in a way that can be understood by the client. These ideas can become a basis for construction drawings that will not offer the same conceptual overview, but that will control detailed execution.

The Josef Hoffmann drawing (page 115) uses an ink line technique suggestive of a Japanese wood-block print with its careful composition and enclosing border line. Such a sketch can be viewed as a work of art in its own right, quite aside from its function as representation of a designed interior.

A stairway in the always intriguing form of a spiral is a classic opportunity for development of unique detail. In this case, color is a key element in the sketch elevation serving to set up a strong contrast between inner and outer form. Here again the detail study (page 117) derives directly from the sketch and converts it to a specific architectural form.

The bathroom window of a Norman Diekman project (pages 118–121) had its origin in thoughts about the round, porthole-like windows of an airplane. The window becomes a reflection of the round washbasin beneath, and vice versa. Placing a window where one is accustomed to finding a mirror creates a visual surprise that has even a touch of humor about it. The rough sketch is converted into a section and elevation drafted sketch detail, itself almost a working drawing ready to be converted to that status through the addition of dimensions, material, finish notes, etc.

In the Zambonini bedroom sketch (page 124), a concept is developed in plan and elevation with a thumbnail perspective in the lower right corner to emphasize the three-dimensional character of the headboard niche proposed. The resulting realized project of the photograph is a direct and literal realization of the sketch concept.

In every case, the role of the sketch is a key to the development of the detail idea, and serves as a vital link in converting the idea into drawings that will be used for actual construction.

An ink-line sketch made by the Vienna Secessionist Josef Hoffman in 1900. It is a study for a room divider and seating area using a drawing technique suggesting a Japanese print popular at the turn of the century.

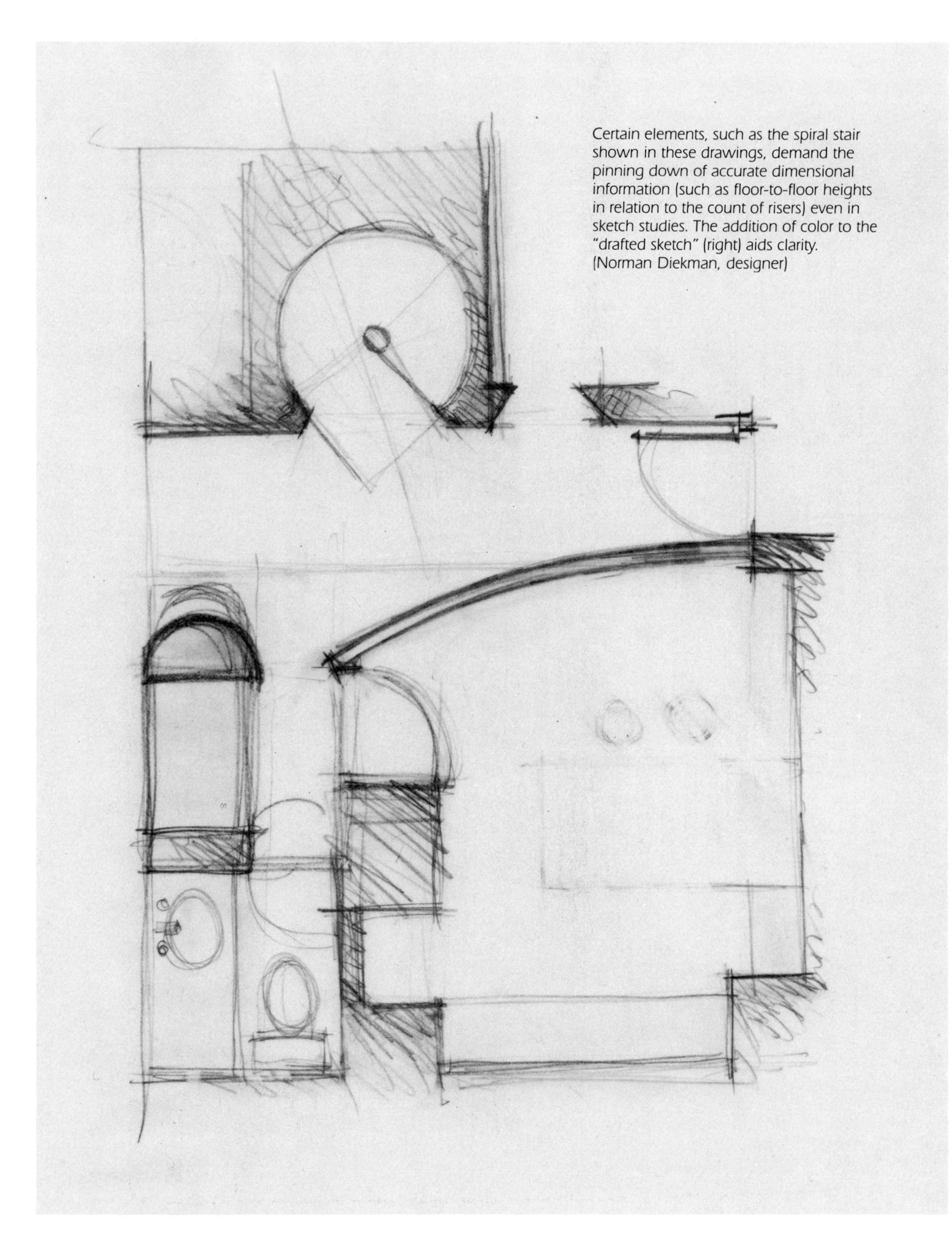

Certain elements, such as the spiral stair shown in these drawings, demand the pinning down of accurate dimensional information (such as floor-to-floor heights in relation to the count of risers) even in sketch studies. The addition of color to the "drafted sketch" (right) aids clarity. (Norman Diekman, designer)

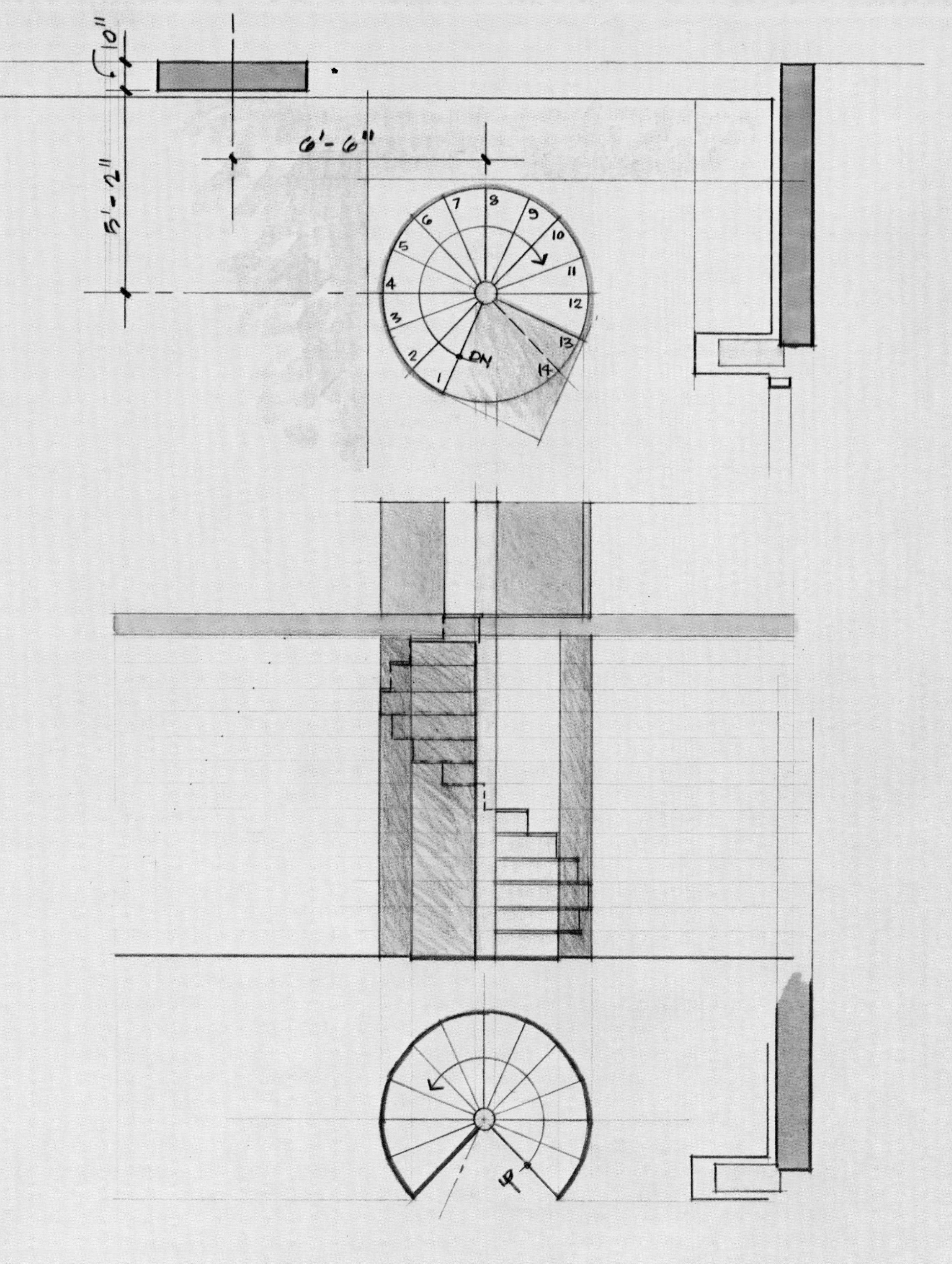

RE
M
CC

PR
SC

NC
16

21

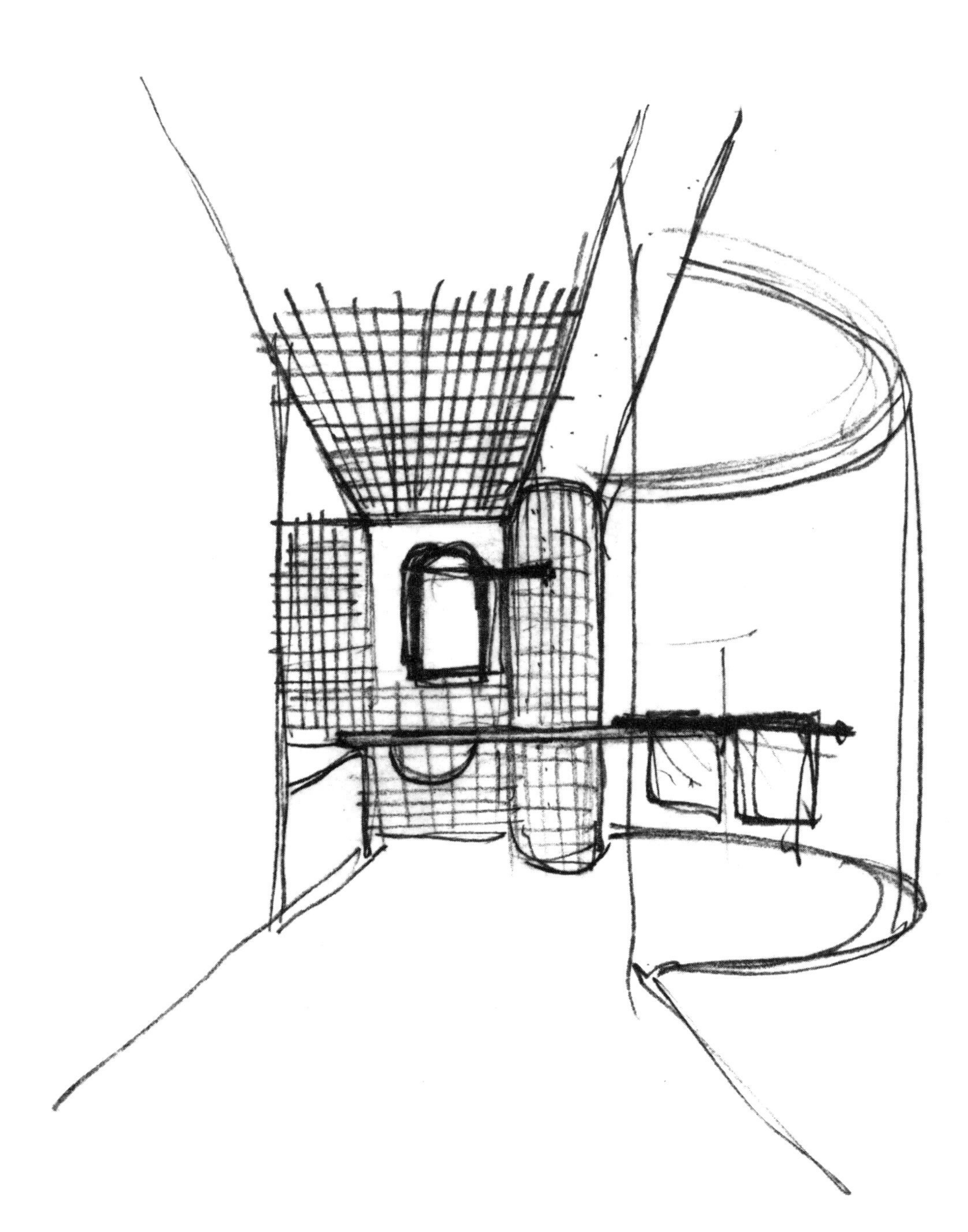

Studies for a small bathroom concentrate on a series of details of washbasin, pivoting mirror, and towel bar within an area that becomes large with the introduction of a curved wall of glass block.

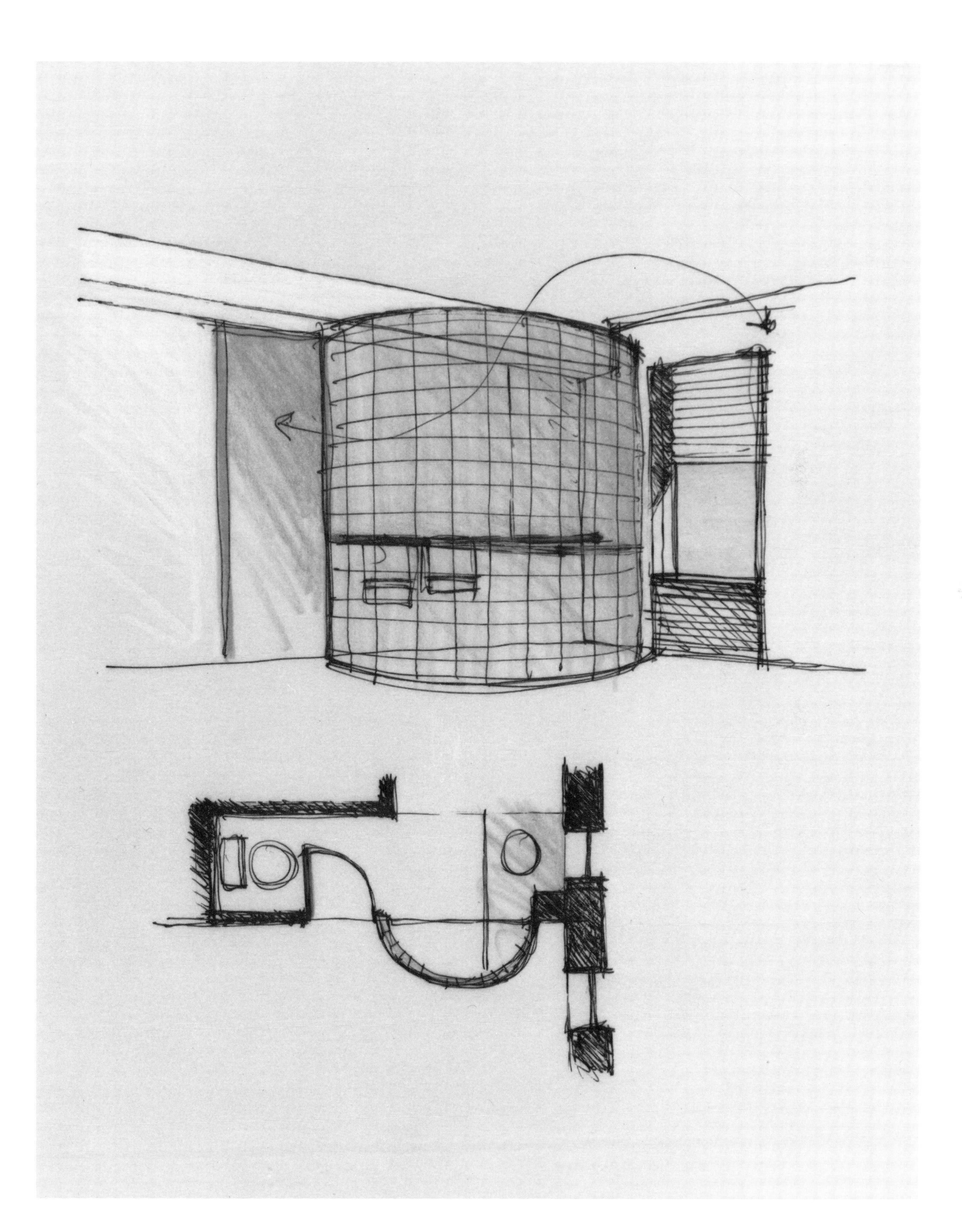

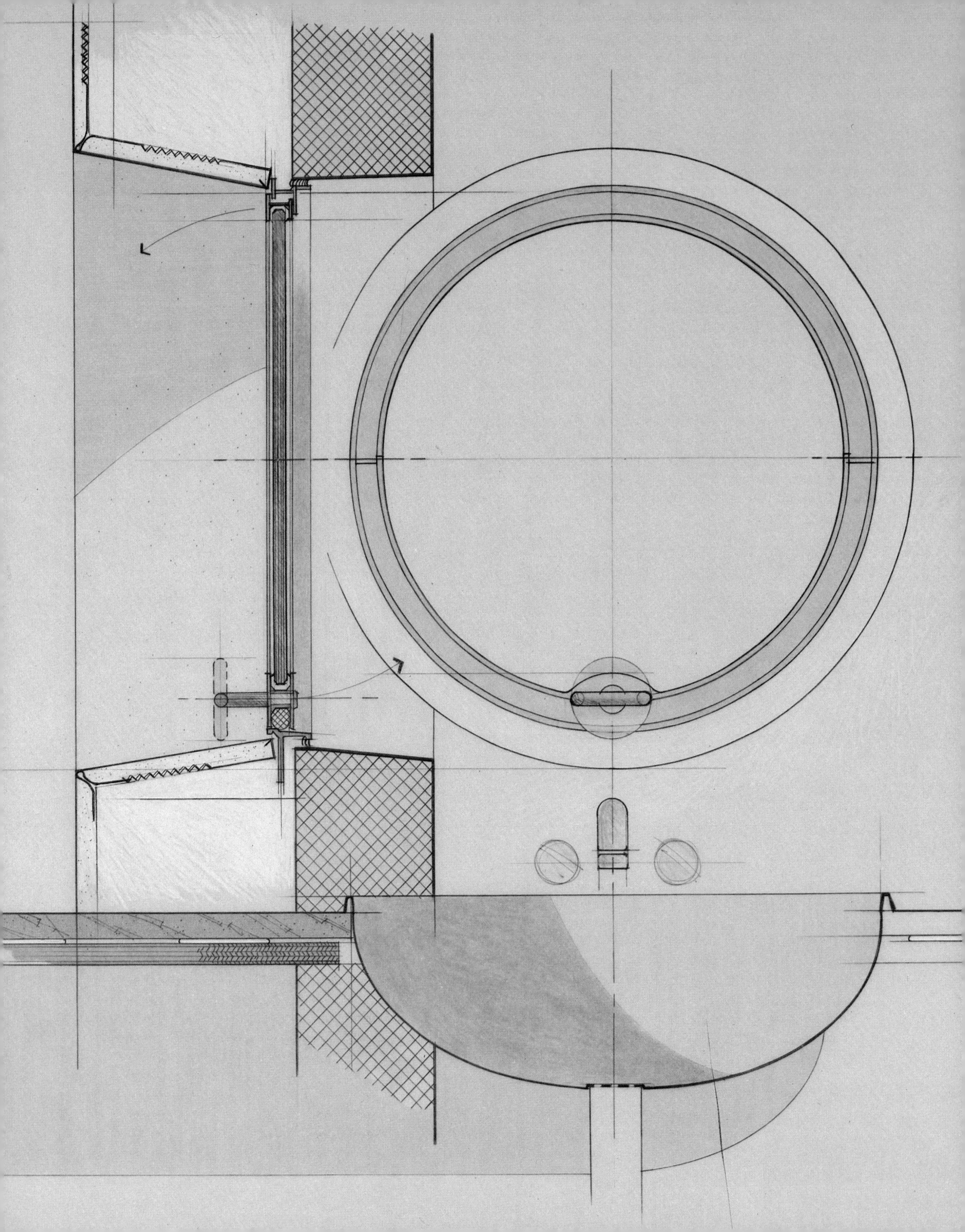

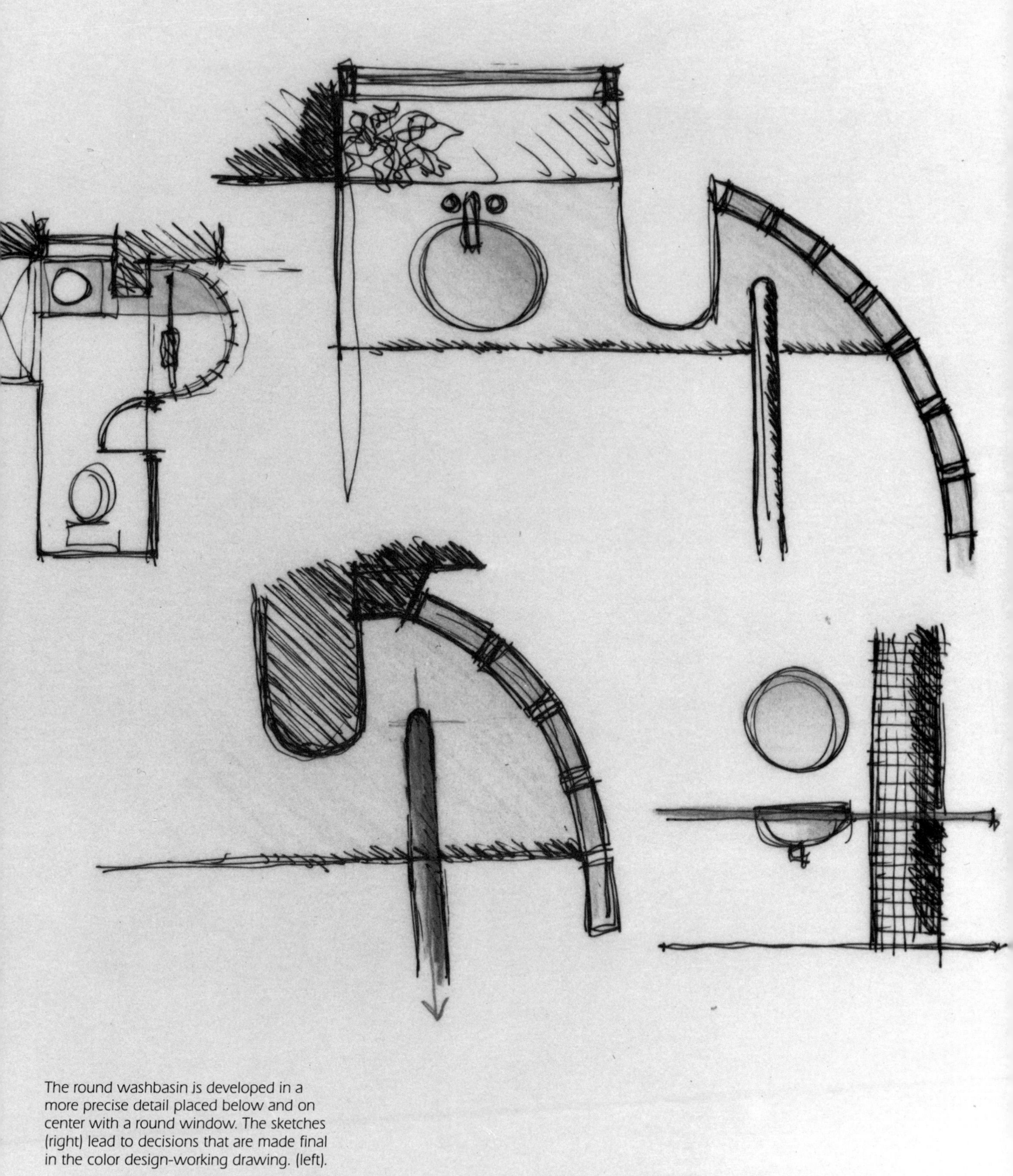

The round washbasin is developed in a more precise detail placed below and on center with a round window. The sketches (right) lead to decisions that are made final in the color design-working drawing. (left).

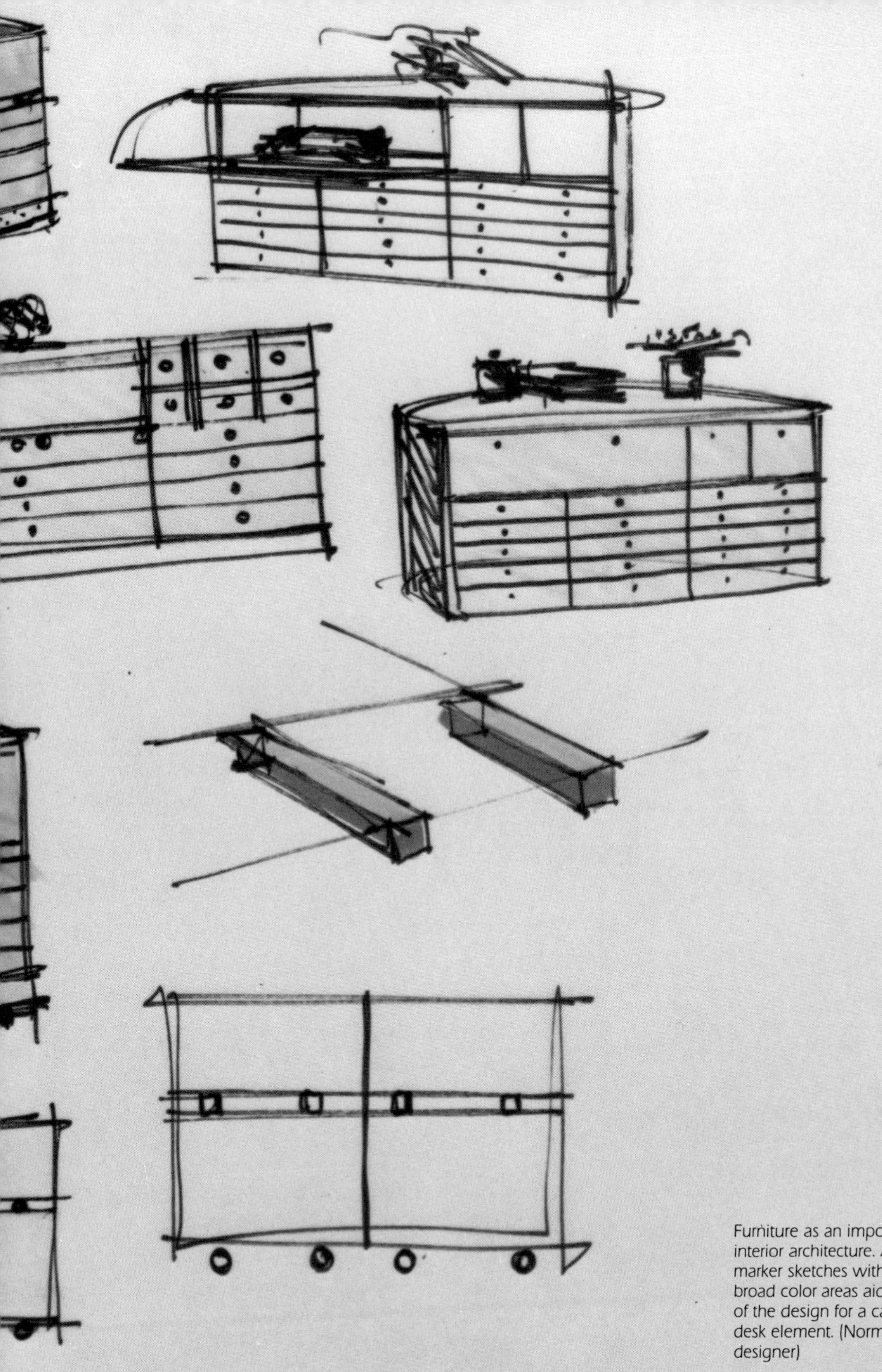

Furniture as an important part of the interior architecture. A series of Pentel marker sketches with design markers for broad color areas aid in the development of the design for a cabinet with a pull-out desk element. (Norman Diekman, designer)

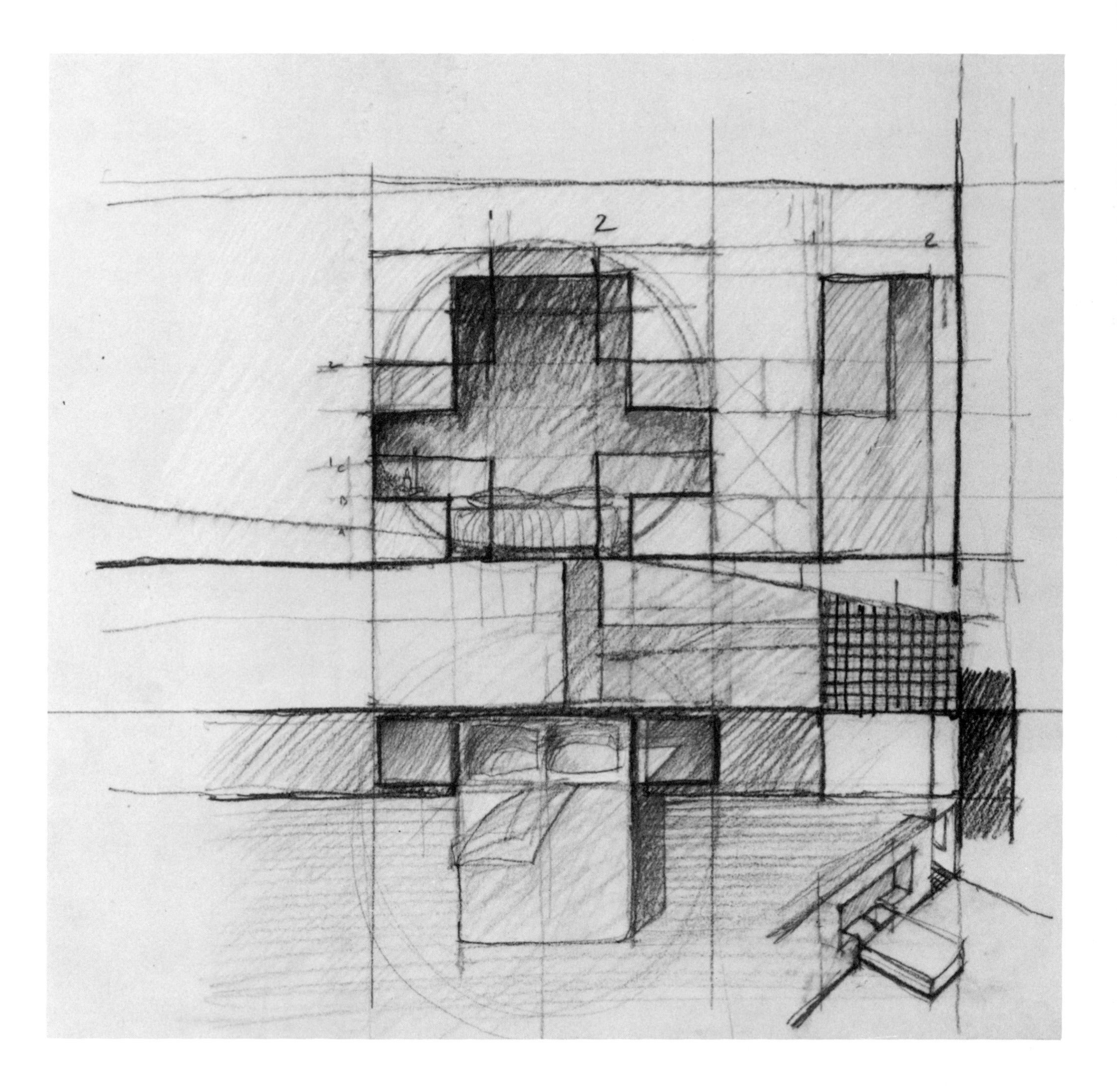

A Giuseppe Zambonini sketch study for a bedroom (left) and the realization of the sketch in the photograph (right). The intricate plan and elevation drawing, developed on the job site, finds its way to actual construction. (Photograph by George Cserna)

7

Sketch Models

Although sketching as a type of drawing is in almost universal use as a technique for every sort of design work, the making of sketch models is less familiar. Models are, of course, in wide use in interior design practice as a presentation device, but the presentation model is usually perfect in detail, highly realistic, and both slow and expensive to produce. It is often the work of specialist model makers and is usually made after the design process is fairly complete so that all details are firmly established. Sketch modeling is quite different. It is quick, direct, often quite abstract (not realistic in material, color, and detail), and it is usually done by the designer as an aid to conceptual thinking.

Although three-dimensional visualization is a skill that every designer tries to develop, there is always a certain gap between design idea, drawings on flat paper (even if in perspective), and three-dimensional space. The three-dimensional reality can be viewed from every angle and is seen through binocular vision as having actual depth and spatial relationships. Architects and industrial designers often make use of sketch modeling to help this kind of design realization, and interior designers are becoming increasingly aware of the usefulness of the sketch model as a creative tool.

Sketching in model form requires acceptance of a degree of roughness similar to that accepted in conceptual drawing. The aim is neither dollhouse cuteness nor architectural precision, but rather access to spatial relationships in a quick but informative way. However rough or sketchy, the sketch model should be to scale—not necessarily accurate in every detail, but correct in overall proportions. Choice of scale is, as with drawings, a matter of selection based on the size of the subject to be modeled (to keep the result manageably small, but large enough to show what is of interest) and the use to be made of the sketch. A usual range would be from ¼″ = 1′-0″ for a whole floor of an office building or a large showroom, to 1″ = 1′-0″ for a moderate-size to small room or group of rooms. Even larger scales (1½″ or 3″ = 1′0″) might be used for sketch models of details; full size is most often used for furniture or other smaller detail elements.

Where an existing space is being dealt with or where a specific new space has been selected (as when an office floor, a loft, or an apartment has been rented or bought), it is useful to have at hand a rough model of the space, to scale, to aid in sensing the space that a floor plan defines. Such a model can be used as a "shell" into which designed elements are inserted as they are developed. It can also serve as a fine way of visualizing color and material relationships. Elements are simply and quickly modeled and inserted into the shell in a temporary, easy-to-change fashion, as the design process continues.

Sketch models of particular areas under study can be made at larger scale as an aid in working out relationships of parts, while rough models of built-ins, special pieces of furniture, and similar details can be a useful first step in design conceptualization. For anyone who has made finished presentation models, the idea of adjusting to rough sketch modeling can be somewhat difficult. The kinds of materials and tools used can help to establish a suitable vocabulary that will avoid the careful precision of both hobby and design professional finished model making. Some of the tools and mate-

Photograph by Jon Naar.

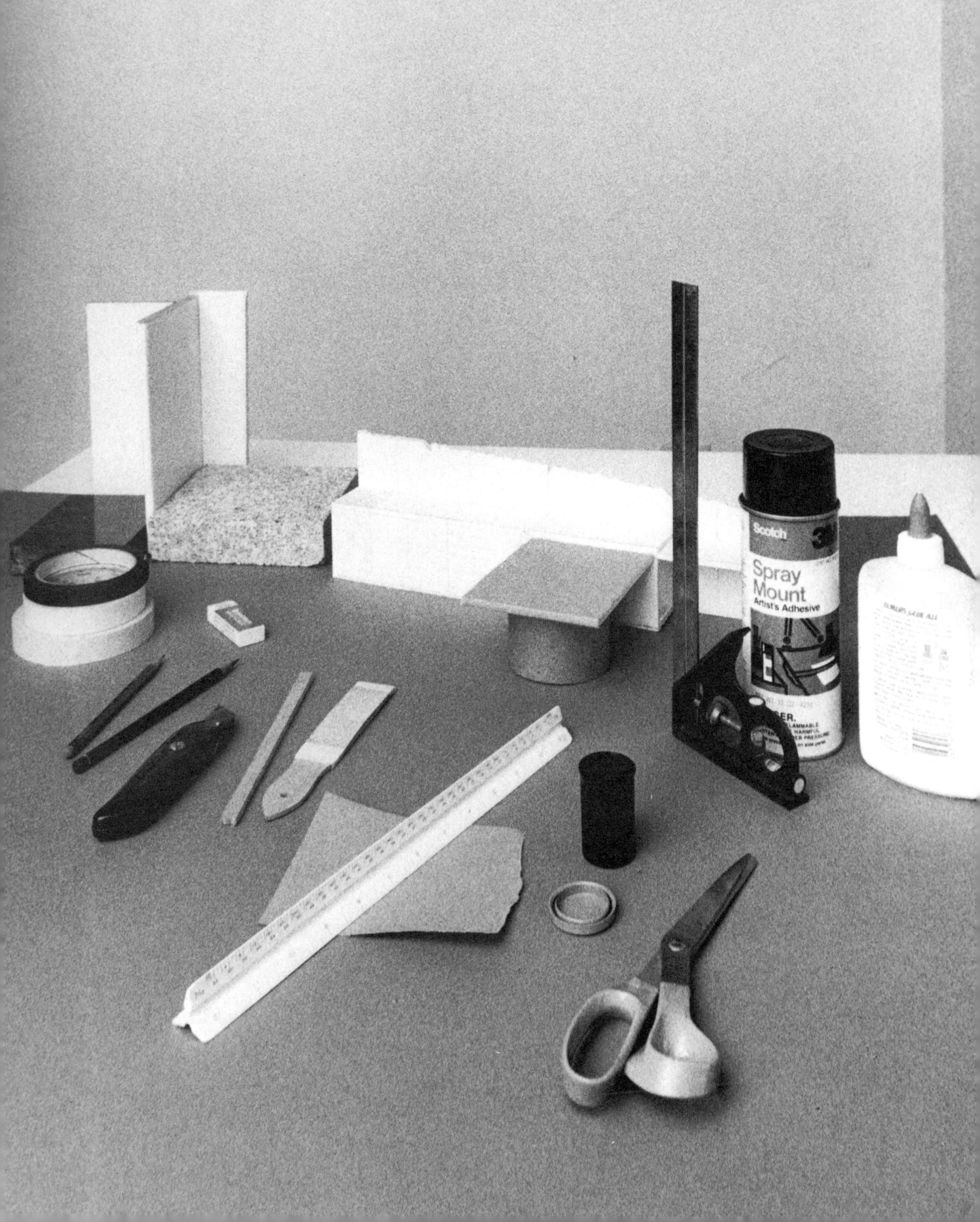
Scotch
3M
Spray
Mount
Artist's Adhesive

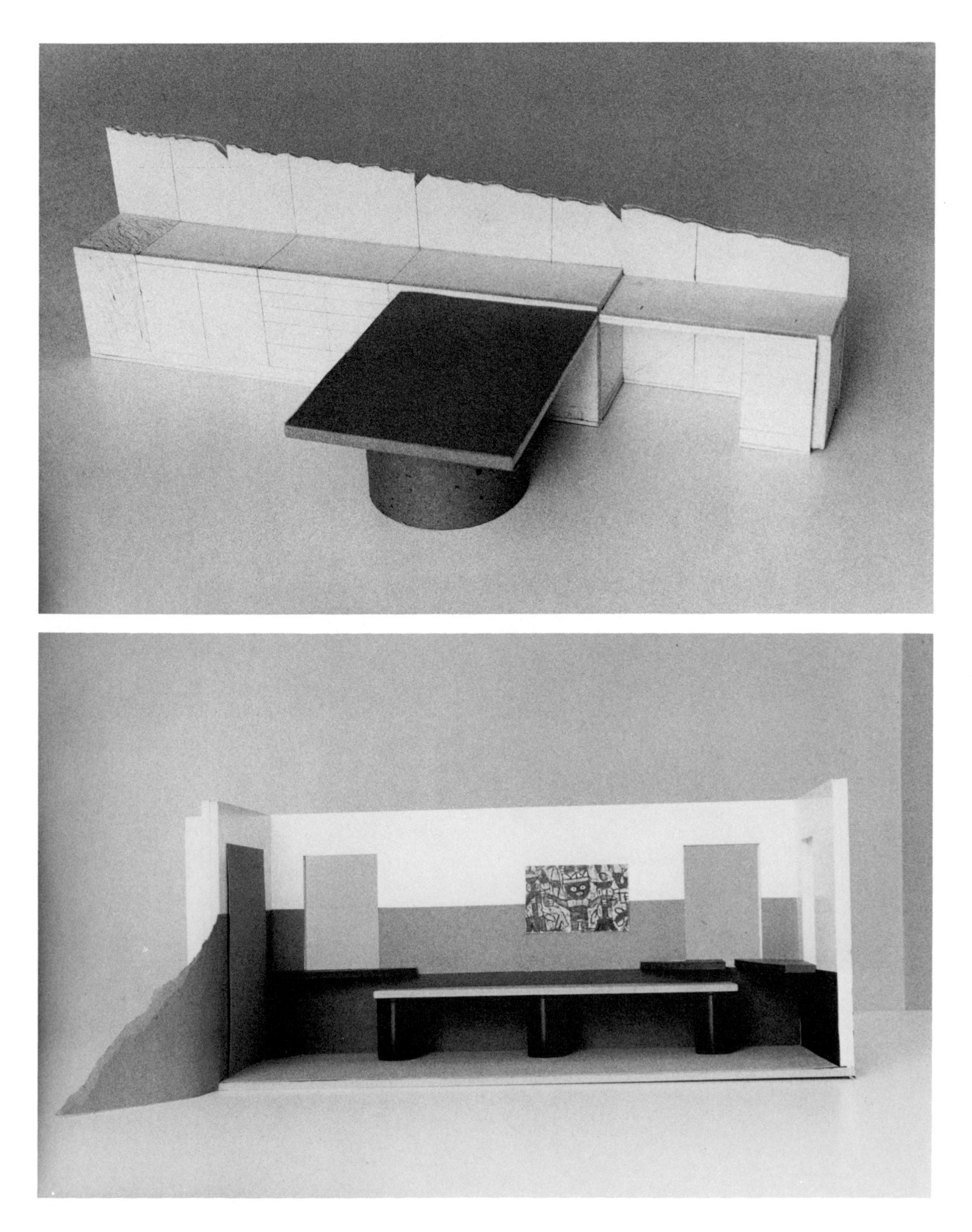

rials are common to both kinds of model making so that everything needed for sketch modeling will probably be on hand anywhere that finished models have been produced. On the other hand, sketch modeling can be undertaken with a minimum of tools and with mostly "found" materials. The following summary of the tools and materials most used will suggest the nature of the sketch-modeling process.

TOOLS

The basic tools are a good shears and one or two kinds of knives, a mat knife and a smaller knife (such as the popular X-Acto knife), perhaps a single-edge razor blade with or without a holder. A metal straightedge is helpful for knife cuts. The basic drafting tools—pencils, triangles, straightedge, and scale—are needed for scale layout. To these basics can be added, as the need arises:

a small dovetail saw

pliers

a wire cutter (may be combined with pliers)

some small C-clamps

a supply of spring clothespins

small paint brushes

a scratch-awl

a few small files (emery boards are particularly useful)

tin snips

A trimming board (the type with a swinging knife cutter arm) is also very convenient for making straight and square cuts in paper or board. Large trimming boards are clumsy and expensive, but a small one (10 or 12 inches) is very useful and can be used for other cutting chores as well.

MATERIALS

A very wide range of materials are useful in making sketch models. Some are familiar studio materials but many are "found" materials collected from scraps, trash, toys and models, or dime or variety store sources. Some bits and pieces from a collection of finished model materials are sometimes useful if they are at hand. Shops that specialize in model-making materials offer a vast range of items that are particularly useful in making finished models but are hardly necessary for sketch models. Special suppliers offer materials for architectural modeling and model railroads, ships, airplanes, and autos. Dollhouse supplies are available in great variety. Most such materials are too detailed (and too expensive) for sketch models, but some can be ideal for a particular use.

The usual basic materials used in making sketch models are:

Cardboard, mat board, illustration board (in several weights, colors, and textures)

Foamcore board (in thicknesses of 1/8", 1/4", and 1/2")

Glues and cements. "White glue" such as Sobo or Elmer's, Duco cement, a wood glue such as Franklin Tite-Bond, contact cement, a 5-minute Epoxy, a "super" (cyanoacrylate) glue

Wood strips. Balsa, basswood, pine in various sizes. Small dowels in 1/8", 1/4", 3/8", and 1/2" sizes.

Acetate sheet and thin Plexiglas, transparent and in a few tints. Plexiglas rod or tubing.

Colored and textured papers such as PMS, Color-Aid, high-gloss flint paper, and charcoal and pastel papers.

Scotch tape—masking, drafting, clear, and frosted. Thin "Chart-Pak" in various thicknesses and colors.

Sandpaper. Finer grits plus "wet-or-dry" and garnet papers. Used both for sanding and as a material.

Wire. Brass and aluminum. Sculptor's armature wire is particularly useful.

Paints. Model paints in small bottles and (for most colors) in spray cans.

Veneer. A few small pieces of most used woods.

To this list, one can add on a vast variety of "found" materials that can be collected in a few boxes and file folders to be at hand as need arises. The possibilities are limitless, but some suggestions might include:

Papers in colors and textures from throw-away brochures, advertise-

Quick design study models using Foamcor board and colored papers together with "found" elements such as film canisters that serve as supports for the desk slab. (Photograph by Jon Naar)

ments, packages, etc. often yield good color papers (trim away print, etc.). If saved and sorted by color, these are a fine source of free materials. Metallics, wood and marble patterns often turn up and can be useful on occasion.

Packages. These yield transparent sheet, metal (aluminum) cans and small items such as bottle caps and film cans for special purpose uses.

Toothpicks (round and flat), soda straws, coffee-stirrers, tongue-depressors, barbecue skewers.

Wire. Coat-hangers and paper clips are favorite sources for wire in various weights.

Odds and ends. Ping-pong and small rubber balls. Beads and marbles. Pins (regular and large heads), brads, and nails. Thread and string. Index cards, report covers, file folders. Packing materials (plastic foam, flexible and rigid corrugated board, plastic bags, and bottles).

Cardboard mailing and similar tubes.

Parts from small toys and model kits. Scrap electric wire. Buttons, snaps, rivets, grommets, washers, and other small hardware items.

As making of sketch models becomes a regular activity, each designer will discover new found materials and will make a habit of watching for and collecting materials that will turn out to be useful at some future time.

MODEL MAKING

The process of making sketch models is as varied and as improvisational as the nature of the materials used. Materials are cut (even torn) to sizes and shapes needed and put together with tape or adhesive as may be convenient. It is often helpful to leave model parts loose (unattached) or only taped in place so that they can be shifted about or changed in form, color, and texture as the design process goes on. A conceptual model is often a good starting point for a design project. It can be of some small part of the project, a "vignette" that serves as a focus or theme, or it may include the total area under consideration. As with a concept collage, concept models may be of bits and pieces snipped or torn from various materials and put together in a quick and rough fashion. Such a model may even be done without thinking about scale, as long as its parts are in an approximately accurate proportional relationship. More often, a few measured dimensions to scale (total width or length and a key height) should be established to make the sketch to scale in a general way, even if details (should any be present) are not measured out.

A concept model may deal with spatial relationships alone, ignoring colors and finishes; it is best, then, to use all white or all gray or neutral-colored materials. If color and material selections are part of the ideas under development, colored papers are usually the best way to introduce these values. Papers may be cut or torn and taped into place on the elements of the model, or the basic materials may be chosen to represent the materials involved. The roughness of the sketch model makes it easy to make and remake changes as ideas develop and as comparisons are tried out.

Another type of early-stage sketch model that is very helpful is a simple box model of the total space being worked on, made to scale. When a plan is available of a rented space (a loft or office floor, for example) where partitioning does not exist, or of an apartment or house where partition changes may be under consideration, a simple model of the "raw space" is very helpful. The plan may be traced onto, or actually pasted down on, a base of cardboard, foamcore, or Masonite. Perimeter walls are then cut out to correct scale height; a supply of long strips can all be cut at once and then cut and folded to make the walls. Columns can be cut from wood strips or dowels, or folded or rolled up from paper or cardboard and glued in place on the floor where shown in the plan. Door and window openings can be cut out to scale in the walls. A "shell" is thus created representing the three-dimensional space in a way that makes visualization easier than it is with only plan and height measurements as reference. New partitions and other elements can now be inserted into the model and moved about, and existing partitions can be cut or removed as changes in the existing space are contemplated. A model of this sort is usually made at ¼″ or ½″ = 1′-0″ for larger spaces, or at 1″ = 1′-0″ for a single room or other small space. The scale of an available floor plan, if at all suitable, will usually decide the scale of the model. As design work progresses, elements of color and material may be inserted and furniture placement may be indicated. Detailed models of furniture are not appropriate to sketch models, but, particularly at ¼″ or ½″ scale, it is often helpful to use simple wood blocks and cut bits of cardboard to form rough approximations of furniture mass and location. Block indication of furniture can be painted in or slips of colored paper can be pasted on to suggest finishes, cover materials, etc. Sometimes simple squares of paper in color, or even cut bits of actual fabrics, can be used to aid in sketch study of color and material selections.

Sketch models at larger scale are useful for studying space and form relationships in specific locations where complex design ideas are being worked out. Elements such as lowered ceilings, level changes and steps, openings of unusual shape, and blocks of built-in or massive furniture can be quickly put together at 1″ or larger scale for study of such problems. The design of special furniture, whether built-in or free-standing, also invites study in sketch model form. Larger scales, such as 1½″ or 3″ = 1′-0″ are useful with the usual materials—cardboard, paper, and foam. Cushions and upholstered elements can be cut and sanded to shape in either balsa wood or plastic foam. The workings of folding, convertible, or other mechanically complex furniture elements are readily studied in this way.

Full-size sketch modeling can also be useful. Most often, only details are taken to this scale. A corner where materials meet, details of molding and reveals and such small items as custom hardware parts can be sketched in cardboard, wood strips, and with miscellaneous materials, found or purchased, as a help in

A sketch model using Plexiglas, colored paper, and cardboard to create dynamic design elements for a prototype table. Also see color illustrations of the same model (page 137). (Design and model by Doris Nieves; photograph by John Pile)

When photographed, a skillfully made sketch model can give a strong impression of an actual space. Camera placement at scale eye level is particularly effective in conveying a sense of reality. (Design and model by Wanda Josefson; photograph by John Pile)

getting things right before moving into drawings and, possibly, prototypes or finished models. Occasionally furniture designs are modeled at full size in cardboard and wood strip—sometimes with astonishing effects of realism. A cardboard chair or table needs to be marked with a warning sign to prevent an unwary visitor from causing an unfortunate collapse!

Sketch models at full size are also ideal for studying the small, accessory items that interior designers sometimes are able to create to complete a particular project. Dishes, glassware, silver, lamps, signs, and similar elements can be sketched in three dimensions in paper, wood, scraps of metal, acetate, or other plastics. Color can be paper, or sprayed or brushed paint; lacquers dry almost instantly and are least likely to warp sketch materials. Such sketches advance the design process with a minimum of time expenditure and cost so that a final, perfect model in real materials can serve as a check on design decisions that have already reached a final, or near final, point.

It is also worth noting that sketch models, like finished models, are an excellent way of communicating design ideas to clients and other laymen. Many people who find drawings mysterious or confusing can understand a model quite readily; more often than not, they also find models attractive and interesting in a way that aids in maintaining communication and obtaining approval to proceed to more developed stages of a design project.

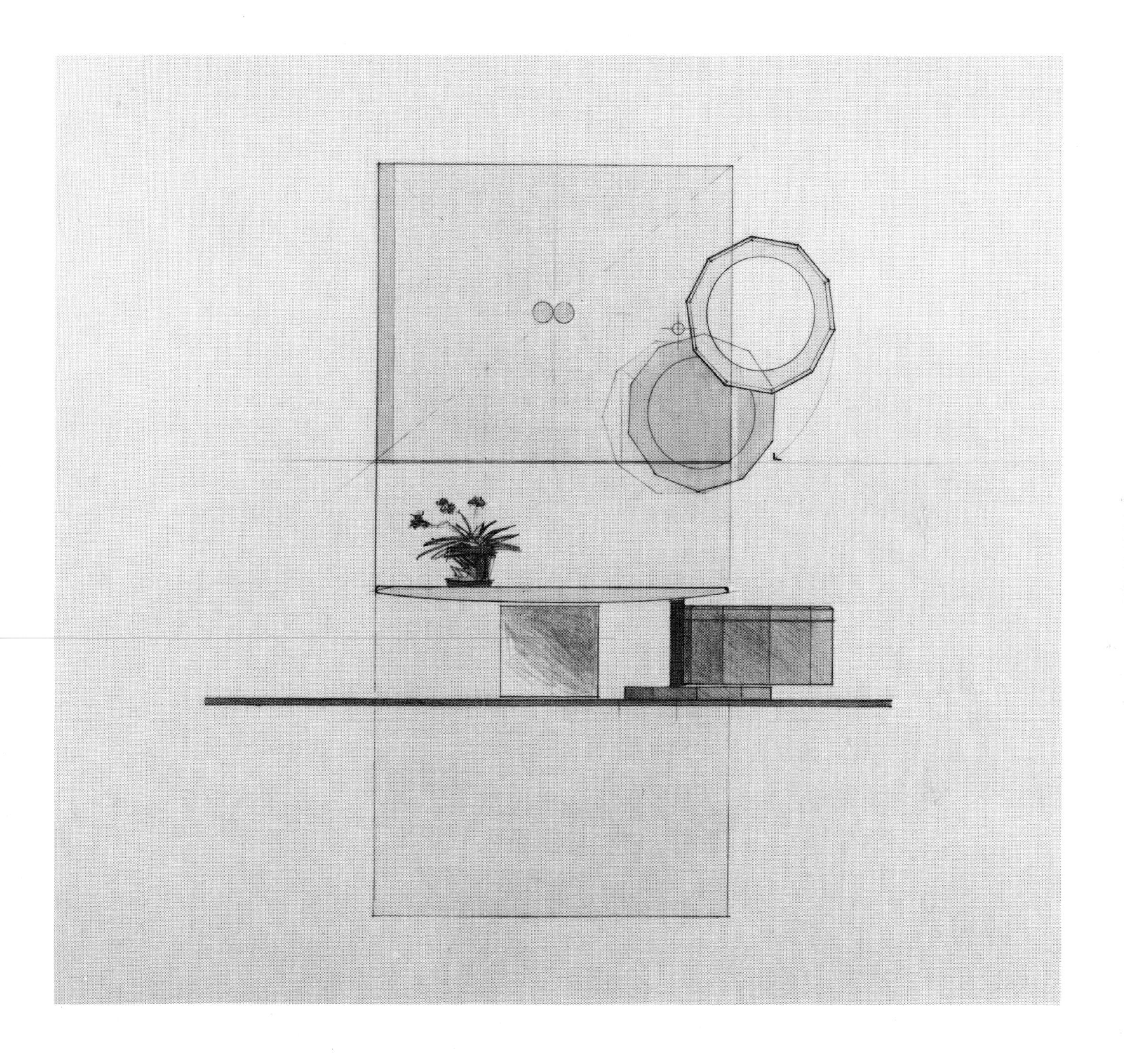

A special extension of the scale model is a full-size model—not a prototype, but still a sketch. Here, colored papers spread out on a sheet of plywood sketch out the form of a proposed coffee table. The chance placement of the dark pillow on the right, intended as a prop to give scale, leads to the development of the small storage unit that appears in the sketch above. (Norman Diekman, designer; photograph by Jon Naar)

A detail drawing of a cabinet pull, (opposite page) together with a simple cardboard and wood sketch model that permits evaluation of the drawn form at full size. (Photograph by Jon Naar)

Design and sketch model (above) by Doris Nieves (see page 131). (Photographs by John Pile)

8

Collected Sketches

The making of sketches is not, normally, an end in itself but rather a step, usually a significant early step, in moving toward realization of built space. Tracing the designer's steps in developing a project can reveal wide variation in process, depending on the scope of a project, the time frame for execution, and the individual designer's way of thinking. Large projects that include major architectural elements usually progress from early sketches to more formal, drafted design drawings, possibly to formal "presentation drawings" and then to "working" or construction drawings that can be used as a basis for bidding, contracts, and construction work.

While these steps are almost inevitable in architectural and engineering projects, interior design projects can often compress the sequence of steps. Simple projects can sometimes be carried forward on the basis of verbal instructions alone, or with sketches and verbal explanations together as the designer's only line of communication with construction staff in the field. More often, even modest projects require somewhat more complete documentation, but it is not unusual to move to client approvals on the basis of sketches and to construction on the basis of informal working drawings that are actually developed sketches. While this may seem to involve some risks, time is saved and there is no evidence that final results suffer from such direct ways of working.

The three projects illustrated here have been chosen to show a variety of project types and the similarities and differences among three design approaches—each incorporating major dependence on sketching as a key tool for design development. Joseph Paul D'Urso has become known for a style that critics often identify with the current concepts of "minimialist" or "high-tech" design (although D'Urso disavows concern with such fashionable notions). Giuseppe Zambonini is currently in practice in New York, where he is involved in the renovation and alteration of lofts. Zambonini is a great believer in design as a process: He integrates all aspects of architecture, graphics, and furniture design. Norman Diekman is concerned with furniture design and the design of related projects but is best known for interior design work, often with a strongly architectural emphasis.

Designers have an unfortunate habit of discarding sketches as they become obsolete during the progress of a project, so that collecting a chronological history of design development in sequential drawings is often difficult or impossible. In the three case histories presented here, the designers have made a point of collecting sketches in the order of their development and have made them available for publication along with some notes on the step-by-step processes that they represent. A few photographs of finished results are also included to give a sense of the relation of the early sketch to the built reality.

JOSEPH PAUL D'URSO

The project illustrated here is a condominium residence in Florida. The sketches are mostly plans, plus a few elevations. There are no perspectives or other "realistic" views at all. All of the sketching is to scale, with ideas developing and changing in time sequence. The medium is pen and ink, used on the familiar thin cream tracing paper that is usually the most favored and the most available material at the designer's drawing board. Some marker color is added here and there, usually not for realistic effect but more as a kind of visual coding to identify and isolate certain elements.

The early sketch at the upper right begins with focus on a certain pivotal grouping in the dining area, where a round table, a curing wall, and a serving unit are grouped in a composition that becomes a key to the development to follow. Marker color makes the planting recognizable as a naturalistic foil to the geometric furniture elements. The lower sketch moves this grouping forward with what may first seem minor changes. The table is now surrounded by chairs that check its seating capacity and give a sense of scale and size. The serving unit shows up with a dotted, diagonal shift indicating consideration of a movable, pivoting role. Most important is the small scribble at the upper right, indicating the intention to place a sculpture in this location. The sculpture—an Ellsworth Kelly—will later develop into a significant anchor and accent in the design of the space.

In the next sketch (page 140) the plan is extended and has become more detailed with the low screen wall that defines the dining area changed in shape in an overlaid tracing sheet. The elevation sketch above gives a further sense of scale by making the height dimension visible. In it, the sculpture has become quite specific while the addition of its red color makes its accent role obvious. The low wall that defines the living area puts in an appearance here and the elevation sketch sets up the form relationships between it and the sculpture.

The same elevation, drawn in part on another overlay (page 141), drops out the low wall at the left and focuses attention on the column immediately to

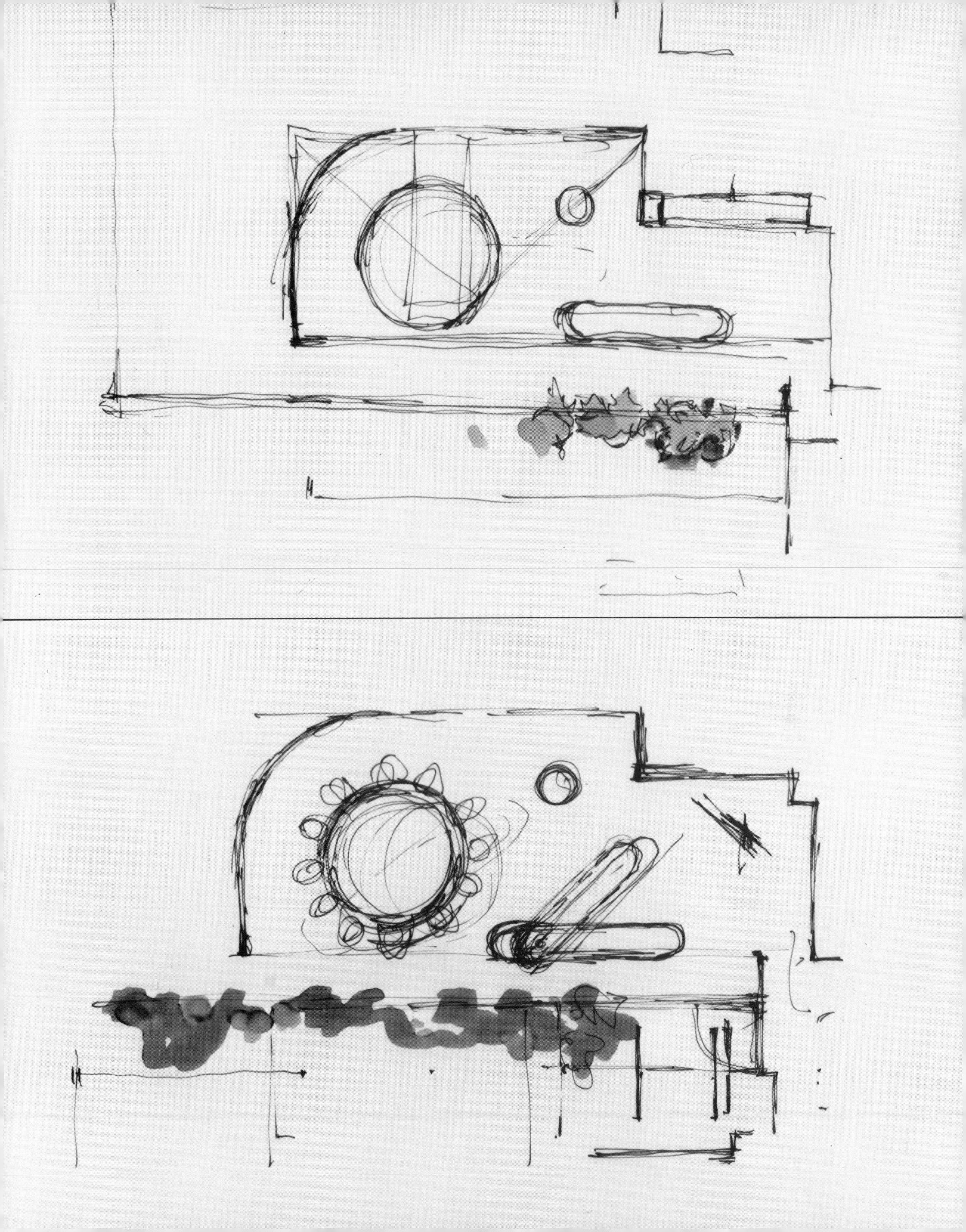

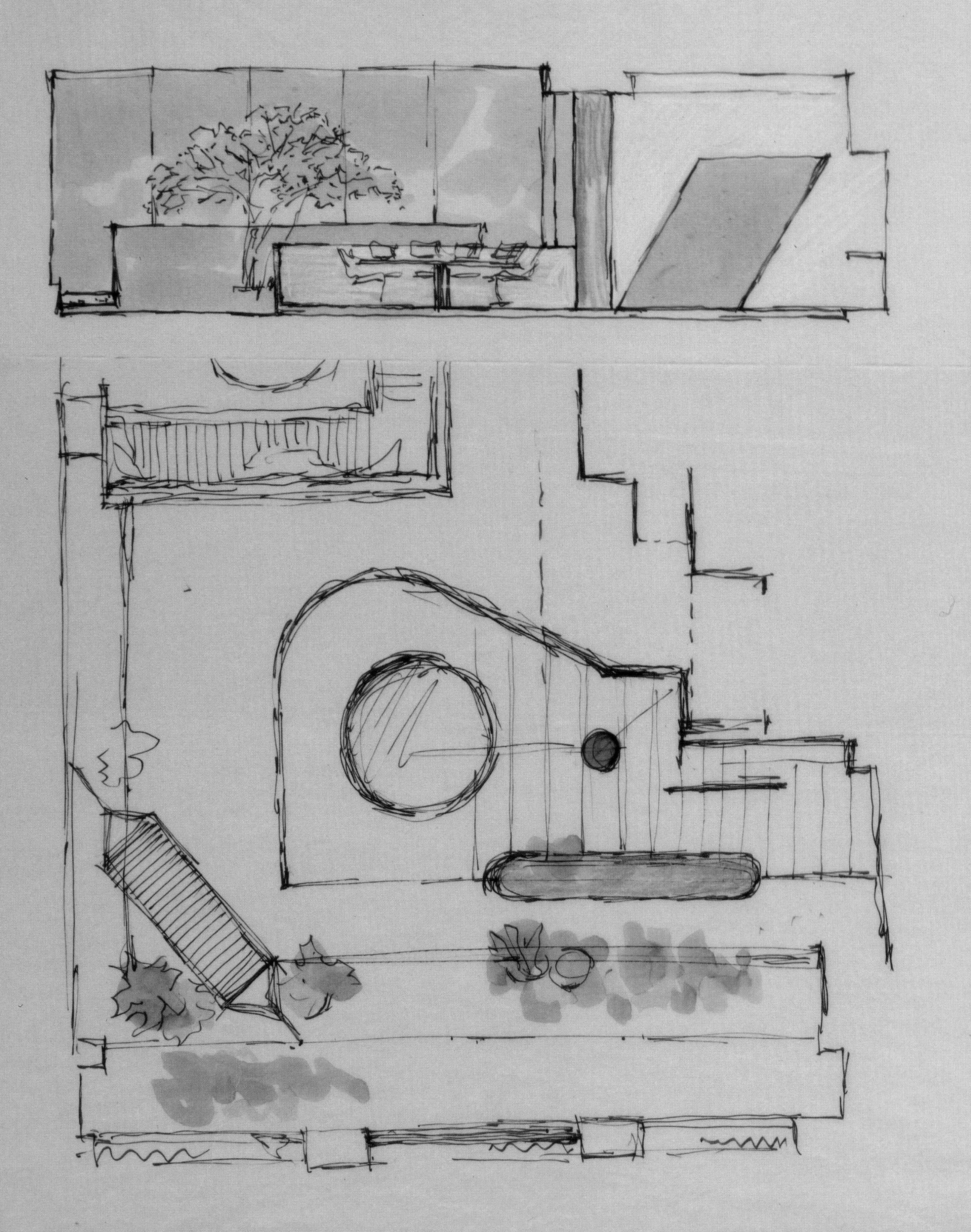

the left of the sculpture in order to consider the column–sculpture relationship in a more specific way. In the more complete floor plan (overleaf) the flow of space up into the living area and on through the spatial circuit to the upper right is developed in more detail. The medium is again pen and ink on yellow tracing paper.

The master bedroom area is studied in the plan sketch on page 144. A greenhouse area is developed along the lower edge of the plan; in it, a chaise (perhaps the famous design of Le Corbusier) has appeared just above with a small, round table. The "racetrack" form (a rectangular block with semicircular ends) that extends to the right has a recall relationship with the serving unit that has been present in the dining area from the first sketch. It appears in end view in the elevation sketch (on page 145) with doors beyond. This drawing explores floor-level change and scale relationships between bed, shelving, doors, and divider.

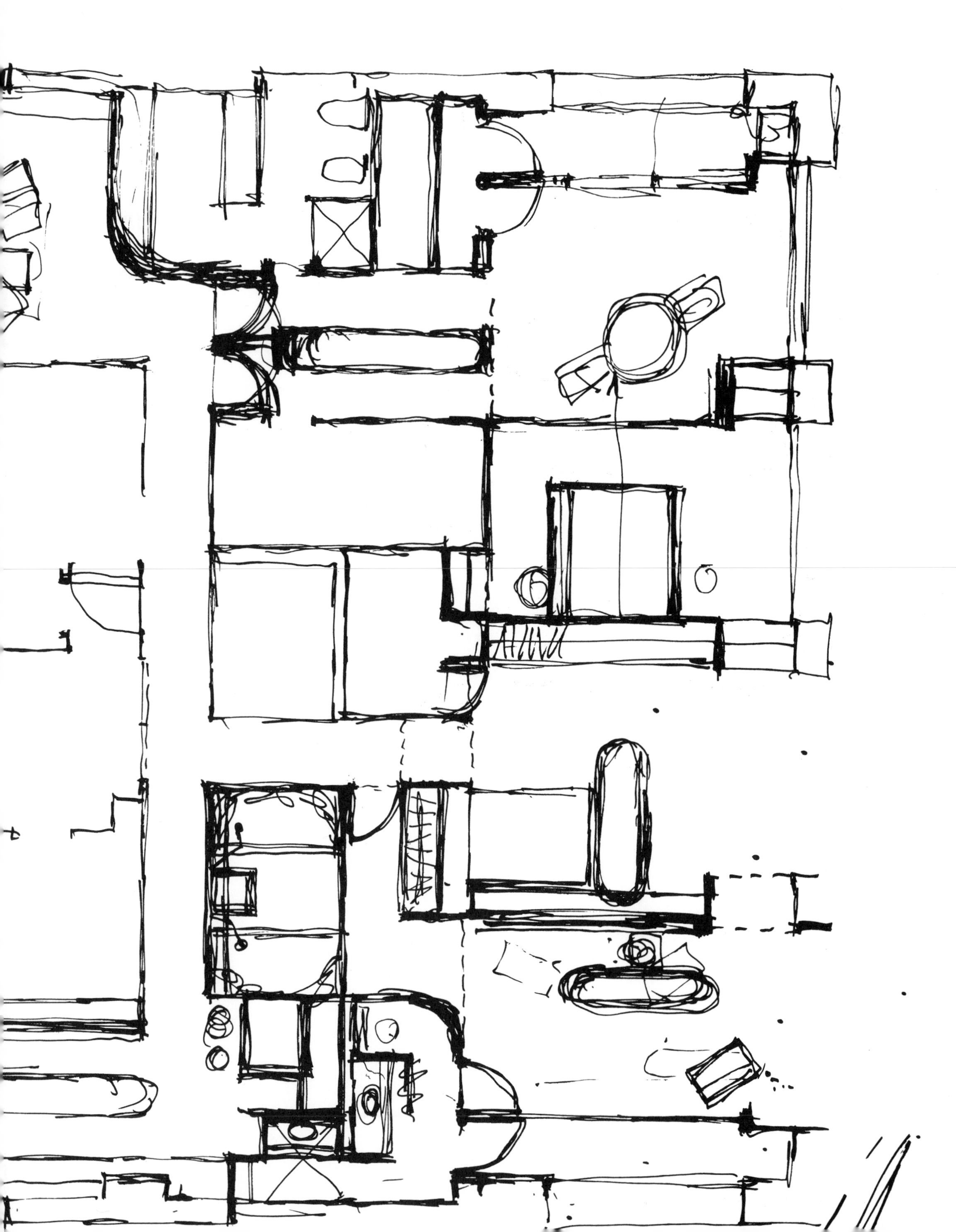

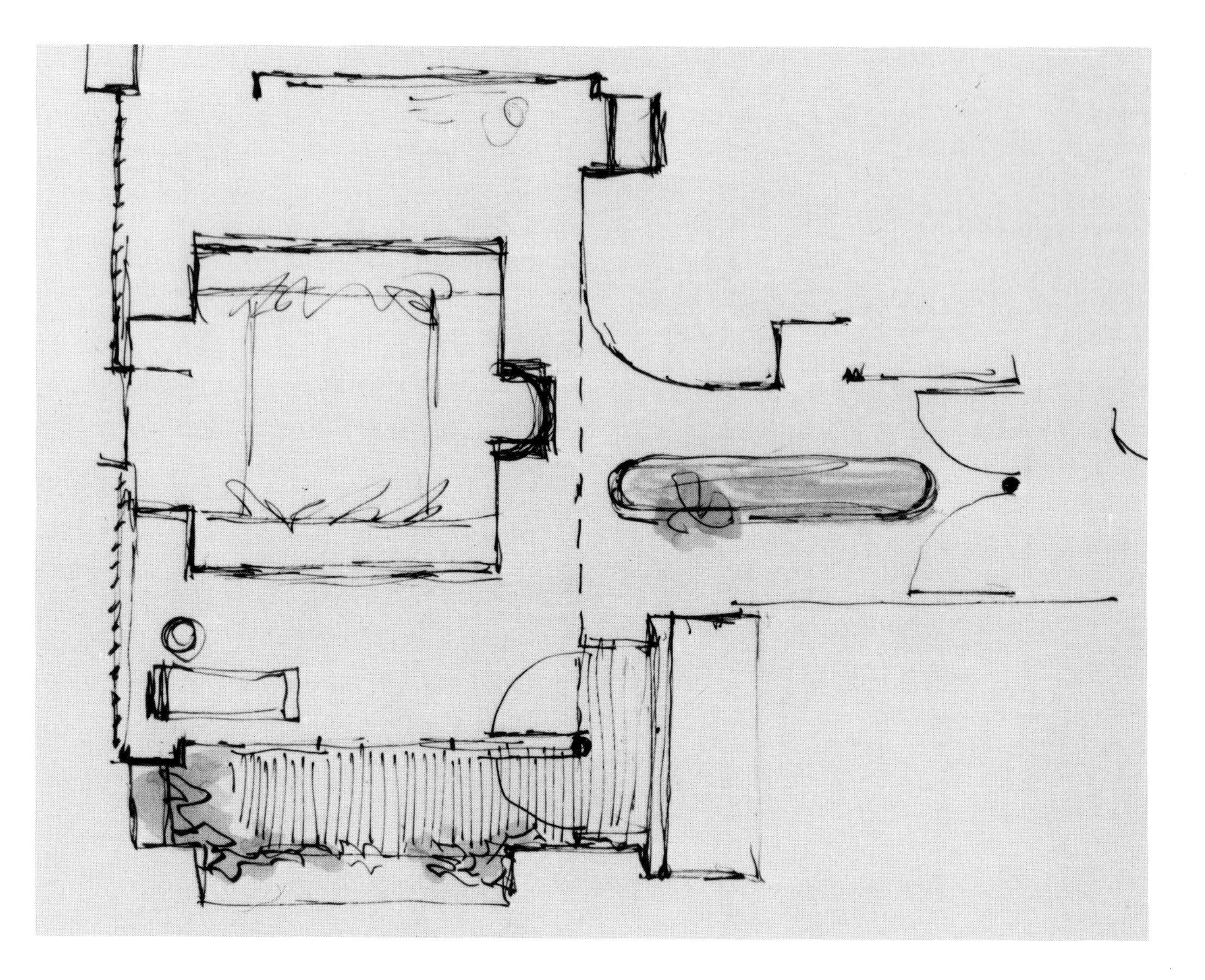

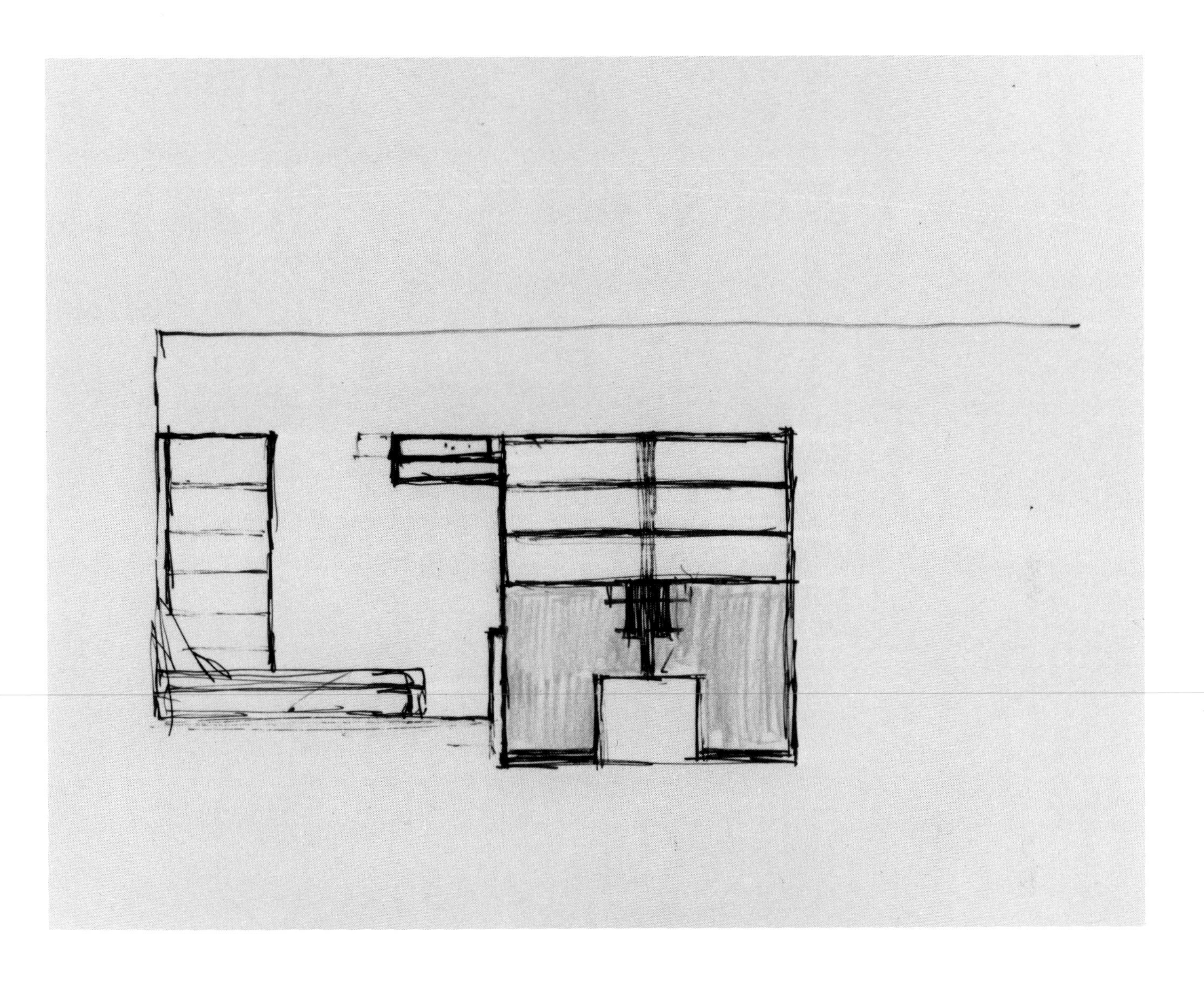

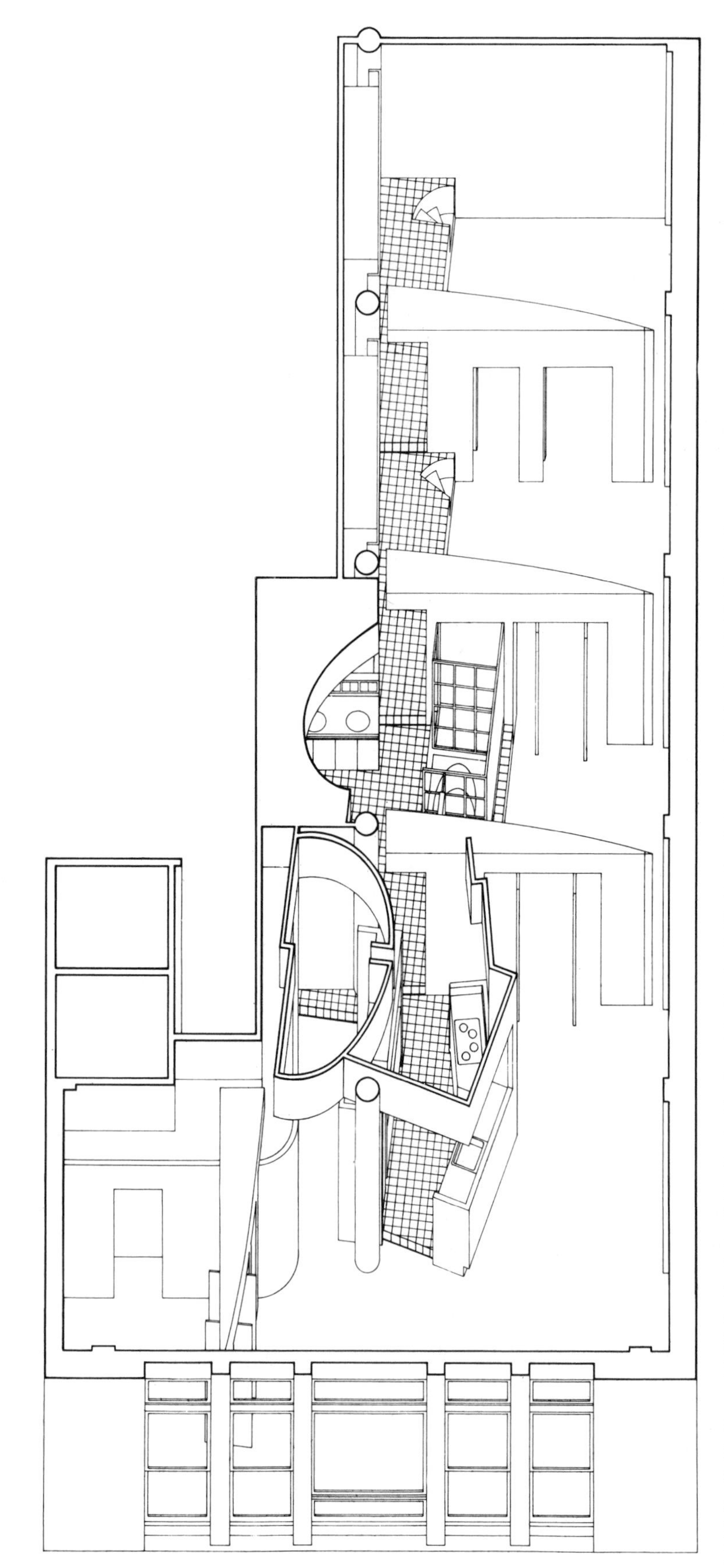

GIUSEPPE ZAMBONINI

In this project, we can trace roots that go back to Giuseppe Zambonini's studies with Carlo Scarpa at the Institute of the University of Architecture in Venice (IUAV) where he took his degree. The project is a loft living space, a lengthwise strip of space in a deep building. In the axonometric drawing at the left we see the space from above and encounter a key conceptual idea—the ribbon of service spaces at the left of the plan, easily identified by the floor-tile pattern with its squaring set at a slight angle.

The cluster of kitchen and bath that begins this band of space can be seen in the first rough plan studies (page 149) where curved forms are introduced in a complex "layering" of spatial elements. In the large plan sketch that follows (pages 150–151) the further layered elements that might be called "blade" forms appear picking up the spacing of the existing columns and making their rhythm a key to the organization of the whole space. The complex axonometric of page 153 then studies the whole space in considerable three-dimensional detail. This might be called a "drafted sketch" in which the straightedge is used for many main construction lines, but scribble and other strictly "sketchy" techniques are used as well to help convey the developing, not yet fully fixed, quality that the design is passing through at this stage.

The full-size detail of page 154 is transitional to the development of construction drawings. It is developed in drawing onto a black-and-white print made from an earlier drawing—again a direction that might be called "layering," superimposition of ideas and elements that goes on in drawing as well as in the conceptual ideas about the design of the actual elements that are to be built. Layering is also involved in the use of color which is built up in layers of color tone.

The photographs of the space as constructed give a sense of the relationship between these somewhat abstract, or at least "diagrammatic," sketch studies and the actuality that they move toward when ideas are transformed into a reality.

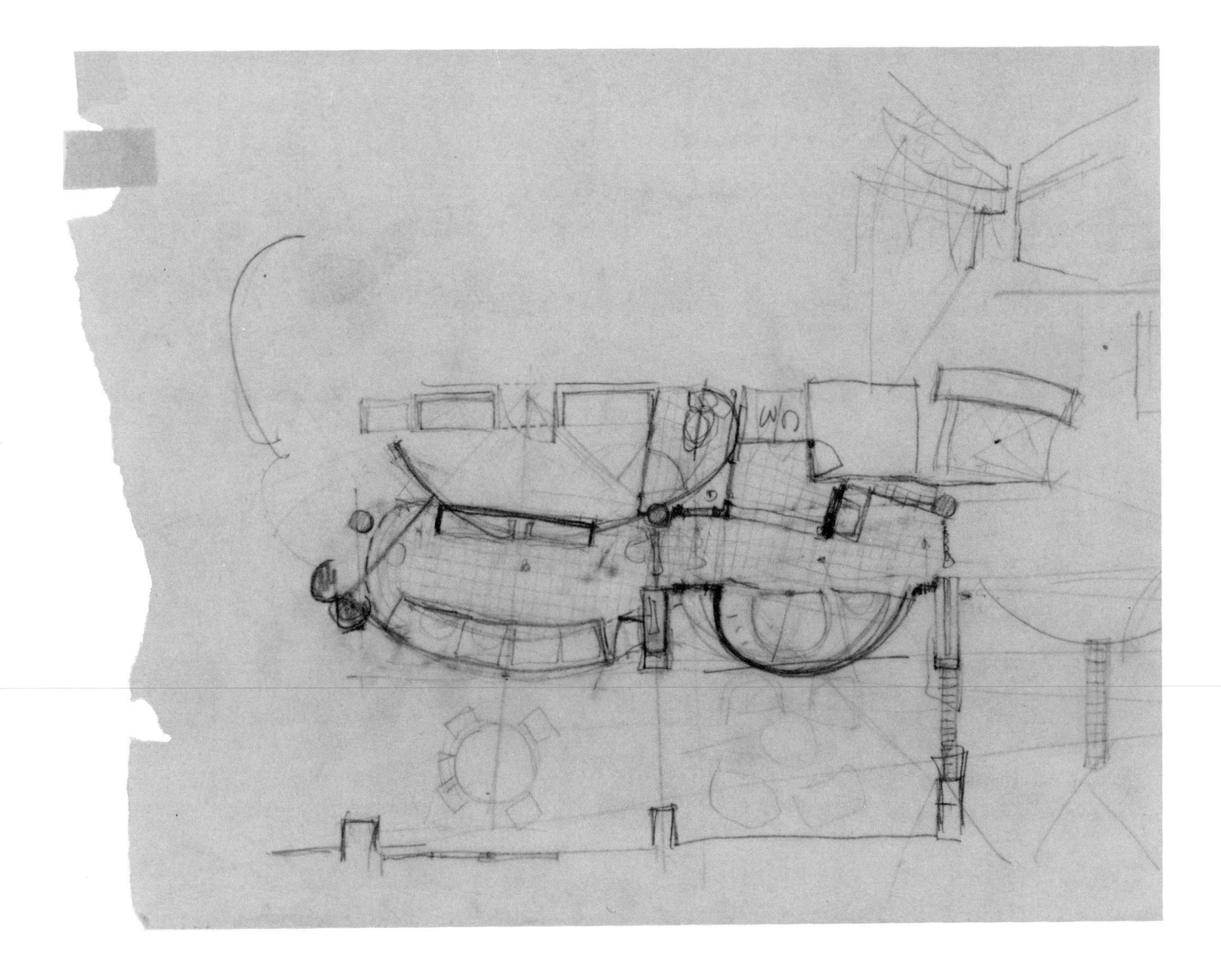
W/C

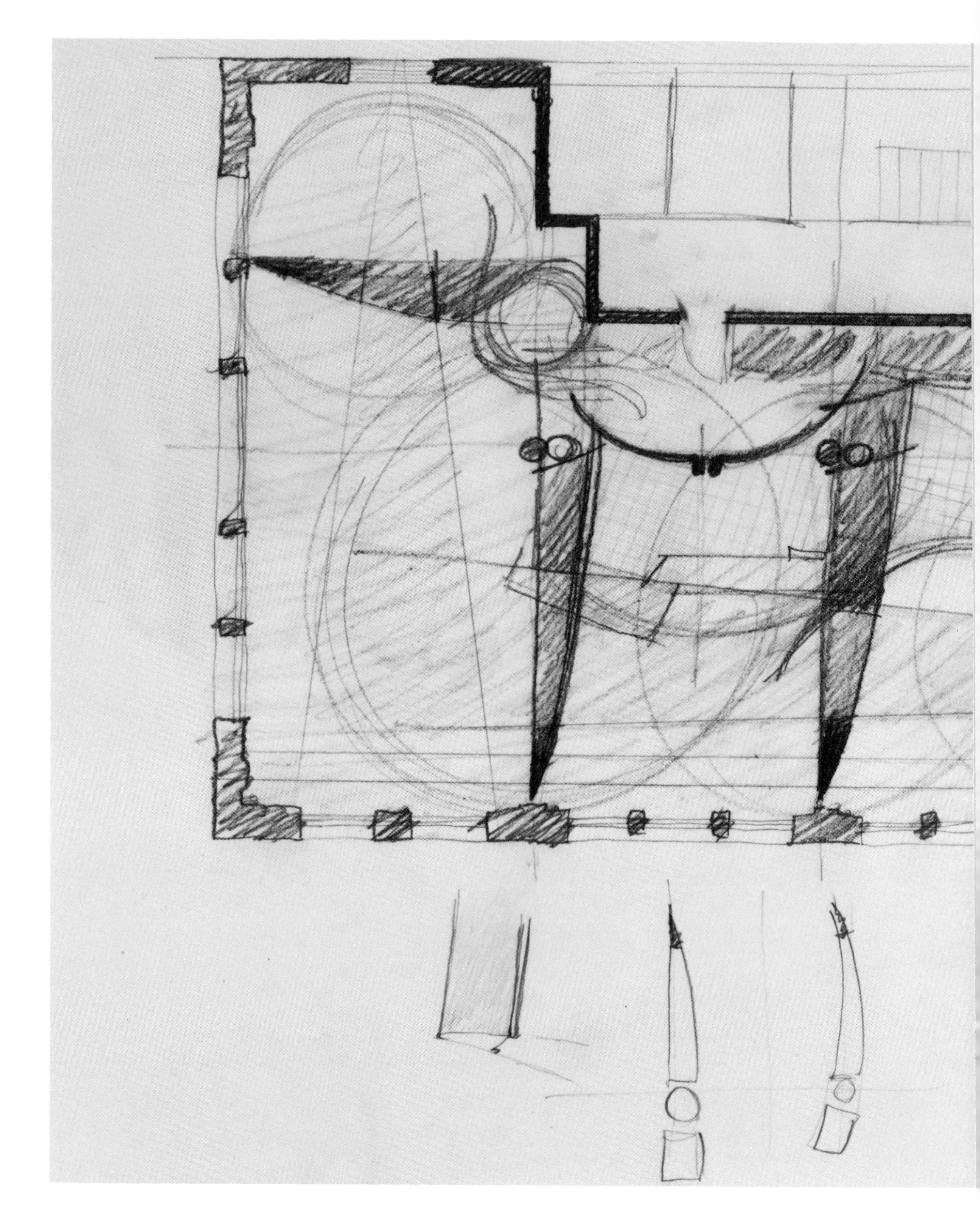

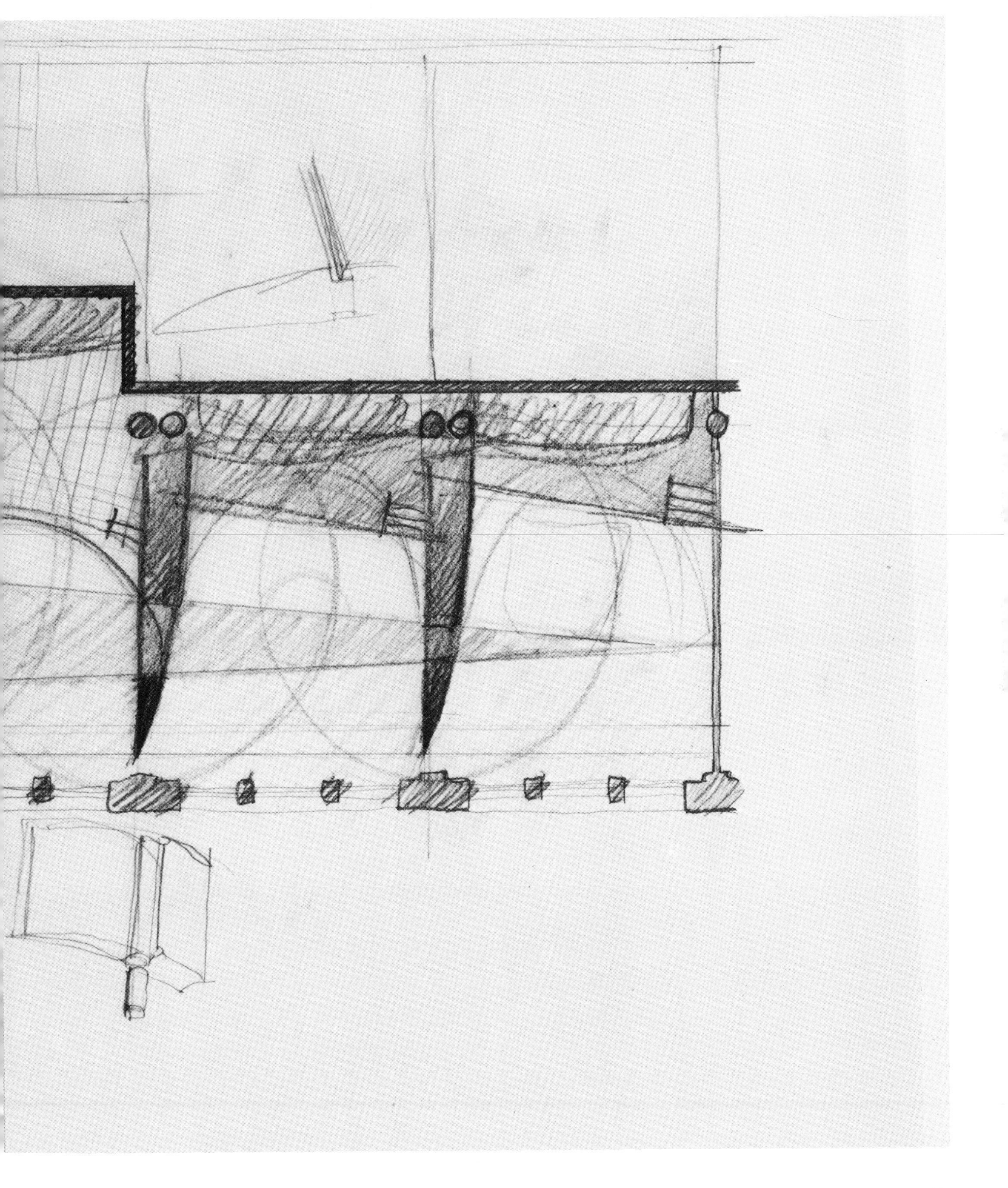

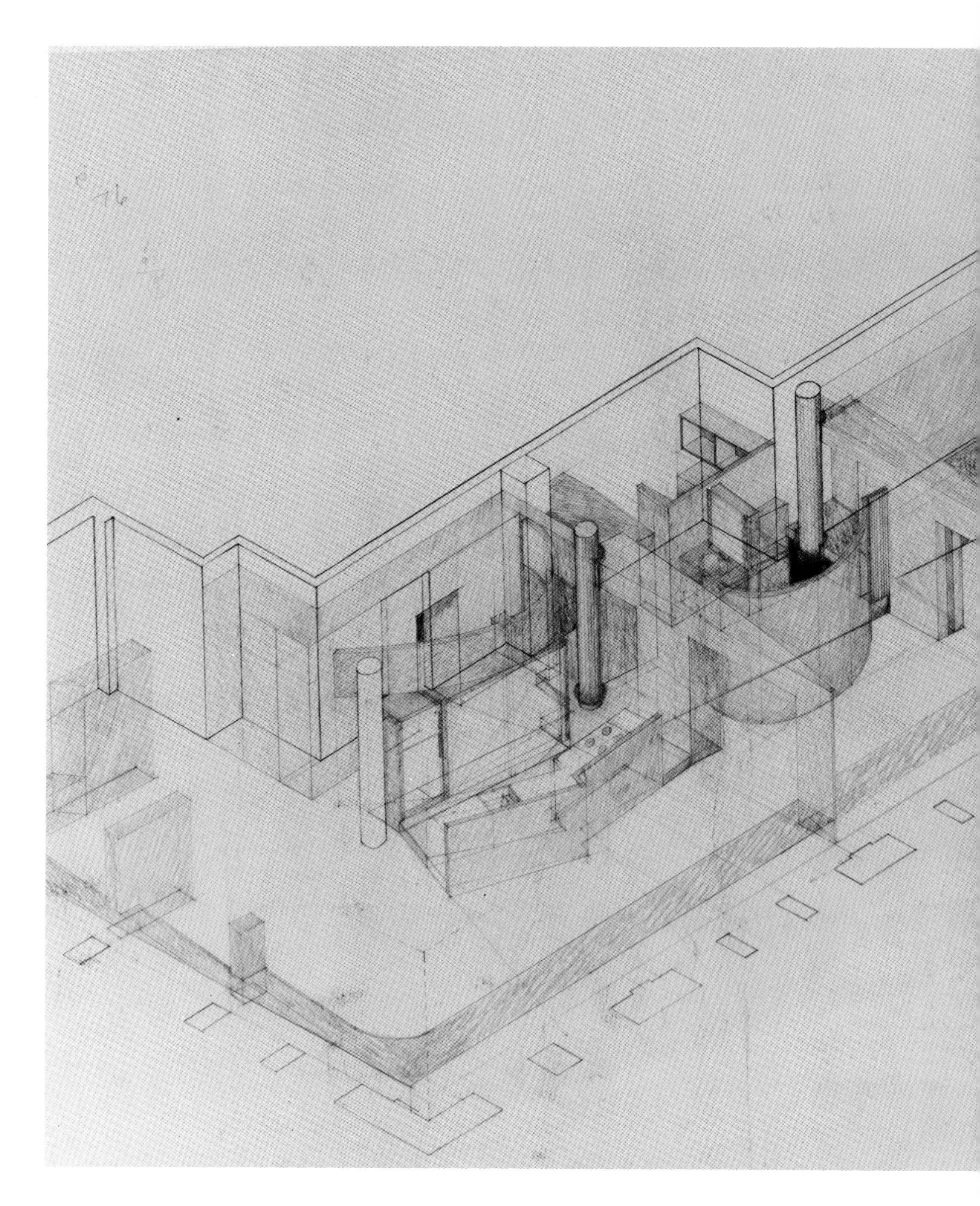

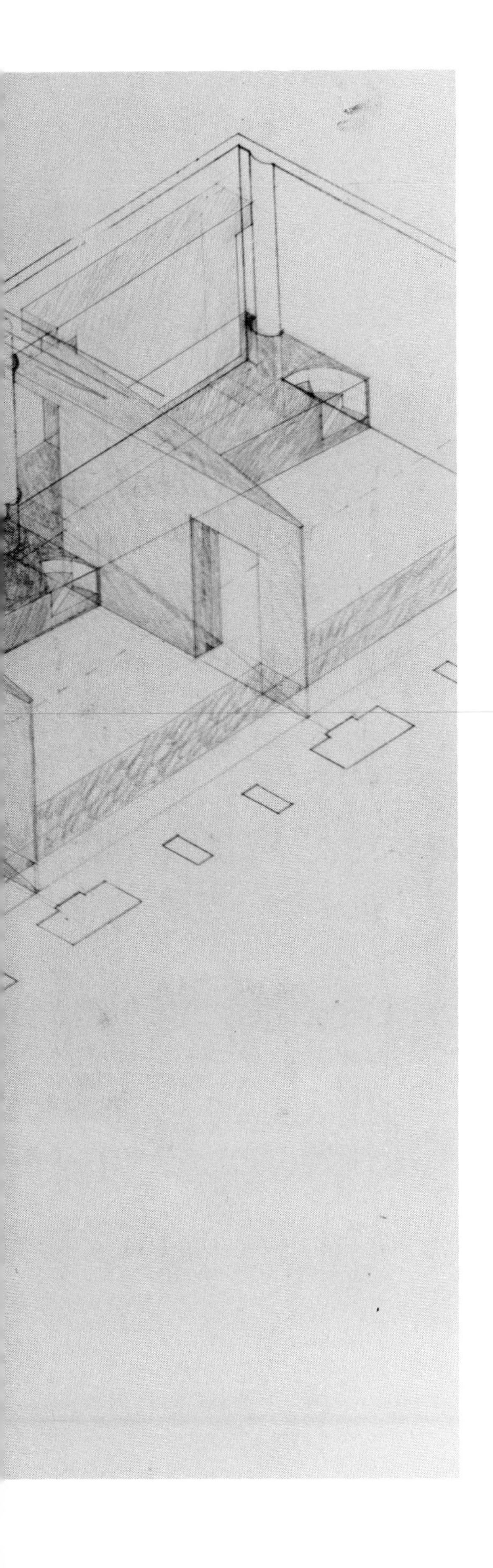

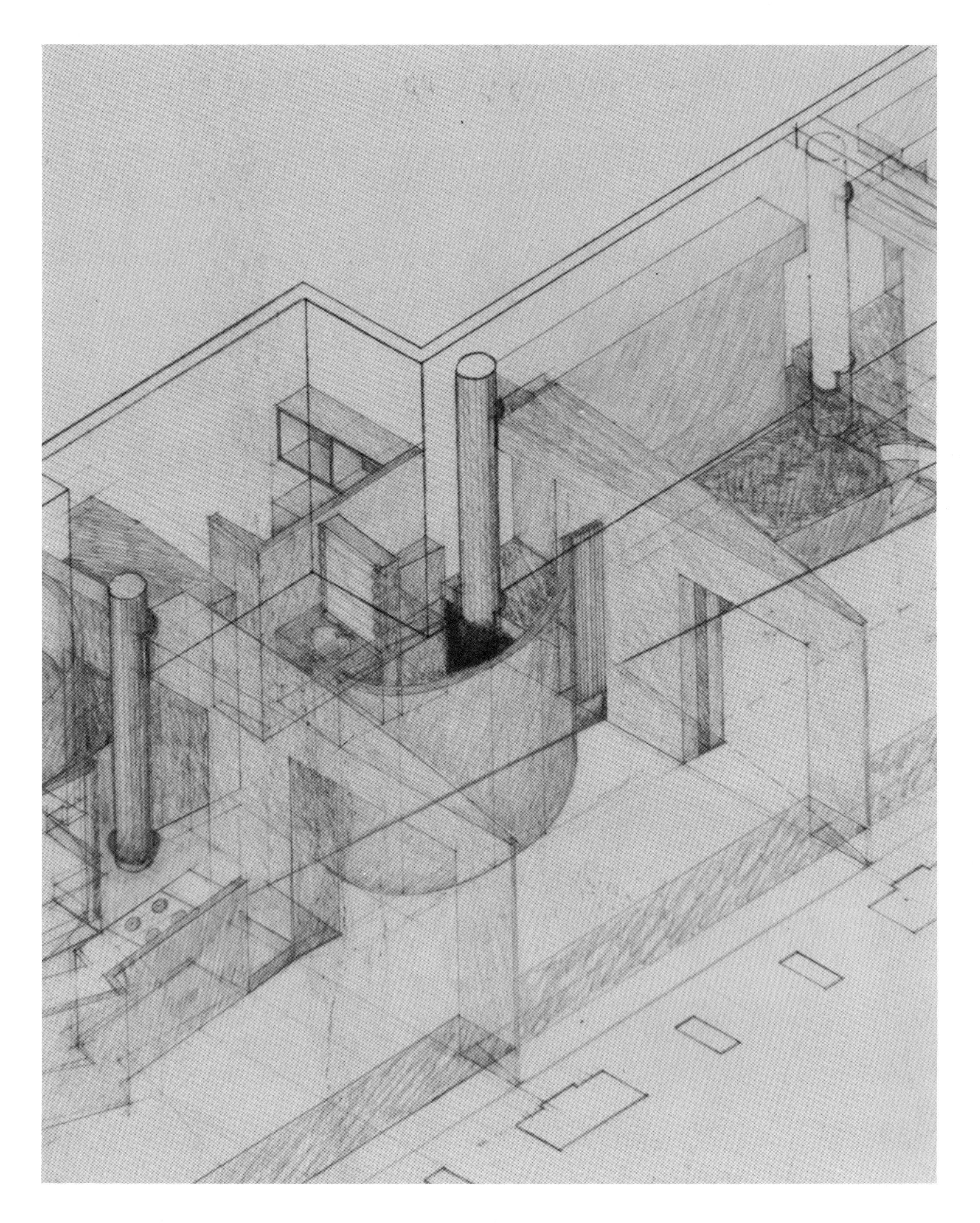

Sleeping area looking back toward living area. Layered space realized as suggested in the preceding drawings. (Photograph by George Cserna)

Cubical form of the kitchen element projects into the living-dining space. "Layers" of space stretch beyond. (Photograph by George Cserna)

Layering of space follows the spirit of drawings with soft green and beige coloring. (Photograph by George Cserna)

NORMAN DIEKMAN

In the assignment illustrated here, Norman Diekman was asked to plan a redesign of a fifteen-year-old suburban house in upstate New York. The first plan sketch (opposite) is a study of the sort that the designer likes to call a "Xerox of the mind." In it, some forms are quite determined and specific, others are ambiguous and sketchy revealing their status as ideas searching additional inspiration. The second set of drawings are on the familiar cream tracing paper, part of it in two layers—the first sketch plus an overlay on top.

Color is used, but its significance is more diagrammatic than realistic. Green tones indicate upholstery, yellow-tan stands for natural wood finishes, while a blue-gray signifies painted wood elements. Other thoughts can be traced in the bits scattered above the plan, plan ideas and, in the center, a fragment of elevation. In the center of the plan (just below the piano) a pair of elliptical forms appear to indicate consideration of two circular openings in the wall—unusual forms that the plan would not otherwise reveal.

After discussion with the client dealing with refinements of the program, further plan sketches extend thinking to the plan of the house showing architectural elements and furniture together. It is an overlay drawn over the first sketch. The idea of a greenhouse now surfaces in the plan of page 162. It is a sort of "daydream" on paper, which triggers possibility for exploration. This plan sketching leads to sectional sketches (page 163) in which the idea is developed further. The idea turned out to be appealing to both designer and client, but cost and time pressures on the project led to a decision to put this idea aside.

A robe-like coat worn by Nineteenth Century Japanese carpenters and seen in an exhibition was the improbable source of the fireplace idea studied on page 164. Another fireplace idea is studied in an elevation sketch on page 165. The upper sketch is a first "instinctive" approach to dealing with the opening itself and its surround and a "broken" corner is suggested as an ending at the left. In the sketch below, this elevation has been simplified (the broken corner is gone) and has become more specific. The paneling at either side establishes a thematic concern with the idea of wainscoting.

Ideas for a family room (page 166) were developed in quick sketches made in the course of a client conference. The skills to do this kind of ad hoc drawing while a client looks on and comments can be very valuable to the designer. Words can often mean different things to designer and client, but drawing has a specific quality that pins down meaning and so expedites reaching agreement on what design direction to take. Approval comes at the very moment when design ideas take form.

The sketch on page 167 deals with development of a private study for the client whose work includes frequent sessions of report writing at home. In the final drawing of pages 168–169; the ideas developed in sketch form move into construction drawings which still make some use of tones and shading to help clarity. Sketching has reached an end destination in moving toward working drawings necessary for actual construction.

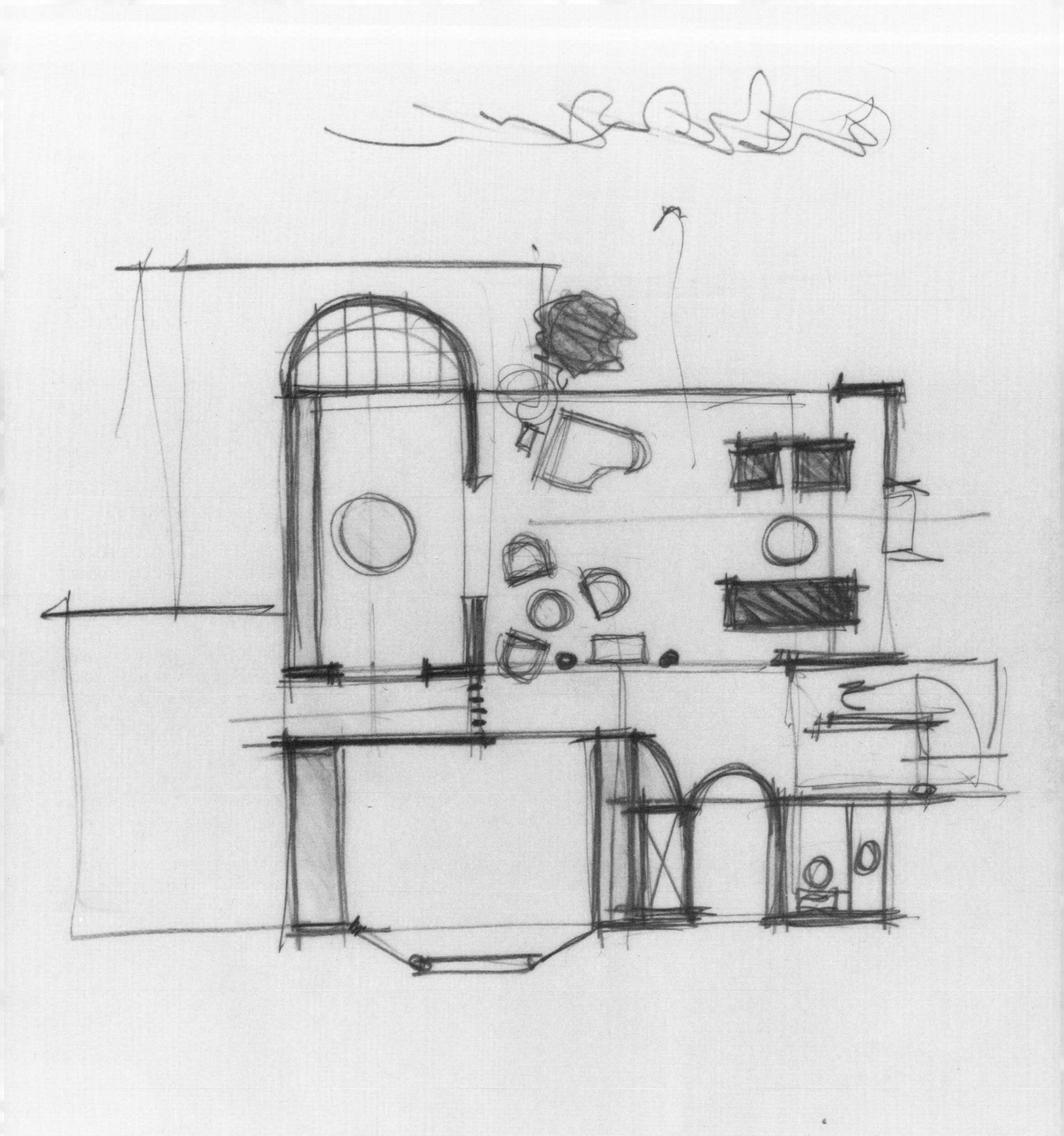

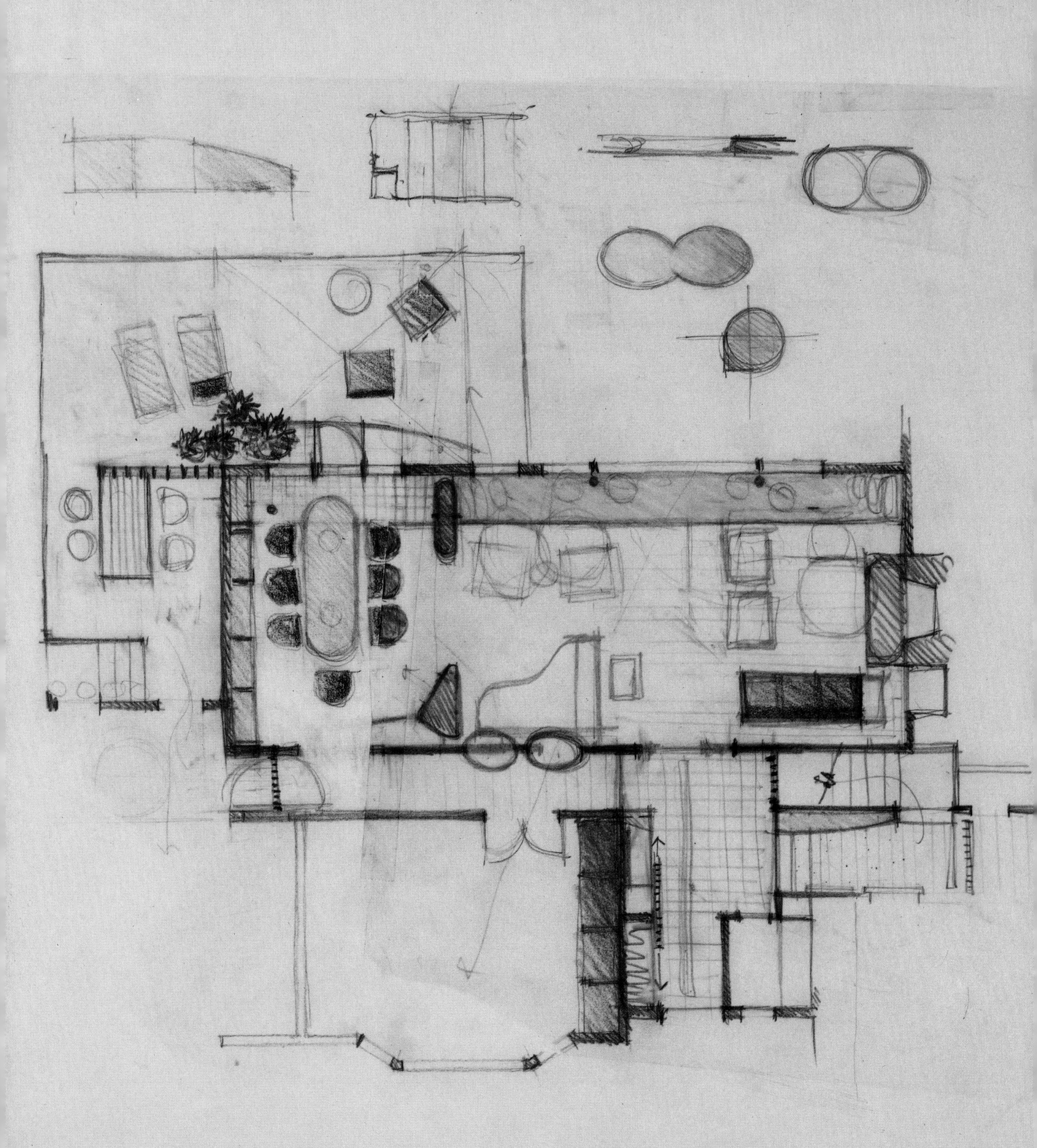

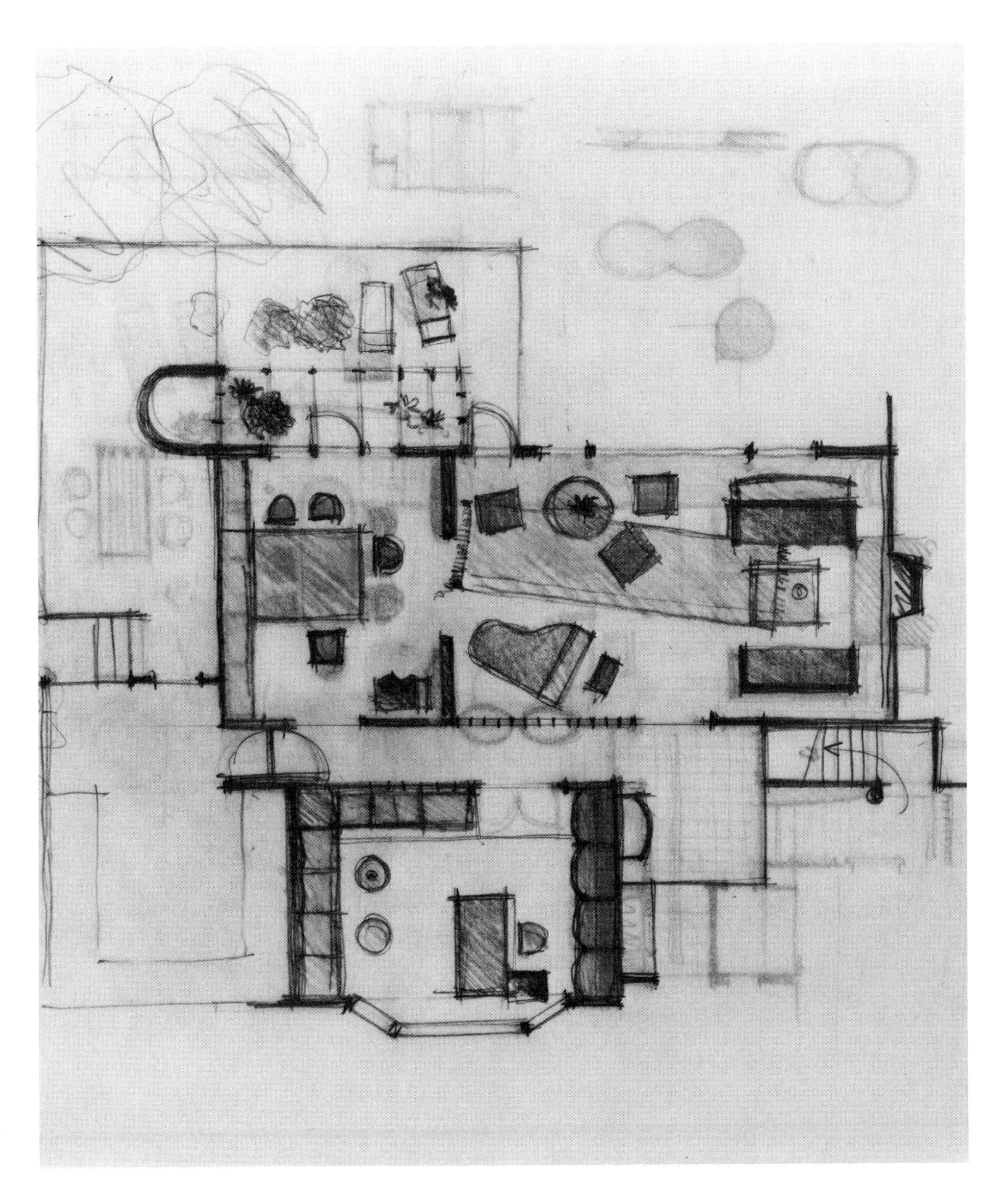

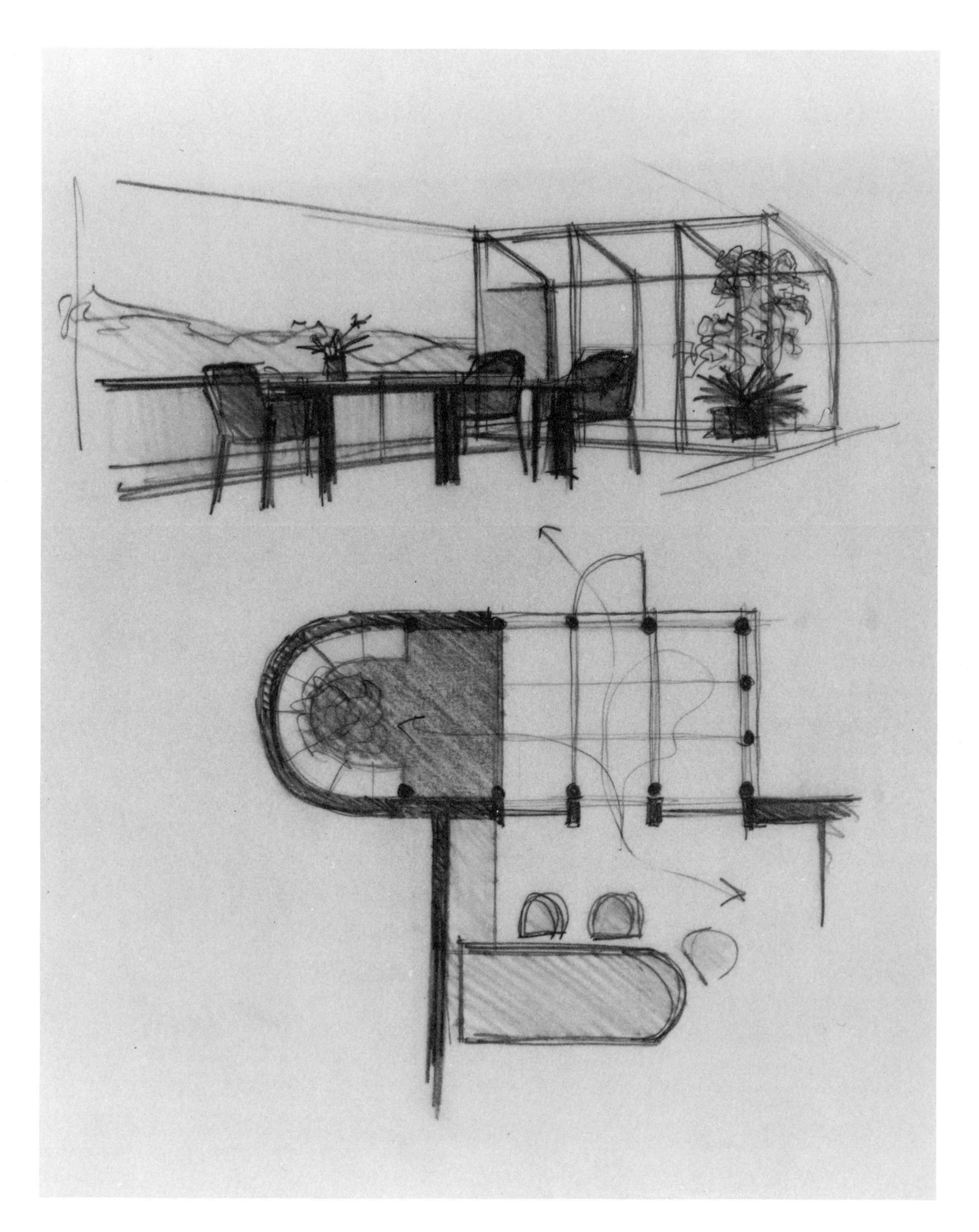

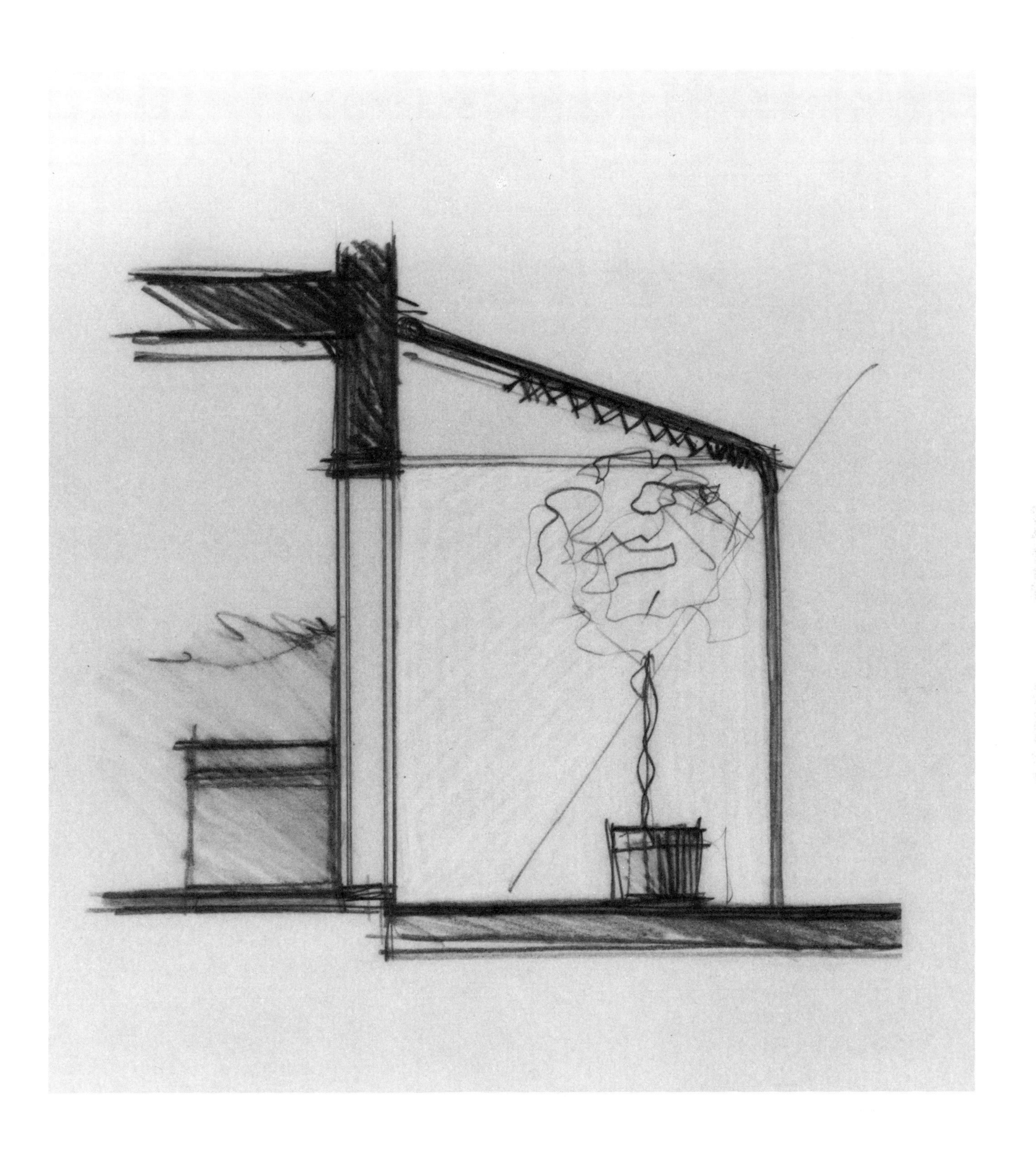

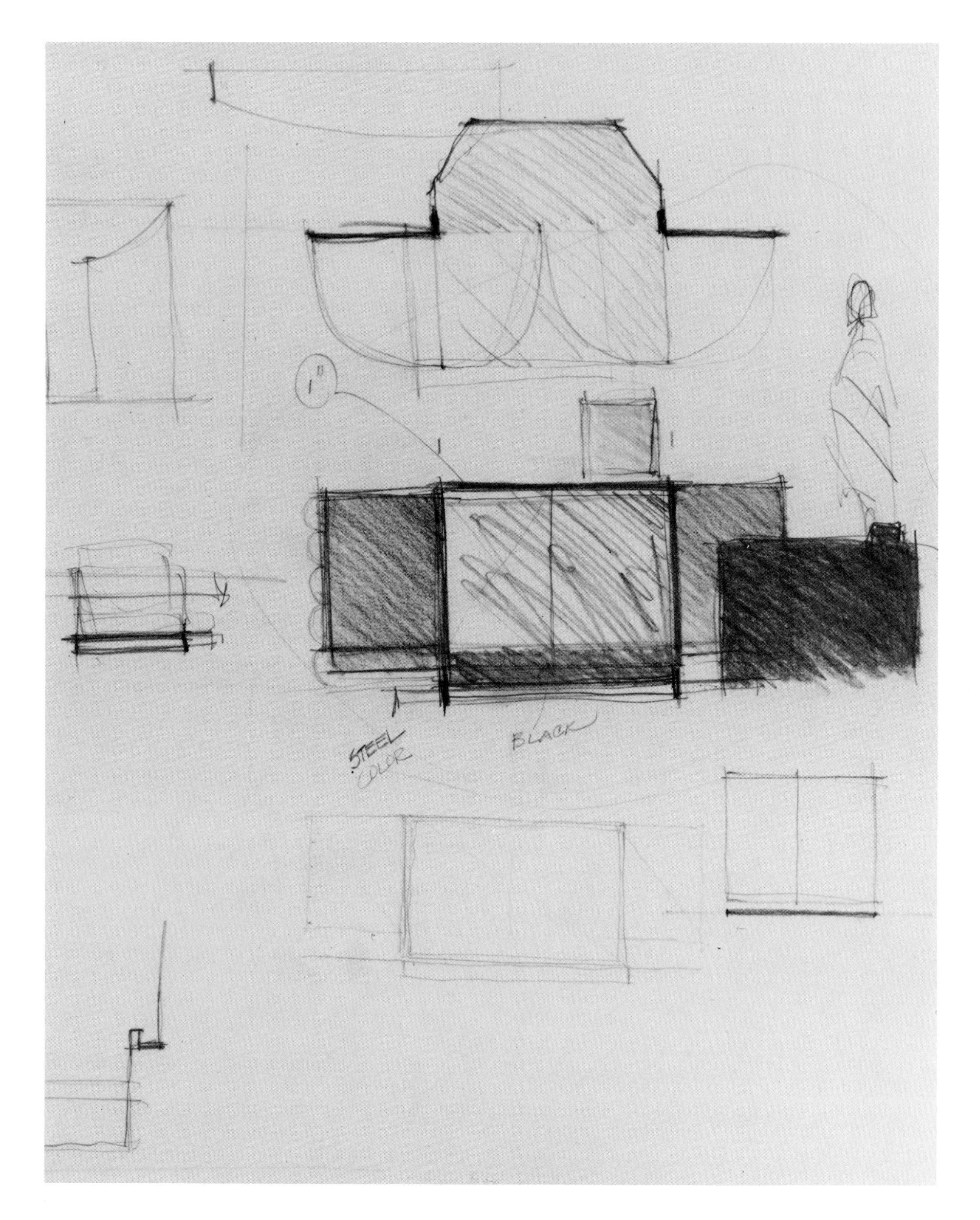
STEEL
COLOR
BLACK

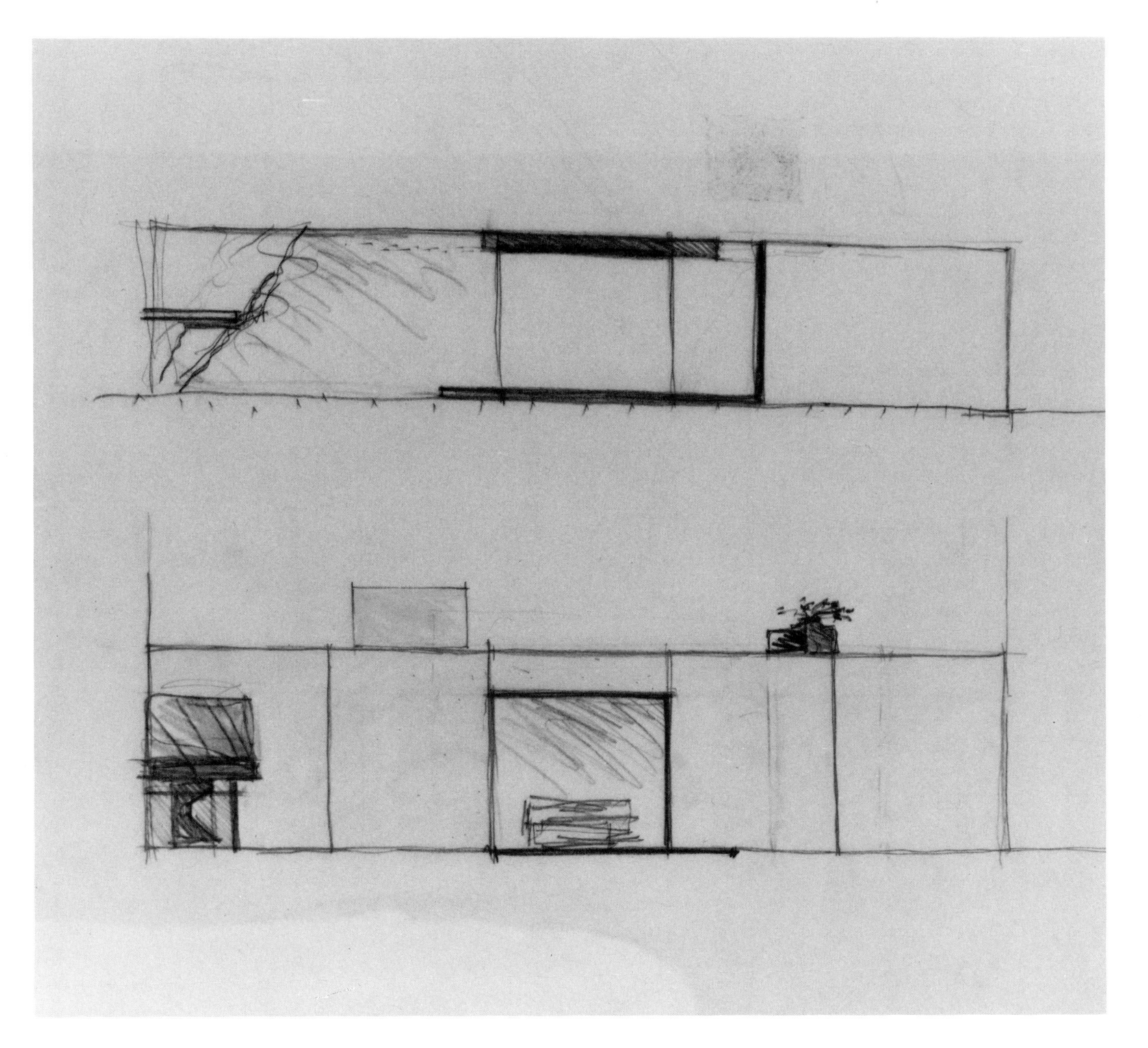

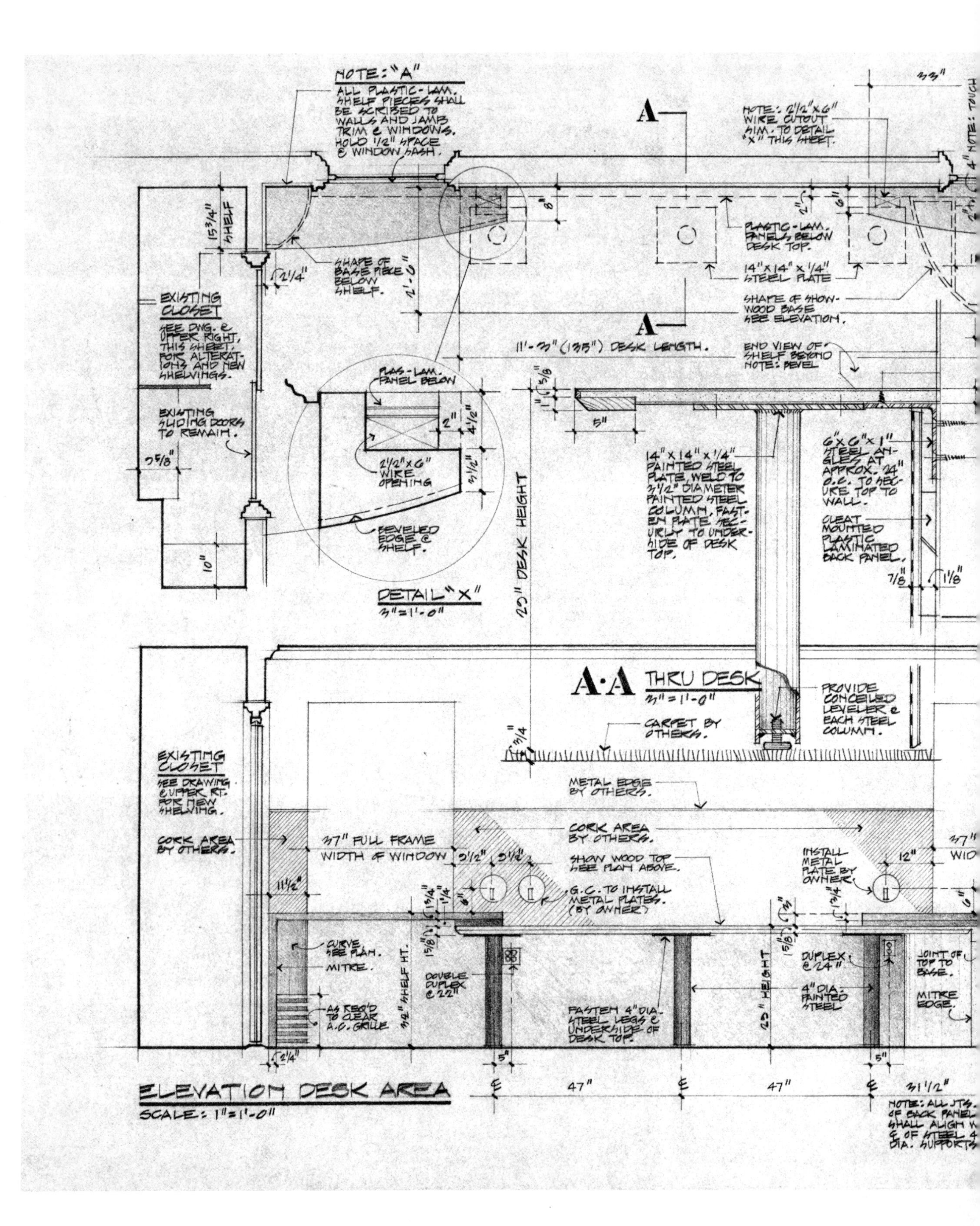
NOTE: "A"
ALL PLASTIC-LAM. SHELF PIECES SHALL BE SCRIBED TO WALLS AND JAMB TRIM @ WINDOWS. HOLD 1/2" SPACE @ WINDOW SASH.
NOTE: 2 1/2" x 6" WIRE CUTOUT SIM. TO DETAIL "X" THIS SHEET.
A
A
SHELF
15 3/4"
2 1/4"
SHAPE OF BASE PIECE BELOW SHELF.
8"
2'-0"
PLASTIC-LAM. PANELS BELOW DESK TOP.
14" x 14" x 1/4" STEEL PLATE
SHAPE OF SHOW-WOOD BASE SEE ELEVATION.
EXISTING CLOSET
SEE DWG. @ UPPER RIGHT, THIS SHEET, FOR ALTERATIONS AND NEW SHELVINGS.
11'-3" (135") DESK LENGTH.
END VIEW OF SHELF BEYOND NOTE: BEVEL
PLAS-LAM. PANEL BELOW
EXISTING SLIDING DOORS TO REMAIN.
2"
4 1/2"
3 1/2"
2 1/2" x 6" WIRE OPENING
BEVELED EDGE @ SHELF.
7 5/8"
10"
DETAIL "X"
3" = 1'-0"
29" DESK HEIGHT
5"
14" x 14" x 1/4" PAINTED STEEL PLATE, WELD TO 3 1/2" DIAMETER PAINTED STEEL COLUMN, FASTEN PLATE SECURELY TO UNDERSIDE OF DESK TOP.
6" x 6" x 1" STEEL ANGLES AT APPROX. 24" O.C. TO SECURE TOP TO WALL.
CLEAT MOUNTED PLASTIC LAMINATED BACK PANEL.
7/8"
1 1/8"
A·A THRU DESK
3" = 1'-0"
PROVIDE CONCEALED LEVELER @ EACH STEEL COLUMN.
CARPET BY OTHERS.
3/4"
EXISTING CLOSET
SEE DRAWING @ UPPER RT. FOR NEW SHELVING.
METAL EDGE BY OTHERS.
CORK AREA BY OTHERS.
CORK AREA BY OTHERS.
37" FULL FRAME WIDTH OF WINDOW
3 1/2"
SHOW WOOD TOP SEE PLAN ABOVE.
INSTALL METAL PLATE BY OWNER.
12"
37"
11 1/2"
G.C. TO INSTALL METAL PLATES. (BY OWNER)
CURVE SEE PLAN.
MITRE.
AS REQ'D TO CLEAR A.C. GRILLE.
32" SHELF HT.
DOUBLE DUPLEX @ 22"
FASTEN 4" DIA. STEEL LEGS @ UNDERSIDE OF DESK TOP.
29" HEIGHT
DUPLEX @ 24"
4" DIA. PAINTED STEEL
JOINT OF TOP TO BASE.
MITRE EDGE.
2 1/4"
5"
5"
47"
47"
31 1/2"
ELEVATION DESK AREA
SCALE: 1" = 1'-0"
NOTE: ALL JTS. OF BACK PANEL SHALL ALIGN W/ ℄ OF STEEL 4" DIA. SUPPORTS

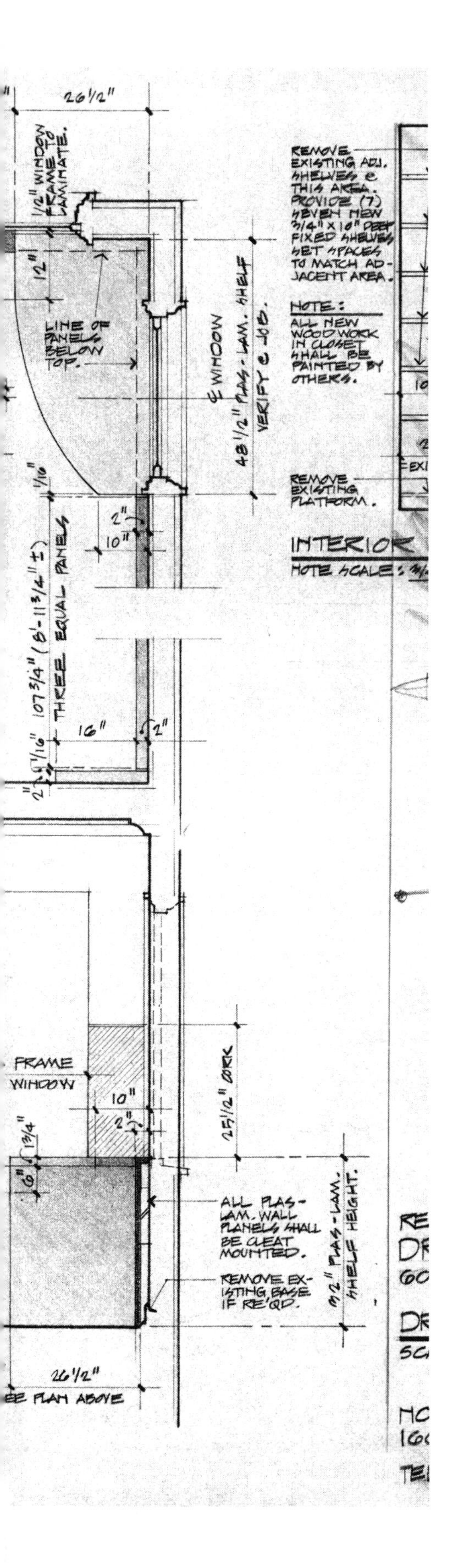
REMOVE EXISTING ADJ. SHELVES @ THIS AREA. PROVIDE (7) SEVEN NEW 3/4" x 10" DEEP FIXED SHELVES SET SPACES TO MATCH ADJACENT AREA.
NOTE: ALL NEW WOODWORK IN CLOSET SHALL BE PAINTED BY OTHERS.
REMOVE EXISTING PLATFORM.
LINE OF PANELS BELOW TOP.
ALL PLAS-LAM. WALL PANELS SHALL BE CLEAT MOUNTED.
REMOVE EXISTING BASE IF RE'QD.
SEE PLAN ABOVE
INTERIOR
NOTE SCALE

Sketch by Rob Krier, courtesy of Max Protetch Gallery

Selected Bibliography

General books dealing with sketching (and, in many cases, with other types of design drawing) are listed in a group, alphabetically, by author. Monographs dealing with the work of a particular designer or architect follow in a listing arranged alphabetically by name of the subject. All of the books listed are extensively illustrated.

GENERAL

Allen, Gerald, and Richard Oliver. *Architectural Drawing: The Art and the Process.* New York: Whitney Library of Design, 1981.

Baynes, Ken, and Francis Pugh. *The Art of the Engineer.* Woodstock, NY: The Overlook Press, 1981.

The California Condition. La Jolla Museum of Contemporary Art, 1982.

California Counterpoint. New York: Rizzoli, 1982.

Ching, Frank, *Architectural Graphics.* New York: Van Nostrand Reinhold Co., 1975.

Diekman, Norman, and John Pile. *Drawing Interior Architecture.* New York: Whitney Library of Design, 1983.

Dortmunder Architekturausstellung 1979, Museumbauten: Entwürfe und Projekte seit 1945. Dortmund: Lehrstuhl für Entwerfen und Architekturtheorie, Abt. Bauwesen, Universität Dortmund, 1979.

Gebhard, David, and Deborah Nevins. *200 Years of American Architectural Drawing.* New York: Whitney Library of Design, 1977.

Gregotti, Vittorio. "Carlo Scarpa, Frammenti 1926/1978." *Rassegna* (July 1981).

Kliment, Stephen, ed. *Architectural Sketching and Rendering.* New York: Whitney Library of Design, 1984.

Klotz, Heinrich, *Moderne und Postmoderne.* Braunschweig/Wiesbaden: F. Vieweg und Sohn, 1984.

Lotus International 27 (1980), 41 (1984), Venice: Gruppo Electa Spa./Rizzoli.

Pile, John, ed. *Drawings of Architectural Interiors.* New York: Whitney Library of Design, 1967.

Die Revision der Moderne—Postmoderne Architektur. München: Presel-Verlag, 1984.

MONOGRAPHS

Raimund Abraham

Raimund Abraham Collisions, New Haven, CT: Yale School of Architecture, 1981.

Raimund Abraham Works 1960–1973. Vienna: Galerie Grünangergasse 12, 1973.

Aymonino and Rossi

Aymonino, Carlo. *Campus Scolastico a Pesaro.* Rome: Edizioni Kappa, 1980.

Conforti, Claudia. *Il Gallaratese di Aymonino e Rossi 1967/1972.* Rome: Officinia Edizioni, 1981.

Aldo Rossi. Bologna: N. Zanichelli Editore, 1981.

Aldo Rossi. Zürich: Jamileh Weber Galerie, 1983.

Aldo Rossi, Opere Recenti. Modena/Perugia: Edit. Panini, 1983.

Mario Botta

Mario Botta, La Casa Rotonda (symposium). Milan: L'Ebra Voglio, 1982.

Rota, Italo, ed. *Mario Botta.* London: Academy Editions, 1981.

Joseph Paul D'Urso

Carlsen, Peter. *D'Urso.* Design Quarterly 124. Cambridge, MA: MIT Press, 1984.

Michael Graves

Dunster, David, ed. *Michael Graves.* New York: Rizzoli International, 1979.

Michael Graves, Esquisse for Fire Houses. Tokyo: GA Gallery, 1984.

John Hejduk

"John Hejduk." *A + U No. 53* (May 1975), pp. 77–154.

"John Hejduk." *Mask of Medusa.* Kim Shicapich, ed. New York: Rizzoli International, 1984.

Josef Hoffmann

Baroni, Daniele, and Antonia D'Auria. *Josef Hoffman e la Wiener Werkstätte.* Milan: Electa Editrice, 1981.

Louis I. Kahn

Louis I. Kahn. New York: Access Press, Inc., 1981.

"Louis I. Kahn." *L'Architecture d'Au Jour d'Hui 142* (1969).

Wurman, Richard Saul, and Eugene Feldman. *The Notebooks and Drawings of Louis I. Kahn.* Cambridge, MA: The MIT Press, 1973.

Le Corbusier

80 Disegni di Le Corbusier. Bologna: Edizioni Ente Fiere di Bologna, 1977.

Frampton, Kenneth, and Sylvia Kolbowski, eds. *Le Corbusier's Firminy Church.* New York: Rizzoli International, 1981.

Une Petite Maison: Le Corbusier. Zürich, Girsberger, 1954.

Mies van der Rohe

Blaser, Werner. *Mies van der Rohe Furniture and Interiors.* Woodbury, NY: Barron's Educational Series, Inc., 1982.

Glaeser, Ludwig. *Mies van der Rohe: Drawings in the Collection of The Museum of Modern Art.* New York: Museum of Modern Art, 1969.

Tegethoff, Wolf, ed. *Mies van der Rohe: Die Villen und Landhaus-projekte.* New York: Museum of Modern Art, 1981.

Carlo Scarpa

Carlo Scarpa Disegni. Rome: De Luca Editore, 1981.

Carlo Scarpa: Il Progetto per Santa Caterina a Treviso 1984. Ponzano: Grafiche Vianello Sri, 1984.

Carlo Scarpa, Opera Completa. Milan: Gruppo Electa Spa, 1984.

Randoli, Marina Loffi, ed. *Scarpa: Il Pensiero il Desegno i Progetti.* Milan: Jaca Book, 1984.

Ettore Sottsass

Di Castro, Federica, Ed. *Sottsass's Scrap-Book.* Milan, Casabella, 1976.

Robert A. M. Stern

Arnell, Peter, and Ted Bickford, eds. *Robert A. M. Stern 1965-1980.* New York: Rizzoli International, 1981.

James Stirling

James Stirling. London: RIBA Publications Ltd., 1974.

James Stirling: Architectural Design Profile. New York: St. Martin's Press, 1982.

Stirling, James. "The Monumental Tradition." *Perspecta 16: The Yale Architectural Journal* (1980), pp. 33–49.

Stirling, James. *James Stirling Buildings and Projects 1950–1974.* New York: Oxford University Press, 1975.

Robert Venturi

"Venturi and Rauch 1970–1974." *A + U No. 47* (November 1974).

"Venturi, Rauch and Scott Brown." *A + U Extra Edition* (December 1981).

Frank Lloyd Wright

Frank Lloyd Wright Drawings for a Living Architecture. New York: Horizon Press, 1959.

Mezzasalma, Nicola, Cinzia Perrotta, and Fabio Della Sala. *Frank Lloyd Wright Drawings 1887–1959.* Florence: Centro Di, 1976.

Index

Edited by Stephen A. Kliment and Brooke Dramer
Designed by Jay Anning
Graphic production by Hector Campbell
Set in 10 point Century Old Style